SYMBOLS OF CANADA

SYMBOLS OF
CANADA

Edited by Michael Dawson, Catherine Gidney & Donald Wright

BETWEEN THE LINES

Toronto

Symbols of Canada

© 2018 Michael Dawson, Catherine Gidney and Donald Wright

First published in 2018 by
Between the Lines
401 Richmond Street West
Studio 281
Toronto, Ontario M5V 3A8
Canada
1-800-718-7201
www.btlbooks.com

Text and cover design by David Vereschagin, Quadrat Communications
Cover illustrations by Josh Holinaty
Photo of editors by Jeff Crawford
Printed in Canada

Library and Archives Canada Cataloguing in Publication

Symbols of Canada / Michael Dawson, Catherine Gidney and Donald Wright, editors.

Includes bibliographical references and index.
Issued in print and electronic formats.
ISBN 978-1-77113-371-5 (softcover).—ISBN 978-1-77113-372-2 (EPUB).—ISBN 978-1-77113-373-9 (PDF)

1. Canada—Miscellanea. 2. Canada—History—Miscellanea. I. Dawson, Michael, 1971–, editor II. Gidney, Catherine (Catherine Anne), 1969–, editor III. Wright, Donald A., 1965–, editor

FC60.S96 2018   971.002   C2018-902796-7
                                        C2018-902797-5

We acknowledge for their financial support of our publishing activities: the Government of Canada; the Canada Council for the Arts, which last year invested $153 million to bring the arts to Canadians throughout the country; and the Government of Ontario through the Ontario Arts Council, the Ontario Book Publishers Tax Credit program, and the Ontario Media Development Corporation.

CONTENTS

INTRODUCTION

Michael Dawson, Catherine Gidney, and Donald Wright

A polar bear stands guard at the Winnipeg airport. Located outside a souvenir and snack shop near Gate 5, and wearing a Royal Canadian Mounted Police tunic and hat, it is a popular draw. But as a playful combination of Mountie mythology and northern fauna, it also belongs to a familiar and instantly recognizable pattern: the display of national symbols at Canada's airports.

Sharp-eyed visitors entering the departure lounge at the London, Ontario airport will note the small plastic beaver nonchalantly going about its business. Vancouver's airport features a black bear that seems to size up passengers before they enter the security zone for international flights. And the Montreal airport boasts two selfie-friendly (and very fluffy) moose wearing—what else—RCMP uniforms.

Because airports draw on, and reinforce, national symbols, they are a convenient starting point for a book about Canada's symbols—their origins, their shifting fortunes, and their many uses. Over forty million passengers move through Toronto's Pearson International Airport each year. Named after Lester B. Pearson, a former prime minister and the winner of the 1957

Canadian symbols standing on guard at Canada's airports.

Nobel Peace Prize, it invokes a prominent national symbol, one rooted in a particular understanding of Canada's military history: the peacekeeper. A plaque in Canada's busiest airport notes Pearson's connection to the flag and Medicare, both national symbols, but reserves its highest praise for his role in resolving the 1956 Suez Crisis, describing him as "one of the twentieth century's great peacekeepers." But Canada's commitment to peacekeeping has waned and, in early 2018, it ranked near the bottom of the United Nations' peacekeeping list, just ahead of Armenia and Samoa but well behind Ethiopia and Bangladesh. Even the United States provided more peacekeepers.

Of course, very few passengers will pause to think about the contradiction between Canada's rhetorical commitment to peacekeeping and its actual role in the world. Instead, they are more likely to spend time in a handful of specialty shops that sell Canadian souvenirs, including maple syrup, hockey sweaters, and postcards featuring the beaver, the northern lights, and Niagara Falls. At Pearson's Rocky Mountain Chocolate store, they

Hudson's Bay Company Trading Post, Pearson International Airport, Toronto, 2017.

The maple leaf theme is so prominent in Canada's airports that travellers using the men's washroom near Gate 60 in Montreal are greeted with this backlit mural.

can enjoy a True North Slab, a chocolate bar with maple-glazed cashews. Between 2012 and 2018 Pearson also boasted a Hudson's Bay Company Trading Post, where travellers could check out a unique line of mittens, toques, and blankets. Citing its "historical role in the development of the nation"—in the fur trade and the exploration of the northern half of North America—the HBC Trading Post even displayed a canoe. In fact, it was for sale.

At Canada's airports, travellers can grab a quick bite in any number of Tim Hortons. Or they can sit down for a meal and catch a hockey game. In its words, the Montreal airport hopes to "shoot and score" with the Avenue des Canadiens, a Montreal Canadiens–themed restaurant. The Edmonton airport, meanwhile, invites travellers to Gretzky's Wine & Whisky. On the off chance that a customer has forgotten who Wayne Gretzky is or what he means to hockey, a wall-sized poster of the Great One lifting the Stanley Cup will remind them. Like hockey, the maple leaf is prominently displayed at Canada's airports too. Canada's two major airlines, WestJet and Air Canada, both incorporate it

into their omnipresent logos, with the latter also trumpeting the perks associated with its exclusive Maple Leaf Lounges.

Of course, Canadian symbols are represented by more than cheap kitsch, stuffed animals, and private lounges. They are also represented in art and in craft. The Ottawa airport carefully displays a birchbark canoe. Built in 1968 by Patrick Maranda, an Algonquin elder from Quebec, it was part of a set: the second was given to Prime Minister Pierre Elliott Trudeau in 1971 as a wedding gift. The Toronto airport displays three large inuksuit, built in the early 1960s by Kiashuk, an artist and storyteller from Cape Dorset, Nunavut. And at the Vancouver airport, visitors can contemplate a totem pole made by Don Yeomans, a Haida artist and master carver. *Celebrating Flight* includes a raven, a whale, an eagle, a bear, and a frog, "all creatures of strength and power in Haida mythology." But it also includes Asian and European motifs and references, making it a symbol of movement and multiculturalism.

This book invites readers to explore the ways in which Canadians employ symbols, are shaped by symbols, and (although this might seem *un*-Canadian) argue over symbols. As they do in other nations, symbols permeate everyday life in Canada. They can be found in classrooms, courtrooms, and museums; they are reproduced on T-shirts, tattoos, and coffee mugs; and they are featured in advertisements, billboards, and product displays. They are in our homes (on Christmas-tree ornaments and in family photo albums) and they occupy public spaces (on monuments and in Remembrance Day services). They can be sources too of light-hearted and self-deprecating humour. Comedians Rick Moranis and Dave Thomas turned "Take off, eh!" into a national punch line. The Frantics invented Mr. Canoehead, the crime-fighting superhero who had an aluminum canoe permanently fused to his head after being struck by lightning in Ontario's Algonquin Park. And popular historian

Above left: Birchbark canoe, Ottawa airport
Above right: *Celebrating Flight* totem pole,
Vancouver airport.
Bottom left: Three inuksuit at Pearson
Airport in Toronto.

and broadcaster Pierre Berton once defined a Canadian as someone who knows how to make love in a canoe. Indeed, Canadian euphemisms for sex often riff on national symbols: "sugaring off," "pulling the goalie," "finding the Northwest Passage," and, "What about a little Double-Double tonight?" In short, symbols are everywhere.

Their prevalence alone makes them worthy of examination. But it is their power and influence that makes them so important. Symbols often serve an integrative and defensive function, uniting an imagined "us" against an imagined "them": hockey is "our game"; Canadian health care is superior to American health care; and Canadians are peacekeepers while Americans are war

Left: From Expo 67, this beaver dressed as a Mountie embodied two Canadian symbols. And it confirms a basic point: Canadians are not born, they are made—in this case by the toys they play with.

Right: Hockey as public space: a hockey-puck bench and Stanley Cup sculpture in downtown Ottawa.

makers, or so we like to tell ourselves. And yet, even though symbols are used to fashion a national "we" and a national "us," they are complicated and contested: the national anthem means different things in English and French Canada; the maple leaf is on Canada's national flag but the *fleur-de-lys* is on Quebec's; hockey has been celebrated both as a Canadian game and as a symbol of French-Canadian survival; the Niagara Falls are as much American as they are Canadian; and the totem pole, lacrosse, and the canoe are wrapped up in the history and politics of colonialism. The canoe, for example, is not just a symbol of Canada, but a symbol of Indigenous resilience and resurgence, making it an object embraced by many nations.

The goal of this book is to show readers how many of the symbols most closely identified with Canada were invented, how they are used, and how they have changed over time. But to say that symbols are invented is not to say that they are created out of nothing. Indeed, Canada produces most of the world's maple syrup; the Canadian Pacific Railway is an actual railway; many Canadians *do* love hockey. Rather, it is to say that symbols are produced, transformed, and employed by individuals, corporations, and the state. They were made and remade at specific moments for specific reasons. For example, more Canadians have heard of Laura Secord than Dollard des Ormeaux. But the decline and subsequent disappearance of Dollard as a symbol reveals a great

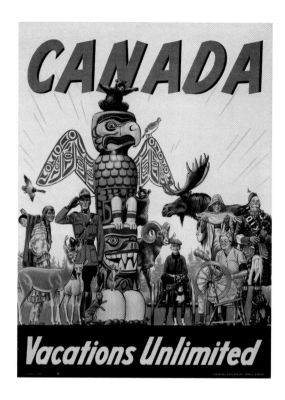

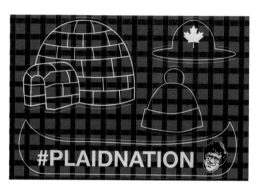

Like tourists of yesteryear, patrons of the Smoke's Poutinerie chain are enticed by a set of familiar "Canadian" symbols.

deal about shifting political priorities and cultural sensitivities in today's Quebec. In short, the fascinating history of symbols allows us to better understand Canada's past and present—and to anticipate and shape its future.

Some symbols began as representations of local experiences but were rendered "national" in scope through the influence of powerful people, commercial endeavours, or the federal government. The origins of poutine, for example, are deeply rooted in Québécois culture but this popular food is increasingly seen not just as a representation of Quebec, but of Canada too. At times, symbols are championed from within the country as desirable representations of national identity and destiny. Singer and

songwriter Gordon Lightfoot celebrated the Canadian Pacific Railway as "an iron road runnin' from sea to sea." At other times, they are reinforced by the perceptions and expectations of visitors from outside the country, by tourists seeking an authentic Mountie on horseback or making a pilgrimage to Green Gables.

Symbols invariably rely upon a process of selection. After all, some aspects of Vimy Ridge are remembered while others are forgotten. Yet understanding what is remembered and what is forgotten can be empowering, giving ordinary citizens the opportunity to stand up to the dangers of blind nationalism and unchecked patriotism. Most importantly, perhaps, symbols are subject to appropriation. Indeed, many symbols are *products* of appropriation. But here, too, there are lessons to be learned and, in some cases, intriguing and positive developments to note as Indigenous peoples successfully reclaim and develop cultural practices that were once outlawed or transformed to suit the interests of European settlers.

Sometimes symbols of Canada are presented individually—a jade inuksuk on a store shelf, for example. On other occasions they are combined in flamboyant and nonsensical ways—a polar bear and a moose sporting police uniforms. In fact, Canadian symbols exist within a web of understanding that connects them to one another and that often reinforces common themes—the struggle to survive in a harsh climate, the challenge of differentiating oneself from a more powerful neighbour, the search for community in an increasingly fragmented world, or the desire to be recognized as a peaceful but powerful nation. The chapters that follow explore these themes—and many others—while highlighting the unexpected twists and turns that have marked each symbol's history.

This book examines some of the most recognizable and influential Canadian symbols; in so doing, it attempts to answer a number of questions. Where did these symbols come from? How have their meanings changed over time? How did their influence rise or fall? How does their popularity prioritize some interests over others? And, perhaps most importantly, in what ways are we consciously and subconsciously shaped by the symbolic landscape we all inhabit?

Closing ceremony of the 2010 Vancouver Olympics: the beaver signifying the nation. Note the mashup of Mounties, lumberjacks, hockey players, a maple leaf, and a canoe.

BEAVER

Colin M. Coates

Can there be a more obvious symbol of Canada than the beaver? No other animal, except for humans, is credited with the creation of the country. (Historically, the codfish might have had something to say, but no one is listening to it.) "The beaver makes everything," said an Innu hunter to Jesuit missionary Paul Le Jeune in the seventeenth century: its valuable pelt could be traded for whatever people desired. Maybe the beaver could even make Canada. Economic historian Harold Innis ascribed the geography of the Canadian state to the fur trade that moved west and north across the northern half of North America between roughly 1600 and 1850. (To be precise, he was writing before Newfoundland joined Canada). Since 1975, the beaver has even been an official symbol of Canada, though its route to that lofty position bears examination. Like any symbol, the beaver presents a number of ambiguities.

Its scientific (Linnean) name seems unambiguously Canadian: *Castor canadensis*. But it shares the adjective with 216 other species in the animal kingdom, 44 plants, 7 bacteria, 4 fungi, and 1 chromista (or algae). Among these species, we find the Canada goose (*Branta canadensis*), the grey jay (*Perisoreus canadensis*),

The first Canadian postage stamp, 1851. At the time, "Canada" referred to the Province of Canada, in the southern parts of present-day Ontario and Quebec.

him to operate through diplomatic channels and dissuade the state legislators in New York from proceeding. O'Sullivan also spoke directly to Faulkner's parliamentary secretary, Gustave Blouin.[3] Faulkner did not respond formally to O'Sullivan's letter until February 5. In the meantime, the young MP seized the opportunity to enhance his own political profile.[4] O'Sullivan saw the potential in this issue; as he would later write, "the beaver was about to be kidnapped by Americans."[5] He appeared on the CBC Radio show *As it Happens*. The tone was jocular, but public reaction was swift. *As it Happens* launched a public petition, commissioned a French horn quartet to play an ode to the beaver, and brought one into the studio. The beaver proceeded to pee on host Alan Maitland.

Thousands of letters and signatures on petitions (over thirteen thousand) poured in. The letters were almost exclusively in English. O'Sullivan drafted a private member's bill. On January 24, 1975, he presented the bill in first reading "to protect the beaver as a popular symbol reserved to Canadians by declaring the beaver a national symbol."[6] By the time the bill reached the debate stage, O'Sullivan had acquired cross-party support. Bill C-373 aimed "to provide for the recognition of the Beaver (*Castor canadensis*) as a symbol of the sovereignty of the Dominion of Canada." This designation technically limited its status as a national symbol, since it provided merely that "when the beaver is used by the Queen in Parliament, it [is] used as a symbol of the country."[7]

Nonetheless, this attempt served to "correct an oversight of history" because it was easy to "find that the strong, tireless and industrious beaver has always been symbolic of our northern homeland."[8] O'Sullivan cited the many ways the beaver had been used as a symbol: as an Indigenous clan sign, a figure carved on totem poles, as part of the Hudson's Bay Company's arms, and the heraldry for Sir William Alexander's short-lived Scottish

the Canadian milkvetch (*Astagalus canadensis*), and the Canada hemlock (*Tsuga canadensis*).[1] Then again, another common name for the animal is the "American beaver."

The process by which the beaver reached its official recognition is the first part of this story. In 1974, New York state senator Bernard Smith launched the idea of making the beaver his state's official animal. This proposal created consternation in Canada. *Toronto Sun* journalist Mark Bonokoski contacted the office of former prime minister John Diefenbaker. Diefenbaker's aide, Keith Martin, turned the story over to his young friend, the twenty-two-year-old member of Parliament Sean O'Sullivan.[2]

O'Sullivan, a member of the Progressive Conservative Party, wrote immediately to Secretary of State Hugh Faulkner, urging

colony of Nova Scotia in 1632. When O'Sullivan stated that the beaver appeared on the first Canadian stamp, another MP interjected: "Before the Queen?" Yes, the young MP replied, "Before the Queen." Switching to French, O'Sullivan added that coins, the coat of arms of the city of Montreal, and fourteen Canadian regiments all boasted the image of the animal.

Trying to head off any opposition, and maybe not wishing to stir up bad feelings from the flag debate of the 1960s, O'Sullivan commented that the beaver and the maple leaf went together. It was true that Oregon, the "Beaver State," had already adopted the animal (though it uses the Latin name, *castor americanus*), and its flag, dating back to 1925, has the beaver on its reverse (the only two-sided state flag). But the Canadian claim was stronger and of broader appeal: it was "a symbol of national significance, well-founded in history and honoured by generations."[9]

Given the limited time allotted to private member's bills, only two others spoke on the issue, both of them from the government side. The bill was referred to committee and quickly passed without a formal vote. In the Upper Chamber, Senator Muriel McQueen Fergusson quoted from the groundswell of supportive letters. From St. Catharines, Ontario: "Please add my name to your list of supporters in regard to our beaver as an emblem. Why don't we use the emblem more? It stands for industry and faith. The little creatures build well. Somehow to me beavers mean Canada." From Halifax: "Keep the beaver Canadian—it is as Canadian as the maple leaf. Maybe even more."[10] The bill passed in the Senate without division, and it received royal assent on March 24, 1975.[11] From that moment, the beaver was a state-sanctioned symbol of Canada.

As O'Sullivan's campaign made clear, Canadians had long used the beaver to represent something more than itself. Bill C-373, spurred by the Americans and aided by CBC Radio, simply recognized that Canadians had bestowed greater prominence on the beaver than such animals as the muskrat or the lynx. Although other animals were hunted and skinned for the fur trade, the best pelts came from the beaver. A seventeenth-century French dictionary associated the beaver directly with Canada when it stated that "more can be found in Canada than in any other location in the world."[12]

Reverse of Canada's five-cent piece since 1937: the ubiquitous beaver.

Cap badge of the Royal 22e Régiment based in Quebec City: the beaver as a military insignia.

Indeed, Canadians use the beaver as a geographical marker more often than other animals. The word "beaver" is used in 689 geographical designations, from Beaver Cove, Newfoundland, to Beaver Creek, Yukon. "Castor" appears 384 times, and if one adds some of the Indigenous words for beaver (*amik*, *amisk*, and *tsá*, for instance), the total exceeds 1,100. In contrast, if we include the French variants of the words, "moose" appears only 575 times, "muskrat" 155, "buffalo" 111, and "lynx" 89. Commercial enterprises also favour the beaver. In the 2017 phone book for Central Toronto, to take one example, twenty-five businesses reference the animal in their title, from Beaver Lock & Key to Beaver Window Cleaners, to, somewhat confusingly, Beaver Fishery. Two Toronto businesses use "Castor" in their name. But there are only three moose, including Moosehead Breweries,

Roots Canada™ logo: The beaver
as a corporate symbol.

one elk, one cod, three bears, and two loons. No other Canadian animal is so well represented as the beaver.

The beaver's iconic status stems from the fact that many of its characteristics appeal to humans. Beavers epitomize northernness, industry, and hardiness. The famous and fanciful image of the upright, hard-working beaver carrying logs to build its dam exaggerates the animal's organizational skills, and yet by any measure, its engineering abilities are impressive. But even using that adjective anthropomorphizes the beaver, as people have been doing for many centuries. One of the earliest historians of Canada thought that the beaver offered an excellent lesson for humans "of foresight, industriousness and dedication to work."[13] A French colonial official likewise wrote of leadership among the beaver.[14]

Other writers focus on the beaver's monogamous nature, though biologists posit that beavers are socially, but not necessarily genetically, monogamous: they reside with the same partner but may have other sexual relations.[15] In the twentieth century, the author and conservationist Grey Owl anthropomorphized the beaver more than most, adopting them into his home and taming them. He wrote a popular children's book, *The Adventures of Sajo and her Beaver People*, assuring the reader that "the delineations of animal character are to be taken as authentic."[16] Grey Owl's beavers are domestic and faithful, more so than that caddish British impostor ever managed to be.

One of the most recent and compelling incarnations of the beaver is as a prototypical environmentalist. With their skills in building dams, and thus in modifying watercourses, beavers create new ecological niches, making them one of the few animals capable of intentionally transforming their environment. For biologist Glynnis Hood, the beaver represents "tenacity, intelligence, and an ability to survive even the harshest climates."[17] The beaver, clearly, is a Canadian.

No less an authority than Joe ("I am Canadian"), speaking on behalf of Molson's Canadian beer, assured television watchers that "the beaver is a truly noble animal." The humour ultimately lay in the comparison to other countries' symbols—the lion, say, or the eagle. But the beaver is only noble to the extent that all animals are intrinsically noble.

Unfortunately, the beaver does not always get the respect it deserves. It is, in its essence, a rodent, and that poses some problems. To be fair, it is the world's second-largest rodent, after the capybara—what better fit for the world's second-largest country? And no one would mistake the beaver, if they saw it in the wild, for a rat or a mouse. Yet as soon as one tries to depict the beaver, one risks misconstruing it for another rodent. In other words, it poses a branding problem.

In an early flag debate in the 1930s, Conservative MP Robert Smeaton White recalled suggestions that the beaver be placed on the flag to symbolize the country. Alas, he reminisced, "while the beaver is a very industrious animal with a good deal of ingenuity and skill, placed upon a flag it too much resembles a rat."[18] Prime Minister R. B. Bennett later defended the use of the maple leaf to symbolize Canada abroad, which allowed businesspeople and the government to avoid using the beaver. "The beaver is difficult to use effectively on certain types of products," he said; "in some instances it looks rather like a rabbit."[19]

As a result, artists tend to accentuate two of the beaver's features to distinguish it from other rodents: its flat tail and its large teeth. They also tend to depict it on land, rather than in the water.[20] Stylized for the closing ceremony of the 2010 Vancouver Olympic Games, and the Parks Canada and Roots Canada logos, the beaver is immediately recognizable. In these iterations, the beaver is not just any rodent.

However, beavers use their impressive teeth to build dams and create floods. Not all their actions, then, are highly compatible with humans' use of habitats. For one current senator, they create problems for cottagers. In 2011, Senator Nicole Eaton achieved some notoriety when she criticized the beaver, a "dentally defective rat" with the effrontery to wreak "havoc on farmlands, roads, lake, streams and tree plantations, including my dock every summer." She suggested replacing the beaver as Canada's national symbol with a more majestic choice: the polar bear.[21] Clearly, not everyone likes the beaver.

Beyond their propensity to act like the animals that they are, damming watercourses and gnawing prized trees, beavers have another strike against them: their ambiguous sexuality. The classical legend about the male beaver's self-emasculating tendencies—the idea that he will chew off his own testicles when fearful of attack—may suit a certain type of ironic Canadian self-deprecation. On a more scientific level, it can be very difficult for

CBC Radio publicity campaign, 1975: the sexualized beaver.

humans to distinguish between male and female beavers. Some scholars, in discussing the beaver as a national and commercial symbol, emphasize the animal's ambiguous sexuality as a way of addressing the difficulties of defining Canadian nationalism.[22]

But the beaver's primary sexual ambiguity lies in its use as a slang reference to female genitalia. When Nova Scotian rapper Classified, in his pastiche of Canadian symbols and clichés, sings, "Our national mascot's a damn beaver / Oh Canada, we love our beaver," he plays on both senses of the word.[23] A Toronto lesbian bar calls itself The Beaver. In 2010, the history magazine *The Beaver* changed its name to *Canada's History* to avoid the problems that the name caused for consumers.[24] CBC Radio once played on the theme by depicting a beaver, presumably male, holding open his raincoat, with the injunction to "Expose Yourself to CBC Radio." Despite this other meaning of its name, the beaver could overcome the sexual connotations and confusions and the negative implications of being a tree-destroying rodent.

The key problem with beavers as a national symbol is somewhat different.[25] Primarily, most of what Canadians commemorate in the beaver is its death. If in the 1930s Harold Innis was correct in seeing the fur trade as outlining Canada's borders, the country's geographical expansion occurred, literally, on the backs of the beaver. It was the stunningly fast extermination of beaver in specific habitats, after all, that led fur traders to canoe further west and north, and which over time provided some basis for French or British claims to the territory.

The extent of the beaver slaughter was astonishing. If one were to rewrite Canadian history from an animal rights perspective, the country would not get off lightly. It has been estimated that in the combined French and British fur trades of the 1720s, a beaver was killed every three to four minutes.[26] Although Canadian historical imagery pays great homage to the French and British fur traders, these men had little direct contact with the live beaver themselves. Rather, they were largely couriers, taking the beaver that Indigenous people had killed to foreign markets. Traders were middlemen in a chain in which Indigenous people performed the most difficult labour. Indigenous people also created the best pelts by wearing them as clothing over the winter and removing the guard hairs. Euro-Canadian traders performed a function not unlike the Salvation Army's recycling of clothing. But their markup was a lot more substantial.

Beaver pelts were used primarily for felt hats, largely for the aristocracy and the military. The French peasant did not own beaver products. Thus, the *Castor canadensis* played its role in shoring up the class system in Europe. This was no small achievement, but how productive the class-oriented production of hats was may still be up for debate.

Spurred by European demand, the over-hunting of the beaver continued well past the fur trade's heyday, and by the early twentieth century, non-Indigenous trappers played key roles. In the late 1920s, Quebec suspended the non-Indigenous beaver hunt, and in the mid-1930s banned the hunt outright, with support from Cree leaders. Later in the century, animal rights groups increasingly opposed the fur trade, a form of activism that did little to help Indigenous people living on reserves. The debate over the beaver's designation as a national symbol in the 1970s inspired some writers to encourage politicians to ban the leg-hold trap and end the trade in beaver pelts.[27]

Cree artist Kent Monkman has recently captured the essence of the ambiguity of the beaver as a national symbol. In a parody of, and ironic commentary on, different genres of art, Monkman's 2016 painting *Les Castors du Roi* riffs off relevant images, including fanciful historical depictions, of the beaver. French and Indigenous hunters savagely murder the beaver with spears, daggers, leg-hold traps, and guns, while church representatives stand idly by. On the right of the canvas, an anthropomorphized

Kent Monkman, *Les Castors du Roi*, 2011: the ambiguous beaver.

beaver prays to a Christian God, while beaver spirits ascend towards heaven.

No national symbol lacks problems. Meanings shift over time, as historic contexts change. Few urban Canadians today have ever seen a beaver. But the beaver warrants recognition, many Canadians have agreed, because it exemplifies a number of admirable human qualities, such as industriousness, technical expertise, and foresight. In its actions, it might even embody an aspiration toward what the Canadian Constitution refers to as "peace, order and good government." The proposal to designate the beaver a national symbol allowed Canadians to debate issues of national identity in a largely playful fashion, safely criticizing a perceived act of American cultural imperialism and reaffirming some fairly vague national characteristics. They engaged in this discussion with gusto. More significantly, the beaver—along with bison and humans, one of the widespread keystone species to inhabit the boundaries of present-day Canada—has uncontestably played a key role in the historical development of the country we know today. Unfortunately, from its point of view, the beaver had to give its life to create Canada.

My thanks to Jessica DeWitt, Richard Dickinson, and Donald Wright for helpful research pointers, and to all the editors for their astute comments throughout the process. Gabriel Hanna of the CBC, Captain Martin Dauphinais of the Royal 22ᵉ Régiment, Elyse Goody of Roots Canada, Louisa Fenner of the Royal Canadian Mint, and Jamie Chirico and Brad Tinmouth from Kent Monkman Studio kindly assisted with permissions for illustrations.

NOTES

1   See Integrated Taxonomic Information System database at itis.gov.
2   Sean O'Sullivan with Rod McQueen, *Both My Houses: From Politics to Priesthood* (Toronto: Key Porter Books, 1986), 96–9; Brock University Archives, Sean O'Sullivan fonds, RG431 (hereafter SO).
3   SO, box 12, file 26, Secretary of State—Beaver Bill, 1974–75. Handwritten note, Dec. 19, 1974.
4   Ibid., O'Sullivan to Faulkner, Dec. 19, 1974; Faulkner to O'Sullivan, Feb. 5, 1975.
5   O'Sullivan, *Both My Houses*, 97.
6   House of Commons Debates, 1975, 2573 (hereafter HofC Debates).
7   SO, box 12, file 27, Minutes, Mar. 12, 1975, 15–34.
8   HofC Debates, 21 Feb. 1975, 3463.
9   Ibid.
10 Senate Debates, Mar. 20, 1975, 686.
11 HofC Debates, Mar. 24, 1975, 4447.
12 Antoine Furetière, *Dictionnaire universel* (La Haye, 1690), s.v. "Castor."
13 Pierre-François-Xavier de Charlevoix, *Journal historique d'un voyage de l'Amérique* (Paris, 1744), 95.
14 Camille de Rochemonteix, ed., *Relation par lettres de l'Amérique septentrionalle* (Paris: Letouzey et Ané, 1904), 21.
15 Dietland Müller-Schwarze and Lixing Sun, *The Beaver: Natural History of a Wetlands Engineer* (Ithaca, NY: Comstock Publishing, 2003), 31.
16 Grey Owl, *Adventures of Sajo and her Beaver People* (London: Lovat Dickson and Thompson, 1935).
17 Glynnis Hood, *The Beaver Manifesto* (Victoria, BC: Rocky Mountain Books, 2011); see also Frances Backhouse, *Once They Were Hats: In Search of the Mighty Beaver* (Toronto: ECW Press, 2015).
18 HofC Debates, Feb. 19, 1934, 726.
19 Ibid., May 18, 1934, 3201.
20 Jody Berland, "The Work of the Beaver" in Thomas Allen and Jennifer Blair, eds. *Material Culture in Canada* (Waterloo: Wilfrid Laurier University Press, 2015), 30.
21 Senate Debates, Oct. 27, 2011.
22 Margot Francis, "The Strange Career of the Canadian Beaver: Anthropomorphic Discourses and Imperial History," *Journal of Historical Sociology* 17, no. 2/3 (June–Sept. 2004): 209–39; Kim Sawchuk and Barbara Crow, "Leave it to Beavers: Animals, Icons and the Marketing of the Bell Beavers" in Enric Castelló et al., eds., *The Nation on Screen: Discourses of the National on Global Television* (Newcastle upon Tyne: Cambridge Scholars Publishing, 2009), 309–26.
23 Classified, "Oh… Canada," on *Self Explanatory* (Sony, 2009).
24 Martin Patriquin, "How 'The Beaver' lost its name" *Maclean's*, Feb. 17, 2010.
25 Berland, "Work of the Beaver."
26 Professor Thomas Wien (Université de Montréal), personal communication with the author, Mar. 30 2017.
27 E.g. Eve Smith to O'Sullivan (received Feb. 26, 1975), SO, box 12, file 27, Secretary of State—Beaver Bill, Part II. Mar.–Apr. 1975.

E. Pauline Johnson (1861–1913), known also as Tekahionwake, was a popular Mohawk poet and performer. She was also an enthusiastic and skilled canoeist. In Johnson's poetry, the canoe symbolizes independence and connection to the land. It also has erotic connotations.

CANOE

Jessica Dunkin

Leanne Betasamosake Simpson's poem "how to steal a canoe" opens with Kwe—the Anishinaabemowin term for woman—"barefoot on the cement floor / singing to a warehouse / of stolen canoes": "bruised bodies / dry skin / hurt ribs / dehydrated rage." Kwe's companion, Akiwenzii—Anishinaabemowin for old man or Elder—calls the place "canoe jail." They pray to the old ones, they rub "drops of water on the spine of each canoe," they smudge. And then, while Akiwenzii distracts the security guard, Kwe takes one of the canoes and drives to Chemong Lake, where she "pulls Her out into the middle of the lake / sinks Her with seven stones / just enough to / fill Her with lake & / suspend Her in wet."[1]

Simpson, a Michi Saagiig Nishnaabeg scholar, writer, and artist, explains the piece in this way:

On one level, "how to steal a canoe" is about returning an old birch bark [sic] canoe to the Mississauga Nishnaabeg people in an honourable way. On another level, this song is about taking back all the things that have been stolen from Indigenous peoples, whether that's land or bodies, knowledge or belongings. It is taking back of our precious selves.[2]

Simpson's poems and stories often begin with a literal narrative, in this case a visit to the Canadian Canoe Museum in Peterborough, Ontario, with her mentor Doug Williams of Curve Lake First Nation to perform a ceremony for a recently repatriated nineteenth-century Nishnaabeg birchbark canoe. The Canoe Museum, with more than six hundred canoes and kayaks in its collection, is a cathedral to canoeing in Canada, a mecca for paddling enthusiasts, and an important site for the production of the canoe as a national symbol.[3] Simpson's framing of the museum as canoe jail and of canoes as living beings disrupts conventional colonial understandings and representations of the canoe.

The canoe is ubiquitous in mainstream Canadian culture, even though many Canadians have never stepped foot into one of these small crafts. A popular visual symbol, the canoe has been the subject of paintings by iconic Canadian artists like Tom Thomson, Emily Carr, and Alex Colville. It appears on the labels of and in advertisements for a diverse range of products, including milk, cigarettes, salmon, and cameras. It occasionally surfaces in political discourse, serving as a useful metaphor in discussions ranging from regionalism and leadership to the economy and Canada-US relations.[4] In anticipation of Stephen Harper's proroguing of Parliament in 2008, Patrick Martin, the NDP member of Parliament for Winnipeg Centre, deployed the canoe to shame the prime minister, then leading a minority government, for his inability to work with the other parties: "If we were all paddling our canoe in the same direction, we could navigate these turbulent waters without this unrest that is unfolding as we speak."[5] The canoe's ubiquity reflects its plasticity as a symbol; in short

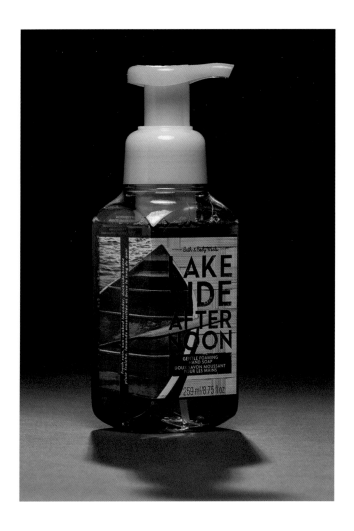

The canoe has been used to sell a diverse range of products, many of them with little obvious connection to the canoe—a testament to the power and plasticity of the canoe as a symbol.

order, it can be made to embody teamwork, leisure, wildness, economic expansion, and indigeneity, among many other things.

The canoe is routinely understood as "one of the great Canadian icons," a tool of diplomacy and cross-cultural collaboration that made this place called Canada possible, a humble craft that connects Canadians to wild places and rewards determination and hard work.[6] Such representations overlook how the canoe as a physical object and symbol has participated in the expansion of a colonial market economy, displacing Indigenous communities and fueling resource extraction. They also allow a very particular activity—contemporary recreational canoeing is dominated by middle-class white people—to stand in for the nation. A closer look at the canoe as an object and symbol, focusing on themes of appropriation and settler colonialism, work and recreation, and Indigenous resilience and resurgence, reveals the multiple divergent meanings attached to the small craft.

The stereotypically Canadian canoe is a red sixteen-foot Prospector. One hundred years ago, it would have been made of cedar and canvas. Today, it is more likely to be molded from a composite like Royalex or Kevlar. It likely has two seats and its occupants propel it with long, single-blade paddles. In reality, there has always been much greater variation in the size, shape, and materials of canoes. This is especially true of canoes built by Indigenous nations.

The different styles of canoe are as numerous as the meanings attached to them, the richness and complexity of Indigenous canoeing traditions reflecting the richness and complexity of Indigenous cultures, cosmologies, and relations with the land. More than tools of transportation, canoes are commonly understood as living things with spirits. The First Nations of the Pacific Coast, including the Coast Salish, Kwakwa̱ka̱'wakw, and Haida, transform giant cedars into ocean-going crafts of different sizes through a process of shaping, hollowing, steaming, and carving.

River canoes are typically made of deciduous trees, using a similar process. Each nation has its own designs, which are uniquely suited to local conditions and uses. Alongside totem poles and plank houses, canoes are a form of monumental art on the Northwest Coast, symbols of clan and community.[7]

The most common traditional canoe style on the continent, owing to the extensive range of *Betula papyrifera* (paper birch),

The canoe is a common trope in Canadian political rhetoric and imagery. In this cartoon from 1993, then-Prime Minister Brian Mulroney is paddling on Harrington Lake in a canoe named Unity with Quebec premier Robert Bourassa, as the latter prepares to cut the craft in half.

The First Nations of the Pacific Coast, including the Haida Nation, transform giant red cedars into ocean-going craft, which are at once symbolic and functional.

This image of three unnamed Eeyouch (Cree) paddlers was taken by photographer A. A. Chesterfield on the Great Whale River in 1903. The photograph captures one of the canoe styles favoured by Eeyouch and Innu builders, which was sharply rockered for manoeuvrability.

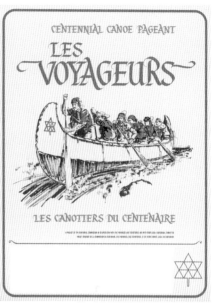

Re-enactments of fur trade history, like the Voyageur Canoe Pageant that took place in the summer of 1967, are one example of the ways in which the canoe has been used to naturalize the claims of settler Canadians to land.

is the birchbark canoe. Here again there is diversity within and between nations, reflecting local materials, needs, and cultures. The Mi'kmaq of the Atlantic Coast build sleek ocean-going birchbark canoes with low, rounded ends that avoid catching the wind and raised gunwales to protect the occupants from waves. One of the canoe styles favoured by the Eeyouch (Cree) and Innu in what is now northern Quebec and Labrador has a steep rise along the keel line so that the bow and stern are as much as a foot higher than the boat's midpoint. This sharply rockered style is highly manoeuvrable and well suited to river travel.[8]

Prior to contact, canoes allowed Indigenous nations across the continent to move through their homelands in search of food, people, and trade goods. Europeans arriving in North America from the sixteenth century onward survived and later flourished because they adopted Indigenous technologies, chief among them the canoe. The canoe enabled explorers, missionaries, voyageurs, surveyors, and settlers alike to travel to the many corners of the continent, which in turn provided them with access to people and resources. The canoe, in other words, enabled the expansion of European economies and the colonial state, expansion that infringed with devastating consequences on the lives, lifeways, and lands of Indigenous peoples.

In Canada, the canoe has long been associated with the fur trade and the romantic figure of the voyageur. The design of canoes used to transport people and pelts across the vast interior of North America from the seventeenth to the nineteenth century was borrowed from Indigenous watercraft. Most were constructed of birchbark held together by spruce root, stretched over a wooden frame, and sealed with spruce or pine gum. However, boats built for the fur trade were often much larger than the birchbark canoes used by Indigenous nations. The largest of the voyageur canoes, the *canots du maître*, were typically thirty feet in length and four to six feet wide at the midpoint. Powered by five to eight paddlers, these canoes could carry up to five tonnes of cargo. With few exceptions, fur trade canoes were built by Indigenous people and Indigenous people, especially the Métis, often paddled the large crafts as they journeyed between metropole and hinterland.[9]

Re-enactments of fur trade history have been and continue to be popular events; a number were held to celebrate Canada's one hundred and fiftieth anniversary in 2017. But the most iconic fur trade re-enactment, and one that was central to the formation of settler canoe nationalism in Canada, took place in the summer of 1967. The Centennial Voyageur Canoe Pageant was a 3,300-mile canoe race from Rocky Mountain House, Alberta, to Montreal. Ten fibreglass canoes painted to look like birchbark and bearing the names of European explorers were powered by teams of six. All of the participants were men; most were white. The Pageant told spectators a story about a nation-state called Canada that grew out of an economic partnership between European traders and Indigenous peoples. More than the mere engine of the fur trade, the canoe reaches across time and space, naturalizing settler Canadians' claims to the land.[10]

The canoe is rarely imagined as a tool of surveillance and state formation, even though it was vital to surveying and mapping the territory that in 1867 became the Dominion of Canada. The Geological Survey of Canada was created in 1842 to generate a detailed geological assessment of northern North America. Prior to the 1930s, when planes took over as the primary surveying tool, canoes, often propelled by Indigenous paddlers, ferried white surveyors and their equipment through the interior. Canoes remained indispensable to surveying well into the twentieth century. Summer students hired by the Ontario Department of Mines in the 1960s were outfitted with sixteen-foot cedar-canvas Prospectors and tasked with compass and pace traversing. The surveys and maps generated in the wake of these canoe journeys produced knowledge about the Canadian territory, which facilitated further white settlement, resource extraction, and industrial development.

For much of the canoe's history, paddling for pleasure was secondary to more utilitarian pursuits, such as harvesting or transportation. Today, however, the canoe is most often imagined as a recreational craft. The recreational canoe has its roots in the mid-nineteenth century. One of the epicentres of this transformation was Peterborough, Ontario. Early white settlers in the area bought birchbark canoes from Anishinaabe builders. Later, they experimented with constructing their own craft in the form of dugouts, also modelled on Anishinaabe boats. Author Susanna Moodie described paddling and sailing for pleasure on Lake Katchewanooka in the 1830s.[11] As early as 1849, settlers in the region were organizing canoe races with separate categories for "Indians" and "white men." A nascent canoe-building industry emerged in Peterborough in the 1860s. By the turn of the century, the Peterborough Canoe Company and others were supplying canoes to paddling enthusiasts near and far.[12]

Waterfront liveries in urban areas made canoes and canoeing accessible to a broader public in the decades around the turn of the twentieth century. The Hicks Family operated a canoe livery on the Humber River in Toronto from the 1870s until the 1950s.

The late nineteenth century marked an explosion in canoeing as sport, recreation, and leisure, what the *New York Times* referred to in 1880 as a "canoe boom."[13] The canoe was everywhere: on the covers of sheet music, in political cartoons, and of course on the water. Many North American cities boasted canoe liveries, where middle- and working-class people could rent a canoe for an hour or an afternoon, and canoe clubs, which brought together paddlers to socialize and compete. While canoeing at this time was a remarkably urban pursuit, enthusiasts could also be found paddling for pleasure in wild places, often accompanied, and in some cases propelled, by Indigenous guides. Increased leisure time, greater disposable income, anxieties about the effects—particularly on white middle-class men—of industrial capitalism and urban living, and a belief in the healing power of nature and exercise, all contributed to the canoe's popularity.

Though inspired by Indigenous designs, early recreational canoeists took special pains to revision the canoe as a craft worthy of middle-class attention and use, a process we might call the "whitening of the canoe." Writers like William Alden, who popularized the canoe in the pages of the *New York Times* in the 1870s and 1880s, worked to distance the "modern" canoe from its Indigenous past by celebrating settler exploits, but

Although the canoe is often imagined as uniquely Canadian, canoeing was also a popular leisure activity in the United States in the decades around the turn of the twentieth century.

more pointedly by differentiating between the "savage" craft of Indigenous nations and the "civilized" canoe paddled by white middle-class men. Settler canoe builders, meanwhile, focused their attention on physical "improvements," using techniques and materials associated with modernity and "civilization."[14]

It is no coincidence that at the same time that Euro-Canadian canoeists were taking to the water in boats appropriated from Indigenous nations, the Canadian state was implementing the

Indian Act, a comprehensive set of laws introduced in 1876 to destroy Indigenous cultures and assimilate the continent's First Peoples into mainstream settler society. Residential schools, forced settlement on reserves, the outlawing of cultural practices such as the potlatch, and the destruction of traditional economies, all profoundly affected Indigenous lifeways, including the construction and use of canoes.

By the 1920s, settler interest in the canoe was waning, perhaps because of the growing number of leisure options available to the expanding middle class and competition from motorized watercraft, which were faster and, to the chagrin of some, noisier. Nevertheless, canoeing remained a popular activity in some circles, including at the youth summer camps that appeared in the early decades of the twentieth century, first in Ontario and then elsewhere in the country. Unlike early proselytizers of the canoe, white camp directors embraced canoeing as part of a broader program of "playing Indian" deemed appropriate for healthy child development.[15] At many summer camps today, the headdresses have been packed away and the Indian Council Rings renamed, but colonial ideologies and practices of cultural appropriation continue to inform campers' experiences.[16]

Wilderness canoeing, which rests on the assumption of wild, unpeopled landscapes, remains a potent symbol of a particular white, middle-class, Central-Canadian identity that has been repeatedly grafted onto the nation. Step through the doors of the Canadian Canoe Museum and one of the first things you will see, enshrined in a glass case with soft spotlighting, is the buckskin jacket with the word "Canada" emblazoned across the shoulders that former prime minister Pierre Elliott Trudeau wore while paddling his beloved craft. (His son Justin donned the same jacket for a sunrise paddle on National Aboriginal Day in 2016.) A committed federalist, Pierre Trudeau represents the apogee of white canoe nationalism.[17]

While it is important to map the appropriation of the canoe by Euro-Canadians, and to detail how the canoe has been a physical and symbolic tool of settler colonialism, there are other stories to tell. Indeed, the renewal of canoeing traditions in Indigenous communities in recent years is part of a larger wave of Indigenous resurgence. Nations are reasserting their sovereignty, reviving traditional economies and forms of governance, revitalizing languages, and reclaiming cultural practices.

Given the centrality of the canoe to many Indigenous cultures, it is no wonder that boatbuilding has been an important part of Indigenous resurgence. In Mi'kma'ki, master builder Todd Labrador has spent years learning how to construct birchbark canoes in the old way. Todd's great-grandfather, Joe Jermey, was also a master builder; he died the year after Todd was born. Though Todd's father Charlie never built a canoe, he was able to pass on what he learned from Joe, such as how to gather birchbark and spruce root, and how to bend wood for the frame. The rest Todd has gleaned through the careful study of photographs, consultations with Elders, and trial and error.[18] Todd has built a number of canoes in community. In 2016, for example, he worked with the Bear River First Nation to construct a birchbark canoe as part of Seven Paddles, a program that seeks to revitalize traditional canoe routes, while also passing on Mi'kmaw culture, traditions, and stories.[19] Similar canoe-building projects have taken place in Indigenous communities from southwestern Ontario to the northern territories to the Pacific Coast over the last three decades.

Canoe travel has been an equally important part of cultural revitalization. Since 1995, for example, the Tłı̨chǫ of Denendeh have organized an annual canoe trip for Elders and youth. Following traditional travel routes through Tłı̨chǫ territory, Wha Dǫ Ehtǫ K'è ("Trails of Our Ancestors") charts a tapestry of named places, each with its own stories that contain knowledge about how to be Tłı̨chǫ and live in respectful relation to the land. Wha Dǫ Ehtǫ K'è, which gives young people the opportunity to hear these stories in place, encourages looking back in order to move forward. By returning to older ways of doing things, youth are grounded in Tłı̨chǫ ways of life and able to chart a way forward for themselves, both as individuals and as a nation.[20]

Many of these examples pertain to individual nations building canoes according to their traditions and travelling canoe routes that crisscross their ancestral territories, but canoes have also brought Indigenous nations together to resist contemporary colonial capitalism in more pointed ways. On Earth Day 1990, Eeyouch and Inuit paddlers from the neighbouring communities of Whapmagoostui and Kuujjuarapik in northern Quebec arrived at Manhattan's Battery Park in a green wood and canvas canoe-kayak hybrid christened *Odeyak*. The six-metre-long craft and its paddlers had travelled by dogsled, road, and river to raise

awareness about an impending hydroelectric project that would radically transform their homeland. Their gambit paid off: New York State pulled out of the agreement with Hydro Quebec and the project was eventually abandoned.[21]

The canoe is an object with a complicated past. It has long been, and continues to be, a physical and symbolic tool of settler colonialism. But it also remains a symbol and tool of Indigenous nationhood, resilience, and resurgence. We see examples of the "taking back of our precious selves" as Kwe secrets a birchbark boat away from canoe jail, as Todd Labrador peels spruce root for stitching, as young people and Elders paddle the waterways of Tłı̨chǫ nèèk'e. For settler Canadians, attending to the past and present of canoe colonialism is an important part of decolonizing the canoe and nurturing respectful relations between Indigenous and non-Indigenous peoples in this country, but it is only a part. To be truly transformative, education must be accompanied

Master builder Todd Labrador with a Mi'kmaw ocean canoe built at Kejimkujik National Park and National Historic site in summer 2015. This canoe is now on display at the Canadian Museum of History in Gatineau, Quebec.

by action. For settler canoeists, this might begin by building relationships and cultivating ethical paddling practices.[22] On whose territory do you wish to canoe? How does that nation understand respectful relations with the land and what are your obligations as a visitor? Is that nation fighting to protect their territory or to gain access to their territory? How can you support them? Of course, these questions are just a beginning. As Leanne Simpson reminds us, the canoe is but one of many things stolen from Indigenous peoples. True reconciliation requires the full restoration of land and lifeways to Indigenous nations.

Many thanks to Bryan Grimwood and Sara Spike for reading and commenting on earlier drafts of this chapter, and to John B. Zoe and Todd Labrador for sharing your canoe stories.

NOTES

1   Leanne Betasamosake Simpson, *This Accident of Being Lost* (Toronto: House of Anansi, 2017), 69. There is an accompanying video for "how to steal a canoe," produced by Amanda Strong and available at player.vimeo.com/video/188380371.

2   Chris Hampton, "Leanne Betasamosake Simpson premieres a video about taking back what's stolen from Indigenous peoples," *Chart Attack*, Nov. 29, 2016, chartattack.com/news/2016/11/29/premiere-leanne-betasamosake-simpson-how-to-steal-a-canoe-video/.

3   For a critical introduction to the Canadian Canoe Museum, see "Recapitulation: The Canadian Canoe Museum," in Misao Dean, *Inheriting a Canoe Paddle: The Canoe in Discourses of English-Canadian Nationalist* (Toronto: University of Toronto Press, 2013), 139–58.

4   Jamie Benidickson, *Idleness, Water, and a Canoe: Reflections on Paddling for Pleasure* (Toronto: University of Toronto Press, 1997).

5   Patrick Martin, "Government Orders Economic and Fiscal Statement Intervention," ourcommons.ca/Parliamentarians/en/publicationsearch?fttarget=0&MaxRowReturn=10000&ParlSes=40&Person=&PublicationTypeId=37&RPP=15&SearchText=&Topic=40417%2c40118&Witness=&xml=1.

6   This is how Bruce W. Hodgins and Bryan Poirier describe the canoe in the opening lines of "Aboriginal Peoples and the Canoe," in Daniel J. K. Beavon, Cora Jane Voyageur, and David Newhouse, eds., *Hidden in Plain Sight: Contributions of Aboriginal Peoples to Canadian Identity and Culture* (Toronto: University of Toronto Press, 2005), 312.

7   David Neal, *The Great Canoes: Reviving a Northwest Coast Tradition* (Vancouver: Douglas and McIntyre, 1995); Hillary Stewart, *Cedar: Tree of Life to the Northwest Coast Indians* (Vancouver: Douglas and McIntyre, 2009), 48–60.

8   John Jennings, "The Realm of the Birchbark Canoe," in Jennings, ed., *The Canoe: A Living Tradition* (Toronto: Firefly Books, 2002), 14–25.

9   Carolyn Podruchny, *Making the Voyageur World: Travelers and Traders in the North American Fur Trade* (Toronto: University of Toronto Press, 2006).

10 Dean, *Inheriting a Canoe Paddle*, 100–1.

11 Susanna Moodie, *Roughing It in the Bush; or, Life in Canada* (New York: George P. Putnam, 1852).

12 Beverly Haun-Moss, "Layered Hegemonies: The Production and Regulation of Canoeing Desire in the Province of Ontario," *Topia* 7 (Spring 2002): 39–55.

13 "The Canoe Boom," *New York Times*, June 19, 1880.

14 Jessica Dunkin, "Canoes and Canvas: The Social and Spatial Politics of Sport/Leisure in Late Nineteenth-Century North America" (Ph.D. diss., Carleton University, 2012).

15 Sharon Wall, *The Nurture of Nature: Childhood, Antimodernism, and Ontario Summer Camps* (Vancouver: UBC Press, 2009); Amanda Shore, "Notes on Camp: A Decolonizing Strategy," 2015, ccamping.org/wp-content/uploads/2015/05/A.Shore-Notes-On-Camp.pdf.

16 Ryan McMahon, "Indigenous Stereotypes Have No Place at Summer Camps," *Globe and Mail* (Toronto), July 7, 2016.

17 Bruce Erickson, *Canoe Nation: Rethinking Canoeing, Nature and Canada* (Vancouver: University of British Columbia Press, 2013); Dean, *Inheriting a Canoe Paddle*.

18 Lindsay Jones, "Wildcat River Family Keeps Mi'kmaq Tradition Afloat," *Globe and Mail* (Toronto), June 17, 2017.

19 Elizabeth McMillan, "Mi'kmaq Artist Builds Traditional Birchbark Canoe in Bear River," *CBC News*, July 25, 2016, cbc.ca/news/canada/nova-scotia/todd-labrador-builds-birchbark-canoe-bear-river-1.3691819.

20 John B. Zoe, ed., *Trails of Our Ancestors: Building a Nation* (Behchokǫ̀, NT: Tłı̨chǫ Community Services Agency, 2007).

21 Hodgins and Poirier, "Aboriginal Peoples and the Canoe."

22 This section is inspired by Chelsea Vowel, "Beyond Territorial Acknowledgements," *âpihtawikosisân*, Sept. 23, 2016, apihtawikosisan.com/2016/09/beyond-territorial-acknowledgments/, and Allison P. Holmes, Bryan S. R. Grimwood, Lauren J. King, and the Lutsel K'e Dene First Nation, "Creating an Indigenized Visitor Code of Conduct: The Development of Denesoline Self-Determination for Sustainable Tourism," *Journal of Sustainable Tourism* 24, no. 8–9 (2016): 1177–93.

Skidegate, Haida Gwaii, in 1878

TOTEM POLE

John Sutton Lutz

An anthropologist, an artist, and a politician walk into a restaurant and . . . we have a great opener for a joke and a brief summary of how the totem pole became recognized around the world as a symbol of Canada. The year was 1929, the anthropologist Marius Barbeau, the artist Group of Seven member Edwin Holgate, and the restaurant the Jasper Tea Room in the iconic Château Laurier. A stone's throw from Parliament Hill, it was the haunt of many parliamentarians, including the prime minister, William Lyon Mackenzie King.

Admittedly, the totem pole is an unlikely candidate for a national icon. Totem poles existed in relatively few First Nations communities in a sliver of what is now British Columbia and southern Alaska, so remote that even in 1910 they could only be reached by several days' boat journey north from Victoria and Vancouver; Indigenous culture was considered by many Canadians, including Prime Minister King, to be "barbaric"; and, finally, totem poles were no longer being carved, and those that survived were in a state of decay, largely because the Indigenous peoples of the West Coast who had carved them were under intense pressure to abandon their culture. (The ceremony needed to carve and raise a totem pole—the potlatch—was actually against the law!) How, then, did these rare and exotic

Totem pole kitsch in a Victoria tourist shop.

the Canadian National Railway (CNR), the totem pole collection at Gitwangak was considered the most photographed site in Canada after Niagara Falls.

The CNR had a formidable ally in the form of Marius Barbeau, a leading anthropologist at the National Museum of Canada. Barbeau believed that Indigenous people in Canada were dying out and that their monumental art needed to be recorded before they entirely disappeared. Like the CPR before it, the CNR used "product placement" to promote tourism and it invited famous artists to travel for free as long as they painted the scenery the company wanted to promote. Barbeau arranged for the CNR to provide free passage to Group of Seven artists A. Y. Jackson and Edwin Holgate, and he served as their guide in Gitxsan territory in the late summer of 1926.[2] They spent a week at Gitwangak, where Harlan Smith, another National Museum of Canada anthropologist, was working on a government-sponsored project to restore, repaint, and relocate the villages' totems alongside the railway tracks, where they would be more visible to tourists.[3]

There were many terrible ironies to this project, a collaboration of the Dominion Parks Branch, the National Museum of Canada, the Canadian National Railway, and the Department of Indian Affairs. The standing poles were being made into a tourist attraction, as a reminder of the past glories of an Indigenous culture that the federal government was actively trying to suppress. The *Indian Act* had been amended in 1884 to ban the potlatch and so suppress Indigenous law and culture. It was amended again in 1914 and 1918 to make it easier to convict British Columbia's Indigenous people of hosting a potlatch—a feast needed to erect a new pole. Successful potlatch prosecutions between the 1910s and the 1930s included a case in Alert Bay in 1921, in which twenty-two Kwakwa̲ka'wakw were sentenced to jail time, and another in 1931 in Gitxsan territory, where Barbeau was working, in which two men were convicted and one sent to prison.

disappearing carvings, many of which were in Alaska, come to be a symbol of Canada?

The story begins in 1913 with the completion of the ill-fated Grand Trunk Pacific Railway (GTPR). The railway, whose president, Charles Hays, went down with the Titanic in 1912, was also sinking under the weight of its accrued debt because almost no one yet lived in the expanse between the northern Prairies and Prince Rupert, BC, except in small First Nations communities.[1] Looking for sources of revenue, the railway turned to tourism. The GTPR's route ran along the Skeena River, through the Gitxsan village of Gitwangak (Kitwanga), one of a very few communities in British Columbia that still had a cluster of standing totem poles. Yes, its more profitable competitor, the Canadian Pacific Railway (CPR), also had grand hotels, as well as sublime scenery, but only the GTPR had totem poles. By 1925, six years after the bankrupt railway had been nationalized as

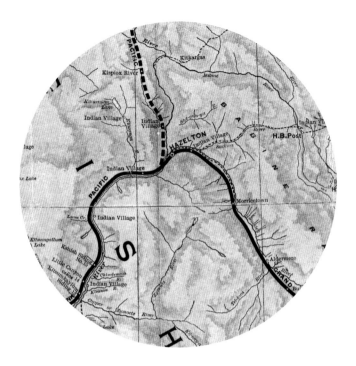

Detail of the Grand Trunk
Pacific route through Hazleton.
Gitwangak is the "Indian Village"
shown west of Hazleton.

The 1920s also saw the extension of the federal Indian residential school program and the beginning of the enforcement of compulsory school attendance designed to eradicate traditional culture.

As Indigenous communities came under new pressure and their population reached its lowest point in the 1920s, Barbeau (ignoring Alaska) identified the totem pole as a distinctive new form of art that was uniquely Canadian—a coming together of Indigenous motifs and culture with the European iron technology used to carve them.

Tourists examining Gitwangak (Kitwanga)
totem poles in the 1920s.

The first drawing of a "totem pole" by John Webber of Maquinna's house in Yuquot from James Cook's 1778 expedition.

Beginning with British explorer James Cook in 1778, visitors have been struck by the power of West Coast Indigenous art forms—including house posts (of which more below) and totem poles. While these monumental carvings existed in various forms before European contact, the arrival of new trade goods and wealth contributed to an explosion of the most familiar totem poles—free-standing outdoor structures—in the mid- to late nineteenth century. By the 1870s, photographs of the Northwest Coast show dozens of these totem poles in front of villages from the Tlingit communities in Alaska, through Haida Gwaii, across to the Nisga'a, Tsimshian, and Gitxsan villages on the Nass and the Skeena watersheds, through the Haisla and Heiltsuk territory, and as far south as the Kwakw̱a̱ka̱'wakw villages on northern Vancouver Island and the islands and mainland shore opposite. One Tlingit village, Tuxekan, had 125 mortuary and memorial poles in 1916, while other communities had more than 70 house, mortuary, and memorial poles standing in the late nineteenth century.[4]

What is now called a totem pole is in fact a story, or series of stories, with a range of distinct purposes and cultural styles carved in three dimensions into a tree trunk stripped of its bark.[5] The earliest pictured is what is known as a house post, painted by John Webber at Yuquot with Captain Cook in 1778.[6] These interior carved poles actually supported the roof beams of the traditional longhouse. Using stylized animal or spiritual figures or crests, these poles told elements of the history of the family or clan that owned the house.

The most familiar of the monumental totems is the house pole, sometimes known as a house frontal pole, a free-standing structure set in front of a longhouse and often with a portal that forms the doorway to the house. Like the house posts, these tell stories about the owners' ancestors, including their deeds, spirit helpers, and clan crests. The poles, according to the Gitxsan and Wetsuweten people, were "the *expressions of ownership* of land [conveyed] through the *adaawk, kungax,* [their stories], songs, and ceremonial regalia." "*Confirmation of ownership* comes through the totem poles erected to give those expressions a material base."[7]

The Haida and the Tlingit also erected a third form of totem pole to mark the death of a distinguished family member. These mortuary poles sometimes held the remains of the deceased. The Coast Salish of southern Vancouver Island and the Fraser Valley carved life-size (or larger) mortuary figures that often represented the deceased or his or her spirit helpers. The Kwakwaka'wakw and the Nuu-cha-nulth, on Vancouver Island's west coast, have historically produced another form of monumental carving: welcome poles, large human figures that stand

near the entrance to a village to welcome guests. The final type of pole was a story pole, narrating a significant event or used to shame or embarrass someone who made the owner angry. In that case, the person shamed was often represented on the top of the pole.[8]

Before the arrival of iron blades, power tools, and motorized transportation, the carving of a pole took several years of work, from the planning, the selection of the right tree—almost invariably a western red cedar—then the felling at the right time of year, the hollowing-out on site, followed by the challenges of transport overland and by sea to its intended location, where the design was ultimately carved. The carving alone might have taken a team many months of full-time work depending on the length and elaboration of the design. The poles were often painted and then a trench was dug to plant the pole. Hundreds of people were, and are, required to raise a large pole, with some people pushing and many others pulling on ropes to bring it into a standing position. Pole raising was, and is, typically accompanied by a potlatch at which speeches are given to tell the story on the pole, praise is bestowed on the owners, and gifts are given to the witnesses in attendance who, in accepting the gifts, certify as true the story and right to the images of the family who raised the pole. Only families who had accumulated large surpluses of wealth could afford to pay for the transport and carving of a pole and the feast required to raise it, so poles were also symbols of prestige and status.[9]

Since the very first arrival of Europeans in the Northwest, there has been an active exchange of Indigenous artistic production and Europeans' industrially produced goods. Indigenous people eager to acquire metal, fabrics, and decorative items traded with sailors eager to have mementos of their visits to the remote Northwest Coast. From the 1820s, Haida were selling elaborate three-dimensional carvings in argillite—a black slate unique to Haida Gwaii—to this small but important market of commercial fur traders and explorers.

The advent of regular steamer service from San Francisco to Alaska in 1883 created an opportunity to capitalize on the unique totem poles still visible from the waters off British Columbia and Alaska. Alaskan visits grew from 1,650 in 1884 to over 5,000 in 1890 as the Pacific Coast Steamship line started to advertise the trip as the "totem pole route" and Alaska as "the land of the totem-pole."[10] Indigenous carvers met the tourist demand for totems with miniature replicas. The earliest known example was carved from argillite and acquired in Victoria by the photographer Frederick Dally in the mid-1860s.[11] Some miniatures were carved by professional artists such as Haida Charles Edenshaw, who was active between 1870 and 1920. Edenshaw's replicas, which were over a metre high, are recognized today as exquisite works of craftsmanship.[12]

For museums, full-size totem poles became the holy grail of ethnographic prizes, and collectors rushed to the Northwest Coast to purchase or, in many cases, simply remove poles from deserted villages without permission, as did some Seattleites who, in 1899, stole a pole from Tongass and erected it in Pioneer Square in their city as a "municipal landmark."[13]

British Columbia was slower to recognize the tourist appeal of the totem pole. In 1903, the Tourist Association of Victoria rejected an artist's suggestion of "an Indian" for the cover of a promotional book because local prejudice against Indigenous peoples had convinced the association "to avoid using Indians in our illustrations as much as possible."[14] By the 1920s, things were changing. In Vancouver, the city had expelled actual Coast Salish Indigenous people from their historic village site in what had become Stanley Park, while a group of citizens in the Art Historical and Scientific Association of Vancouver were attempting to create a mock northern Indian village on the same site to attract

The Landsberg store selling totems and Indigenous art, Victoria, 1901.

tourists. They succeeded in purchasing four Kwakwa̱ka̱'wakw totem poles and erected them on the former Squamish village site, establishing it as one of Vancouver's premier tourist attractions. In 1936, the association added three new poles, and in 1941 Victoria opened Thunderbird Park, its version of an outdoor totem pole museum, which was also located on a former village site.[15]

The demand for low-cost miniature totem poles for the tourist market exceeded the willingness of West Coast carvers to provide such commodities, and so businesses, like Seattle's Ye Olde Curiosity Shop, found in the 1920s that they could supply poles carved in Japan from cow bone.[16] Today, the carved wooden totems sold in tourist shops are imported from Indonesia, and resin or plastic poles, cast in standard molds, are sold at almost every tourist shop in Canada, alongside their miniature northern cousin, the inuksuk.

But back to the story of the making of a national icon: in 1927, the year after Jackson and Holgate visited the Skeena poles and, significantly, the sixtieth anniversary of Canadian Confederation, Marius Barbeau co-organized a show with the National Gallery of Canada—the "Exhibition of Canadian West Coast Art: Native and Modern"—that brought totem poles to the political, cultural, and tourist capitals of Canada. Prime Minister Mackenzie King attended the opening in Ottawa in 1927.[17] The show travelled to Montreal and Toronto in 1928 and introduced both the totem pole and the as yet unknown Emily Carr—whose work frequently featured totem poles—to the national scene alongside the artifacts of West Coast Indigenous people.

"History in Canadian art was made," wrote the Toronto *Globe*, "showing what a tremendous influence the vanishing civilization of the West Coast Indian is having on the minds of Canadian artists."[18] Holgate's woodcuts, Jackson's illustrations, and Carr's new fame all spread the image of the totem as part of the patrimony of Canadian culture and a unique representation of the country. At the same time, Mackenzie King and his colleagues in Parliament were doing their part to erase First Nations from Canada. Having earlier banned the potlatch needed to raise totems, in 1927 Parliament prohibited Indigenous people from hiring lawyers to reclaim their land.

Yet the totem had caught the national imagination. Within a year, the first totem pole to grace a Canadian postage stamp appeared. The pole, the *Spesanish* (or Half-Bear Den) from Kitwanga, had been copied from a photograph by Marius Barbeau.

But Barbeau was not done. He convinced the CNR to commission Holgate to redesign the Jasper Tea Room in its signature hotel, the Château Laurier, in the "Skeena River Indian style."[19] Opened to great acclaim in 1929, this restaurant in the heart of Ottawa's cultural and political centre had the pillars designed as faux totem poles, and applied totem motifs to the lamps and

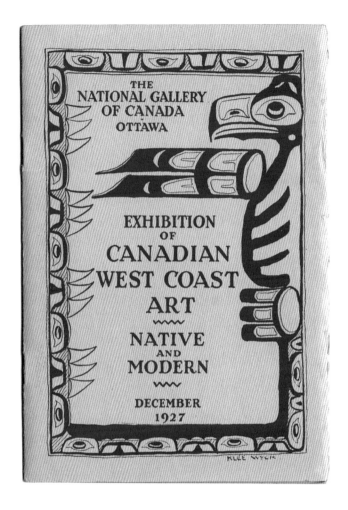

1927 exhibit catalogue designed by Emily Carr—and signed with her *nom de plume*, Klee Wyck—introducing totem poles to the Canadian art world.

This 1928 stamp was the first exposure most Canadians had to totem poles. The stamp shows Mount Hurd framed with the Spesanish (Half-Bear Den) pole from a photo by Marius Barbeau.

other features. Writer Merrill Dennison described it as "the most Canadian room in Canada," while Barbeau described it as "the symbol of our growing aspirations toward nationhood and a culture that will be our own, our contribution to the world at large."[20] In the eyes of both the media and the arts establishment, the totem had been bequeathed to the whole nation by a disappearing race.

In the end, the artist and the anthropologist were elated but the politician disgusted. Prime Minister King, a regular at the Tea Room, had called the 1927 West Coast Art exhibition "barbaric," an adjective he also later used to express his view of totem poles. For his role in creating the Jasper Tea Room, King thought Holgate should face eternal damnation.[21]

While totem poles had definitely arrived as part of the national imagination, if not a part of the prime minister's, they had not yet hit the road as Canada's international ambassadors— but that was about to change. The 1929 opening of the Jasper Tea Room coincided with the onset of the Great Depression and the attendant, and dramatic, drop in tourism. R. B. Bennett, by then prime minister, created a Senate Committee in 1934 to promote tourism. Within months the Canadian Government Travel Bureau was born and in 1935, fifty years since the potlatch had been banned, it published its first promotional booklet. Aimed at American tourists, *Canada, Your Friendly Neighbor Invites You* had on its cover, among many other iconic symbols of Canada, two totem poles.[22] It was the symbol's breakout appearance as a piece of national tourist promotional material. Two years later, when Canada created its pavilion for the Paris International Exhibition, a totem pole stood beside the main door.[23]

In Canada, the revival of totem pole carving began in Vancouver in the 1940s with Ellen Neel, granddaughter of the famous Kwakwaka'wakw carver Charlie James. While this had largely been a male pursuit, Neel began carving model poles in 1946 in Vancouver after her husband had a stroke. In 1948, the Vancouver Parks Board offered Neel space for a carving studio and shop in Stanley Park, not far from the "Totem Park." While Neel mostly carved miniature totems for tourists, including an order of five thousand from the Hudson's Bay Company stores, she also carved some of the first new standing poles to be produced in British Columbia in the twentieth century, including a sixteen-foot pole for the University of British Columbia (UBC) and a large pole for the annual Pacific National Exhibition. In 1949, UBC also invited Neel to restore some poles in its Museum of Anthropology. She did so for a year, but preferring to create her own, she introduced her uncle Mungo Martin to the museum. Martin worked at the museum from 1949 to 1951, when he was hired by Wilson Duff of the British Columbia Provincial Museum in Victoria to restore its poles and to carve replicas.[24]

Jasper Tea Room, Château Laurier, designed by Edwin Holgate in the "Skeena River Totem Pole" style and opened in 1929.

Martin's hiring coincided with the removal of the potlatch prohibition from the *Indian Act*. During the decade that he was chief carver at the BC Provincial Museum, he also carved numerous new poles for the museum, as well as for provincial and federal celebrations. He trained a new generation of carvers, who formed the basis for a renaissance of totem pole carving in the 1960s and 1970s. Martin also formalized an entirely new form of totem that might be called the "Commemoration Pole." To commemorate the centenary of British Columbia's creation as a colony in 1858, Martin was commissioned to create two identical thirty-metre poles, one to be raised in Vancouver on the grounds of the Maritime Museum and the other to be given to Queen Elizabeth and raised in Windsor Great Park. To mark Canada's one hundredth birthday in 1967, the BC Centennial Committee commissioned twenty poles to be placed around the province.[25]

Totem poles appear with other icons on the first federal tourist-promotion literature.

Ellen Neel carving a pole in her Stanley Park studio in 1953.

Totem in the Grand Hall of the Canadian Museum of History across the Ottawa River from Parliament.

And in 1971, to mark the centenary of British Columbia's entry into Confederation, more totems were commissioned—this time thirteen fifteen-foot-high poles—as gifts to each of the other provinces and territories and one for Confederation Park in Ottawa.

Today, totem pole kitsch, plastic miniatures, and totem emblems are on everything from tea towels to water bottles, and from pepper shakers to Playmobil kits, and they can be found in virtually every tourist shop in Canada. But there is also a new generation of full-sized totem poles—monumental structures commissioned by governments, museums, corporations, and First Nations communities—that serve as towering pieces of art, and which tell a different story than that told by Barbeau and Holgate in the 1920s.

This new generation of three-dimensional story poles celebrates revitalized Indigenous cultures, a recovery from the dark years of residential schools, hopes for reconciliation, and the artistry of new generations of skilled Indigenous carvers. Appropriated by Canada in the 1920s, today they have been reclaimed by First Nations artists, both for their own celebrations and for commemorations across Canada and around the globe.

Now, when an anthropologist, an artist, and a politician have a serious interest in totem poles, they take a short stroll from the Château Laurier across the Ottawa River. There, outstanding works from the world's largest collection of totem poles, the celebrated masterpieces in the Great Hall of the Canadian Museum of History, glare with fixed wooden eyes directly at Parliament, where politicians had tried for so many years to suppress Indigenous culture while appropriating Indigenous art.

NOTES

1   Ironically, Hays perished while on his return to Canada to open the Ottawa link in his railway's chain of luxury hotels—the Château Laurier—where the totem story reaches its climax.

2   Sandra Dyck, "'A New Country for Canadian Art': Edwin Holgate and Marius Barbeau in Gitxsan Territory," in Rosalind Pepall and Brian Foss, eds., *Edwin Holgate* (Montreal: Montreal Museum of Fine Arts, 2005), 55.

3   See Douglas Cole, *Captured Heritage: The Scramble for Northwest Coast Artifacts* (Vancouver: UBC Press, 1985), 270–9; Ronald Hawker, *Tales of Ghosts: First Nations Art in British Columbia, 1922–61* (Vancouver: UBC Press, 2003); David Darling and Douglas Cole, "Totem Pole Restoration on the Skeena, 1925–30: An Early Exercise in Heritage Conservation," *BC Studies* 47 (autumn 1980): 39–48.

4   Viola Garfield and Linn Forrest, *The Wolf and the Raven: Totem Poles of Southeastern Alaska* (Seattle: University of Washington Press, 1948), 8.

5   The carved figures may or may not include a reference to spiritual beings who might be considered "totems."

6   Aldona Jonaitis and Aaron Glass, *The Totem Pole: An Intercultural History* (Seattle: University of Washington Press, 2010), 264–6.

7   Julie Cruikshank, "Oral Traditions and Oral History: Reviewing Some Issues," *Canadian Historical Review* 75, no. 3, (1994): 412. Emphasis in original.

8   Richard Feldman, *Here Before the Raven Caws: The Mystery of a Totem Pole*, (Indianapolis: Indiana Historical Society, 2012), 12–24, and Hilary Stewart, *Looking at Totem Poles* (Vancouver: Douglas and McIntyre, 1993), 24–30.

9   Ibid.

10 Jonaitis and Glass, *The Totem Pole*, 62–3.

11 Peter L. McNair, "Early Totem Poles," in McNair and Alan Hoover, eds., *The Magic Leaves: A History of Haida Argillite Carving* (Victoria: British Columbia Provincial Museum, 1984), 112.

12 McNair, "Early Totem Poles," 113–4.

13 Cole, *Captured Heritage*, 309.

14 Michael Dawson, *Selling British Columbia: Tourism and Consumer Culture, 1890–1970* (Vancouver: UBC Press, 2004), 211–2.

15 Jonaitis and Glass, *The Totem Pole*, 81–3.

16 Michael D. Hall and Pat Galscock, *Carvings and Commerce: Model Totem Poles 1880–2010* (Saskatoon: Mendel Art Gallery, and Seattle: University of Washington Press, 2011), 166, 195.

17 Dyck, "New Country for Canadian Art," 53; William Lyon Mackenzie King, Diary, Jan. 11, 1927. Library and Archives Canada (LAC), MG26-J3.

18 Leslie Dawn, *National Visions, National Blindness* (Vancouver: UBC Press, 2014).

19 Dyck, "New Country for Canadian Art," 64–5.

20 Jonaitis and Glass, *The Totem Pole*, 152.

21 William Lyon Mackenzie King, Diary, Jan. 11, 1927. LAC, MG26-J3; Barbeau to Holgate, May 16, 1929 in Canadian Museum of History, Marius Barbeau Correspondence Fonds Holgate, Edwin, Box B204, f.19.

22 Daniel Francis, *Selling Canada* (Vancouver: Stanton Atkins & Dosil, 2011), 154.

23 Mackenzie King described it as "barbaric." See King, Diary, June 24, 1937. LAC, MG26-J3.

24 Phil Nuytten, *The Totem Carvers: Charlie James, Ellen Neel, and Mungo Martin* (Vancouver: Panorama Publications, 1982), 57; B.C. Indian Arts Society, *Mungo Martin: Man of Two Cultures* (Sidney, BC: Gray's Publishing, 1982), 20.

25 "Totems Mark Haida Route," *Roadrunner* 3, no. 3 (September 1966).

aAron Munson, *Isachsen*, 2018. To explore isolation, loneliness, and the psychological effects of extreme wind and cold, artist aAron Munson spent a week at Isachsen, a decommissioned weather station on Ellef Ringnes Island, Nunavut, where his father had been stationed in 1974–75. Isachsen is 1,200 kilometres from the North Pole.

NORTH

Donald Wright

He was a hero of the British Empire when he led an 1845 expedition to locate the Northwest Passage, a sea route across the Arctic that would connect Europe to Asia. But things didn't go according to plan and Sir John Franklin and his men were never seen again. What happened to them? How could they have been so stupid? Did they resort to cannibalism? Was it scurvy, lead poisoning, or exposure that finally killed them? No one really knows, making the Franklin expedition an enduring mystery and the subject of endless speculation, especially in English Canada. Novelists, poets, and musicians have turned Franklin into a symbol of masculine conquest, stubborn resilience, and romantic futility and, in the process, they have transformed the Franklin expedition into a national myth, a usable story to be told and retold in any number of ways with any number of meanings.

Of course, the search for Franklin wasn't only an artistic search, it was an actual search, and in 2008 Parks Canada and its partners attempted to do what no one had been able to do: locate the HMS *Erebus* and the HMS *Terror*, Franklin's two wrecked ships. But after five searches in six years, doubt began to set in. Prime

Minister Stephen Harper, however, refused to concede defeat and, in 2013, he committed his government to discovering the fate of Sir John Franklin's Arctic expedition before Canada's sesquicentennial. A year later, in September 2014, a team of researchers located the wreck of the *Erebus* in just eleven metres of water in Queen Maud Gulf, not far from where Inuit oral history said it would be. There was a lot of hand shaking and back slapping; even the Queen sent her congratulations. It was, said one team member, like winning the Stanley Cup. At an event to mark its discovery, the prime minister linked the *Erebus* to Canada's Arctic sovereignty and referred to it as "part of our country's broader northern narrative and northern identity," adding that "we are answering the age-old call of the North, keeping faith with the explorers and adventurers who have gone before us, and breaking trails for the generations of Canadians yet to come."[1] Harper's brief address drew polite applause from the Royal Canadian Geographical Society. After all, Canada is a northern country. Any map will tell you that, a point not lost on a young Northrop Frye.

One of Frye's earliest memories was learning the geography of Canada on a large, flat map at school in the late 1910s and early 1920s. But that map distorted Canada's geography, making the North appear much larger than it really was. Frye described it as "an immense ghost" looming "over the tiny inhabited strip along the border." And he believed that it had shaped the Canadian sensibility or outlook: the Canadian question isn't, "Who are we?" he said, but, "Where is here?"[2]

Riffing on Frye's famous question, where does the South end and the North begin? At the forty-ninth parallel separating Canada from the United States? Or at the sixtieth parallel separating the Yukon, the Northwest Territories, and Nunavut from British Columbia, Alberta, Saskatchewan, and Manitoba? Or somewhere in between—in, say, cottage country north of Toronto? Now a summer playground for the very rich, Muskoka

As a schoolboy, literary critic Northrop Frye studied Canada on a large, flat map and was haunted by the enormity of the North.

was, in the late nineteenth century, transformed into an instant North, a quick antidote to the ostensibly feminizing and enervating influences of the city. For his part, historian Arthur Lower believed that the North began where the pavement ended. Reverting to what he called the "primitive," and seeking to recharge his masculinity on long canoe trips in the "north country," he left the "festering" city almost every summer.[3] Still, very few Canadians actually live in the North, and even fewer live in a log cabin, making the North less a place and more an idea, a set of images, and even a "state of mind."[4] Writer Stephen Leacock admitted that, not only had he never been to James Bay, he had no intention of ever going. "But," he quickly added, "somehow I'd feel lonely without it."[5]

Ultimately, the North is a symbol, something Canadians ritually invoke to describe themselves to themselves and to others, and to differentiate Canada from the United States. Confederation-era politician George Alexander, for example, hoped that one day Canada would take its place among the nations of the world as "a great Northern Power";[6] author and nationalist Robert Grant Haliburton employed crude racial theories to argue that, because northern climates produce "hardy," "healthy," and "virtuous" men with an instinct for "freedom," "liberty," and "the rights of property," a great national spirit would be nurtured "in the icy bosom" of the "frozen north";[7] Robert Stanley Weir included a reference to "The True North strong and free" in his patriotic song that became the national anthem; Tom Thomson and the Group of Seven painted the North and, according to the mythology that quickly enveloped their work, painted a nation; Donald Creighton called his popular history of Canada *Dominion of the North;* Prime Minister John Diefenbaker referred to Canada's national destiny as a northern destiny; producer Bernie Finklestein founded True North Records in 1969 with a mandate to record and distribute Canadian music by Canadian musicians; comedians Rick Moranis and Dave Thomas donned plaid shirts, toques, and heavy winter coats to become Bob and Doug McKenzie, a couple of loveable hosers with their own talk show, *The Great White North;* meanwhile, countless marketing campaigns have used northern tropes to sell everything from beer and chocolate to sex toys and equity funds, threatening to turn the North into a tired and overworked cliché.

At the same time, writers have used the North to explore loneliness and nothingness. In "Death by Landscape," Margaret Atwood considers the enormity of Canada's Near North, a place where a young girl can simply vanish off the edge of a cliff and disappear from time, swallowed by a massive and indifferent landscape, leading her friend (and the story's protagonist) to reflect years later on the landscape paintings of Tom Thomson and the Group of Seven. They aren't landscape paintings, she decides, because "there aren't any landscapes up there," at least "not in the old, tidy European sense, with a gentle hill, a curving river, a cottage, a mountain in the background, a golden evening sky. Instead there's a tangle, a receding maze, in which you can become lost almost as soon as you step off the path."[8]

In "Stone Mattress," Atwood uses the Far North as the perfect place to commit the perfect murder, the body left "to the ravens and the lemmings and the rest of the food chain." Against the backdrop of "fjords gouged by glaciers over millions of years," "who will remember Bob?"[9] The rhetorical question implies its own answer: no one. For his part, singer-songwriter and Christian Bruce Cockburn cannot bear the thought of an empty universe. In "Northern Lights," he finds spiritual comfort in a night sky "full of rippling cliffs and chasms / That shine like signs on the road to heaven." Poet Karen Connelly, however, doesn't find consolation, spiritual or otherwise, when she returns in winter to her childhood home on the Prairies, "a white frozen world." Kneeling to kiss the ice, she cuts her lip while snow angels "haunt the air."[10]

Quebec, too, sees itself through its North, and it even has its own word to describe its northern identity: *nordicité.* Invented by geographer Louis-Edmond Hamelin in the 1960s, it originally meant the degree of northernness as measured by, among other things, latitude, temperature, and snowfall. But in the Quiet Revolution and the reinvention of Quebec and of Quebec nationalism, it became a convenient shorthand for a fundamental aspect of Quebec history, culture, and identity, and Hamelin became "one of the great thinkers" of the Quiet Revolution.[11] In 2005 the newsmagazine *L'Acualité* included "nordicity," in addition to "cold" and "winter," in its list of 101 words that describe Quebec, making nordicity a repudiation of Voltaire's flippant 1759 remark that New France wasn't worth the effort and expense, that it was simply "quelques arpents de neige," or a few acres of snow.

Franklin Carmichael, *The Upper Ottawa, near Mattawa*, 1924. "We have everything out of which to build ideas and traditions," Carmichael wrote in 1933. "To fail to make use of them would simply be throwing away a priceless heritage of spirit and material."

Lawren S. Harris, *Beaver Pond*, 1921. "There are no backgrounds in any of these paintings, no vistas," Margaret Atwood writes, "only a great deal of foreground that goes back and back, endlessly, involving you in its twists and turns of tree and branch and rock."

Jean Paul Lemieux, *Le visiteur du soir/The Evening Visitor*, 1956.
"In my landscapes and my characters," Lemieux said, "I try
to express the solitude we all have to live with, and in each
painting, the inner world of my memories."

Quebec writers and artists have transformed the North into a national symbol: the boreal cold and sombre northern nights in Louis Fréchette's epic poem *La legende d'un peuple* paint a romantic image of the fur trade and the exploration of a continent;[12] the snow-covered villages and scenes of winter life in the paintings of Cornelius Krieghoff draw on the history of settlement in the St. Lawrence River Valley; *Le visiteur du soir*, *Une femme en hiver*, and *Le rapide*, among other paintings by Jean Paul Lemieux, evoke history, memory, people, and winter—or, in a word, nordicity; and the lyrics of Gilles Vigneault's 1964 song capture what it means to be Québécois, making "Mon Pays" a folk anthem. "Mon pays, ce n'est pas un pays, c'est l'hiver," he said. My country isn't a country, it's winter. Vigneault's country isn't Canada either. In fact, he refused to let the 2010 Vancouver Winter Olympics use his song in the opening ceremonies, fearing that it would be played against the backdrop of a Canadian flag or in a "setting that effectively promoted Canada as a country that included Quebec."[13]

In 2012, *Urbania*, the Montreal-based hipster magazine of pop culture, dedicated an entire issue to winter as "a seminal element of our collective identity." Winter, the editors said, "is more than dates on a calendar, it's a state of mind," and in celebrating winter we are celebrating "ourselves as a people."[14] Of course, Quebecers have been celebrating winter for a long time. In the late nineteenth century, Montreal and Quebec organized fantastic carnivals to transform the cold into a virtue and to attract tourists, although it wasn't until 1955 that the Quebec Winter Carnival became a permanent fixture. In turn, its mascot, Bonhomme Carnaval, became an instantly recognizable symbol of Quebec, his red toque and arrow sash channelling, according to Carnival organizers, "les héros de notre histoire."[15] Like all invented traditions, the Carnival describes itself as

Bonhomme Carnaval poses with singer Anne Murray, who is on cross-country skis. One of Murray's best-known songs is "Snowbird," with its reference to a "snowy mantle cold and clean."

Isidore started its own winter carnival. Believing it was a symbol of French Canada, the organizers used Bonhomme Carnaval as a mascot. When it was told to stop, that Bonhomme belonged to the Quebec Winter Carnival, St. Isidore altered its Bonhomme by adding a blue stripe and a wild rose to his toque, two features of the Franco-Albertan flag. It wasn't enough, and in 1992 St. Isidore chose a new mascot altogether, a great horned owl.[17]

In today's Quebec, according to its leading scholar of the North as an idea, "considerations of the north are bound up with the need not so much to differentiate [Quebec] from other cultures, but to define a new unifying symbol of identity acceptable to the Inuit, First Nations, the French-speaking majority and immigrants, who see the cold, snow, and winter as symbols of a collective challenge and experience."[18] Maybe. But Daniel Chartier excludes Anglo-Quebecers from his Quebec, confirming the larger purpose of national symbols to define *and* differentiate, to include *and* exclude. According to Louis-Edmond Hamelin, "le père de la nordicité,"[19] Quebec's "intensité nordique," its awareness of being northern, is more acute than in other provinces, something that the Parti Québécois summoned in the 1995 referendum.[20] The long, meandering preamble to Bill 1, the act laying the legal framework for sovereignty, deliberately linked Quebec's winter to Quebec's independence, the ultimate project of definition and differentiation, of inclusion and exclusion. "We know the winter in our souls," the preamble says. "We know its blustery days, its solitude, its false eternity, and its apparent deaths. We know what it is to be bitten by the winter cold."[21]

Quebec poet Pierre Morency once said that "le nord n'est pas dans la boussole il est ici."[22] The north is not on the compass; it is here. Governor General Adrienne Clarkson often quoted this line, the image speaking to her intuitive understanding of Canada. When she made the North a theme of her tenure, no one was surprised: what could be more Canadian than the

time-honoured and as inspired by "the traditional Québécois way of life."[16] But behind such "time-honoured" Québécois traditions as "Selfies with Bonhomme" lies a commercial imperative to fill local coffers and sell cheap souvenirs. In short, the Carnival is a business and, like all businesses, it protects its proprietary interests. In the early 1980s, the Franco-Albertan community of St.

Queen's representative sleeping in an igloo, riding a dogsled, and ice fishing?[23] Because the North is so intimately connected to who Canadians are, Clarkson said, for Canadians to deny the North is to engage in "a form of self-contempt."[24] And yet, to accept uncritically the North as a symbol is to engage in a form of self-delusion.

There are at least two Norths, one for Canada and one for Quebec. Both are geographically indeterminate, and both are invested with history, identity, and destiny. Yet both are also connected to real questions of colonialism. The poetry of Louis Fréchette romanticizes the voyageurs as the "brave children of New France" who were prepared to go even to the North Pole to plant the flag, a symbol of occupation and possession.[25] The paintings of Tom Thomson and the Group of Seven are premised, in part, on the erasure of Indigenous peoples and the awful logic of emptiness, that the land was empty and waiting to be claimed. And "Laurentian Shield" by F. R. Scott centres on what he called the North's emptiness and its "waiting" for history to arrive and for a new language to emerge: "Cabin syllables, / Nouns of settlement / Slowly forming, with steel syntax, / The long sentence of its exploitation."[26]

In this way, the invention of the North as a symbol in Canada and Quebec was linked to the colonial project of possession— both the psychic and legal possession of the North—and that project was in turn linked to resource extraction, first fur and later timber, iron ore, hydroelectricity, and now oil and natural gas. In his groundbreaking 1977 report on the Mackenzie Valley pipeline, Justice Thomas Berger reminded Canadians that the North wasn't only a resource frontier; it was also a homeland, in this case, "the homeland of the Dene, Inuit, and Metis." In other words, there is a third North: an Indigenous North. But if Berger urged caution and pleaded for time, he did not suggest that Canada should "renounce" forever its northern gas and oil, or what he called "*our* northern gas and oil."[27] Fast-forward thirty years, when Canada launched the Northern Strategy to unlock the North's "enormous economic potential" in 2007; a few years later, Quebec launched Plan Nord, an "ambitious" agenda to develop its northern resources.[28] Together, the Northern Strategy and Plan Nord fit a larger historical pattern: the North's colonization and "the long sentence of its exploitation."

Read against the backdrop of climate change, F. R. Scott's "long sentence" could be a prison sentence, with Canada and Quebec imprisoned in the logic of a carbon economy based on resource extraction and unlimited growth. What will the North as a national symbol in Canada and Quebec look like under conditions of runaway climate change? That is a difficult question to answer. However, climate change is now appearing in culture: in 2017, Exile Editions released *Cli Fi: Canadian Tales of Climate Change,* a short-story anthology; Bonhomme Carnaval's biggest dream is to reverse global warming; and Quebec neofolk band Les Cowboys Fringants juxtapose the suffocating heat in the present to the snow in the past in "Plus Rien." But maybe it's the wrong question to ask. A better question might be: What will the North look like under climate change where, because of Arctic amplification, temperatures are increasing faster than anywhere else? In *The Right to be Cold*, Inuit activist Sheila Watt-Cloutier paints a stark picture: "The Arctic ice and snow, the frozen terrain that Inuit life has depended on for millennia, is now diminishing in front of our eyes."[29] In *Climate Change*, Inuit artist Elisapee Ishulutaq depicts a bright sun, a melting igloo, and a solitary figure contemplating a tree growing where a tree has no business growing.

The 2014 discovery of the HMS *Erebus* was the lead story on the evening news: at long last, more clues and the promise of more answers. A history buff with a northern obsession, Stephen Harper described the discovery as "historic," and he referred to

Elisapee Ishulutaq, *Climate Change*, 2012. Just a few years ago, climate scientists described the rate of warming in the Arctic as "unprecedented." Having run out of adjectives, they now describe it as "crazy, crazy stuff."

the Franklin expedition as "a great Canadian story."[30] But that story ended badly, a combination of hubris, ignorance, poor planning, and bad luck dooming Franklin and his men from the very beginning. As the planet warms and the ice melts, will the Canadian story end any differently?

NOTES

1 "Prime Minister Stephen Harper talks at RCGS Erebus reception," YouTube video, from speech given at the Royal Ontario Museum, Mar. 10, 2015, youtube.com/watch?v=0SUR4GDMohk.

2 Northrop Frye, "View of Canada," in Jean O'Grady and David Staines, eds., *Northrop Frye on Canada* (Toronto: University of Toronto Press, 2003), 467.

3 Arthur Lower, *Unconventional Voyages* (Toronto: Ryerson Press, 1953), vii–viii.

4 Louis-Edmond Hamelin, *Canadian Nordicity: It's Your North, Too* (Montreal: Harvest House, 1979), 9.

5 Stephen Leacock, "I'll Stay in Canada," in *Funny Pieces: A Book of Random Sketches* (New York: Dodd, Mead, 1936), 291.

6 George Alexander, *Parliamentary Debates on the Subject of the Confederation of the British North American Provinces* (Quebec City, 1865), 82.

7 Haliburton also believed that southern climates produce "enfeebled" men with "the instincts of the brute." See R. G. Haliburton, *The Men of the North and Their Place in History* (Montreal, 1869), 10, 8, 2, 6. Almost no one today subscribes to climate determinism. However, in a short essay on the cold, Quebec explorer and Royal Canadian Geographical Society Fellow Bernard Voyer wrote: "Il [le froid] nous a fait qui nous sommes. Merci. Le froid, c'est le défi, l'obstacle qui fait l'homme plus intelligent, plus créatif, plus fort. Il

fait les meilleurs ingénieurs, car l'appareil qui fonctionne à -20 fonction-nera partout." See Bernard Voyer, «Froid,» *L'Acualité* 30, no. 20 (Dec. 15, 2005): 70.

8 Margaret Atwood, "Death by Landscape," in *Wilderness Tips* (Toronto: McClelland and Stewart, 1991), 128–9.

9 Margaret Atwood, "Stone Mattress," in *Stone Mattress: Nine Tales* (Toronto: McClelland and Stewart, 2014), 220, 222.

10 Karen Connelly, "I Kneel To Kiss The Ice," in *This Brighter Prison: A Book of Journeys* (London, ON: Brick Books, 1993), 73–5.

11 Daniel Chartier and Jean Désy, *La Nordicité du Québec: Entretiens avec Louis-Edmond Hamelin* (Quebec City: Presses de l'Université du Québec, 2014), 3.

12 Louis Fréchette, *La legende d'un peuple* (Paris, 1887). In Fréchette's case, it was a conscious repudiation of Voltaire. See "Sous la statue de Voltaire," in *La legende d'un peuple*. Available online at ebooksgratuits.com/pdf/frechette-p6.pdf.

13 John Furlong, *Patriot Hearts: Inside the Olympics that Changed a Country* (Toronto: Douglas and McIntyre, 2011), 185.

14 "L'hiver est fini, vive l'hiver," *Urbania* 33 (Spring 2012): 4. Translation mine.

15 "Bonhomme Carnaval," carnaval.qc.ca/carnaval/bonhomme-carnaval.

16 "Our History," carnaval.qc.ca/carnaval/our-history.

17 Gisèle Bouchard, "C'était aussi notre bonhomme: discours autour d'un symbole perdu," *Rabaska* 2 (2004): 91–106.

18 Daniel Chartier, "The North and the Great Expanse: Representations of the North and Narrative Forms in French-Canadian Literature," *British Journal of Canadian Studies* 19, no. 1 (2006): 34.

19 Réginald Harvey, "Louis-Edmond Hamelin, père de la nordicité," *Le Devoir* (Montreal), Aug. 6, 2011.

20 Louis-Edmond Hamelin, "Nordicité," *L'Acualité* 30, no. 20 (Dec. 15, 2005): 119.

21 *An Act respecting the future of Québec*, Quebec National Assembly, 1995.

22 Pierre Morency, "lieu de naissance," in *Season for Birds: Selected Poems* (Toronto: Exile Editions, 1990), 56.

23 On Clarkson's visit to Nunavik in northern Quebec, see "The true north, strong and free," *Globe and Mail* (Toronto), Mar. 24, 2011.

24 Adrienne Clarkson, "Speech on the Occasion of a Doctor honoris causa from St. Petersburg State Mining Institute," St. Petersburg, RU, Sept. 30, 2003, archive.gg.ca/media/doc.asp?lang=e&DocID=4025.

25 Fréchette, *La legende d'un peuple*, 87.

26 F. R. Scott, "Laurentian Shield," in *The Collected Poems of F. R. Scott* (Toronto: McClelland and Stewart, 1981), 58.

27 Thomas R. Berger, *Northern Frontier, Northern Homeland: The Report of the Mackenzie Valley Pipeline Inquiry* (Toronto: James Lorimer, 1977), vii, xxvii. Emphasis added.

28 See "Canada's Northern Strategy," available online at northernstrategy.gc.ca, and "Plan Nord," plannord.gouv.qc.ca/en/vision-2/.

29 Sheila Watt-Cloutier, *The Right to be Cold* (Toronto: Allen Lane, 2015), viii.

30 "Lost Franklin expedition ship found in the Arctic," *CBC News*, Sept. 9, 2014, cbc.ca/news/politics/lost-franklin-expedition-ship-found-in-the-arctic-1.2760311.

Discovered in 1945 on King William Island, North West Territories (now Nunavut), were the skeletal remains of a handful of the men on the Franklin expedition.

"Our Country & Our Game": emblem of the National Lacrosse Association of Canada, designed by John Henry Walker, c.1867. Notice the sun shining on an abundance of national symbols: the lacrosse sticks, the beaver, and maple leaves, with the British flag flying protectively overhead.

LACROSSE

Gillian Poulter

It's far from controversial to claim that sport is a marker of national identity—after all, Canadians today have no problem identifying ice hockey as a potent symbol of Canada. But it might be more surprising to learn that in the late nineteenth century it was lacrosse that was hailed as "Canada's National Game." Yet lacrosse was not originally a sport; it was the sacred Indigenous ritual of *baggataway* or *tewaarathon*, performed for a variety of spiritual purposes. How, then, did *baggataway* become the modern, organized sport of lacrosse and an official symbol of Canada and of Canadians? Colonial appropriation played a key role in this development, as did a nascent desire to differentiate English-Canadian identity from its British counterpart.

What we have come to know as lacrosse was played throughout North America long before European explorers and settlers set foot on the continent.[1] The forms differed somewhat, as did the purpose of the game, but all were played in accordance with ancient belief systems. Under the supervision of a spiritual leader, balls and sticks were imbued with magical properties, and players underwent purification rituals before the game. Lacrosse was first taken up by British colonists in Montreal, so it was the

35122

Messrs. Beers and Stevenson playing lacrosse, Montreal, QC, 1868. Part of a series of photographs taken for the frontispiece of W. George Beers's book *Lacrosse: The National Game of Canada.* This pose demonstrates throwing and goalkeeping. Notice the length and shape of the stick, which would have been purchased from local Indigenous producers.

long Haudenosaunee stick with its triangular flat pocket made of leather and gut webbing, crafted and used by players from nearby reserves at Caughnawaga (present day Kahnawake) and St. Regis (Akwesasne), that became the model for the stick used in today's game.[2]

When early explorers and French missionaries first encountered *baggataway*, they likened it to what they knew, comparing it to tennis or an early form of badminton, even though it was played—unlike these European racquet sports—by any number of participants over an equally indeterminate expanse of land. It is commonly thought that a French missionary, Father Le Mercier, gave lacrosse its name in the 1630s when he likened the shape of the stick to a bishop's crozier, but it was more likely because the term *jouer à la crosse* referred in France to any game played with a curved stick and ball. Although they found Indigenous toboggans, canoes, and snowshoes indispensable, lacrosse proved to be of little interest to French settlers. British colonists, however, embraced it enthusiastically.

The first recorded lacrosse match played by white players in what would become Canada occurred in August 1844.[3] Evidently, members of the Montreal Olympic Athletic Club had been visiting the nearby First Nations' reserves to watch games and wanted to try it themselves. They fielded a team of seven players against five Caughnawaga men ... and lost handily! Occasional matches were played over the next decade, but the game was really only taken up seriously when several white clubs were formed in the 1850s. An exhibition game played for the Prince of Wales during his visit in 1860 promoted the game further, and the formation of the National Lacrosse Association in September of 1867, just after Confederation, led to a huge explosion of interest. By November 1867, the number of lacrosse clubs in existence had jumped from ten to eighty, with over two thousand members in Halifax, Quebec, Toronto, Hamilton, Paris, Brantford, and smaller towns throughout Central Canada. The sport spread westward and eastward in the next decade, and by 1884 there were an estimated twenty thousand players registered in clubs across the country and countless others playing informally in streets and parks.[4]

The Montrealers saw it as a lively, aggressive, and competitive game to play and watch, needing only a good dose of British-style regulation and discipline to turn it into a suitably manly sport. As recent or first-generation middle-class British immigrants, they espoused Muscular Christianity and the values of pluck, stamina, discipline, and fair play made famous by Tom Hughes's novel *Tom Brown's School Days,* published in England in 1857. The rules and regulations developed by the Montreal Lacrosse Club and formalized in *Lacrosse: The National Game of Canada* by W. George Beers, a Montreal dentist, sports enthusiast, and ardent nationalist, became the guidebook for the game throughout North America and beyond. Beers's rules provided the elements of discipline and fair play deemed to be missing in the Indigenous game yet so essential in British eyes; both literally and symbolically, they brought the Indigenous game and its players under colonial control. In effect, Beers "tamed" the game. As he explained: "The Indians' old fierce baggataway has shared the fate of the Indian himself. It has lost its wild and wanton delirium, and, has become tamed into the most exciting and varied of all modern field sports."[5]

Beers claimed that lacrosse was a distinctive game, different from British cricket or American baseball, and as such was a sport that could be claimed as "Canadian." [6] Some of the British colonists in Montreal were disgruntled at the lack of recognition they received when they travelled abroad. They resented being identified as Americans, and felt looked down upon as "colonials" in Britain. Although many wanted to retain their connections with Britain and the Empire, they sought ways to distinguish

themselves as Canadians, and sport is one of the cultural practices by which identity can be constructed.

Published in 1869, Beers's book responded to the call for a new national identity for the new Dominion. He drew a distinction between imported "British" sports such as cricket and curling, and "Canadian" sports such as snowshoeing, tobogganing, and lacrosse. As Beers proclaimed: "It may seem frivolous, at first consideration, to associate this feeling of nationality with a field game, but … if the Republic of Greece is indebted to the Olympian Games; if England has cause to bless the name of cricket, so may Canada be proud of lacrosse."[7] The success of his proselytizing can be judged by the widespread acceptance of his oft-repeated assertion that lacrosse had been proclaimed Canada's national game by the new federal Parliament in 1867—a claim that researchers have been unable to substantiate. Nevertheless, Beers took every opportunity to underline this claim, not least in the title of his book and the design of the banner for the National Lacrosse Association, formed in 1867 at Beers's instigation. It was also echoed in the words of a sprightly parlour song from the 1870s entitled "La Crosse: Our National Game."

Beers was well aware that white audiences were fascinated by Indigenous players, and he relied on this to draw big crowds for the two tours he organized in the British Isles. The first, in 1876, was conceived with the objective of introducing the British to Canada's national game. A team of "Canadian Gentlemen" from the Montreal Lacrosse Club played sixteen matches in Ireland, Scotland, and England against a team of Indigenous players from Caughnawaga. An invitation to play for Queen Victoria increased the tour's prestige, and Beers made sure to include it in the advertising. The Indigenous players' primitive "Indianness" was emphasized by their exotic and colourful uniforms. They entertained the crowd with snowshoe races on grass, "war dances,"

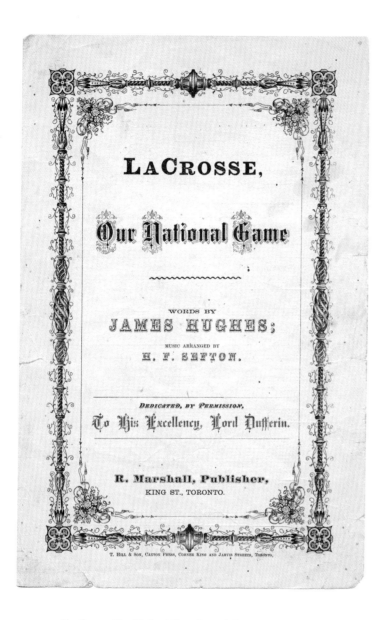

Our National Game

Though Base Ball and Cricket, the bat and the wicket,
Have charms, there is no game can claim, boys,
To yield such large measure of profit and pleasure,
As La-Crosse, our own National Game, boys.

Chorus:
Oh! 'Tis a wonderful game, boys,
'Tis a life-giving, joy-giving game, boys,
Then let us unite in singing to night
Success to our National Game, boys.

With spirits high bounding, and cheers loud resounding,
La Crossers assemble to play, boys;
Their steps are the lightest, their smiles are the brightest,
For thoughts of their game make them gay, boys.

Chorus

How graceful and steady all stand when they're ready,
How anxious are all at the face, boys;
But when the game's started they all, happy-hearted,
Unite in the grand rubber-chase, boys

Chorus

Then with dodging and checking, defending, attacking,
With running, and sometimes a roll, boys;
With catching and throwing, the sport is kept going
Till the ball is sent home through the goal, boys

Chorus

And if muscle and mettle be wanted to battle
For Canada's national fame, boys;
No sons will be truer, than we will be to her,
Who practice our National Game, boys.

Chorus

"La Crosse, Our National Game": words by
James Hughes, music arranged by H. F. Sefton,
c. 1872–78. The song was sung at club meetings
and charitable concerts organized by Montreal
sports clubs.

the "green corn dance," and mock "powwows." As one historian has commented, James Fenimore Cooper, author of *The Last of the Mohicans,* "could not have contrived a more colourful image of stereotypical Indianness for these early 'Harlem Globetrotters' of lacrosse."[8]

The objective of his second tour, undertaken in 1883, was, according to Beers, "to make Canada better known and appreciated in the Old Country," and to attract potential British emigrants to Canada. Although the federal government did not directly fund the tour, it provided thousands of emigration pamphlets and paid for speakers to rouse interest in settling Canada's North-West Territory. Notably, this tour represented the first time in Canada's post-Confederation history that sport was used for expressly political purposes. The chance to see real "savage Indians" was again a big attraction, and the teams played sixty-two matches in forty-one towns and cities across the British Isles. This time the white players were the "native Canadians": they were playing a game that had by now established itself as Canadian; the players' identity as Canadians was underscored by the immigration pamphlets given out at every match; and their frequent wins over the Indigenous team were ostensible proof that British colonists had "conquered" the "savages." It was not coincidental that the tour took place while Indigenous tribes across the North West were being forced onto reserve lands under the control of the federal government—thus making the Prairies "safe" for European settlement. The British audiences' disappointment when the real Mohawk players did not live up to their bloodthirsty fictional stereotypes was held up as further evidence of the civilizing effect of British colonialism.

The Canadian identity that Beers and other nationalists envisaged was distinctly white, English-speaking, and male. Despite the Indigenous origins of lacrosse, Indigenous players were pushed out of the sport; once white players had learned

Sakatis Aientonni, Baptiste Canadien, lacrosse player, Montreal, 1876. Indigenous players were commonly identified by both their "exotic" Indigenous names and their Christianized names. Aientonni was one of the Caughnawaga players on the 1876 tour.

The Canadian Lacrosse Team in England; Game at Kennington Oval, London, 1876. The team of "Iroquois Indians" wore eye-catching red-and-white striped jerseys and knickers with white hose, and each sported a beaded cap with scarlet feathers and a belt and sash made of blue velvet, as can be seen in Sakatis Aientonni's portrait. In sober and "civilized" contrast, the "Canadian Gentlemen" wore white jerseys, grey tweed knickers, and dark brown hose.

all they could from them, they were deemed dispensable. Illustrations from the time acknowledged the game's historical antecedents, but Indigenous players were progressively excluded by rules banning professionals. Since they were customarily paid for their expenses, Indigenous players did not qualify as amateurs and thus were banned from white clubs, although this did not stop some organizations from illicitly hiring Indigenous "ringers" who could pass as white players.[9]

The sport was of little interest to French-speaking Montrealers, who constituted only a small proportion of the members of the elite clubs dominated by English-speaking businessmen and members of the professional class. As colonized people themselves, they probably didn't share Beers's patriotic enthusiasm for Canada's place within the British Empire, and they may have been respectful of the Catholic Church's disapproval of organized sports in general.[10] Lacrosse was also mostly unavailable to women, who were valued in Canada as spectators, but not as players. However, women's lacrosse was played in the nineteenth century in British girls' boarding schools, possibly as a result of Beers's tours. It was valued there as an "unselfish" and "graceful" passing game, requiring speed and skill, but no body contact, and therefore suitable for girls. It spread to the United States when British-trained alumni were recruited to teach at elite schools there. In recent decades, American women's lacrosse has grown enormously, largely as a result of government-imposed equity regulations.

The image of lacrosse as Canada's national game was certainly popularized in the late-nineteenth-century press. In issues of the *Canadian Illustrated News* published between 1869 and 1883, illustrations of lacrosse and snowshoeing (Canada's distinctive summer and winter sports, according to Beers) far exceeded those of any other sport. As a writer in a Boston paper in December 1878 declared of lacrosse, "for years this exciting sport has been identified with Canadian life."[11] Ephemeral items in archival collections are another important indication that the sport was widely known. Sheet music for "La Crosse Galop" by J. Holt, its companion, "La Crosse Quadrilles" by C. P. Woodlawn,

and an arrangement of "La Crosse Waltzes," were published in Toronto between 1867 and 1884. Music for piano entitled "The lacrosse jersey" by Nellie S. Smith and "Lacrosse polka" by L. Fred Clarry were published in 1892. An English company, Huntley and Palmers Biscuits, depicted a lacrosse scene on its trading cards in the late 1870s. Victorians could purchase decorative "scrap" (the ancestor of today's scrapbooking stickers) showing a variety of sportsmen, including a lacrosse player. One such scrapbook keeper took great pains to cut out and rearticulate the arm of a rather risqué, semi-clothed female figure, replacing the original Cupid's bow and arrow with a lacrosse stick. At the turn of the

La Crosse: cover art for sheet music, c.1867. Lacrosse sticks and a ceinture fléchée frame the image of an early game between an Indigenous and a white team, thus recognizing the game's Indigenous origins.

Female Lacrosse Player: an altered cut-out in one of the scrapbooks kept by Montreal sports enthusiast, H.W. Beckett. The original strings and arrow from Cupid's bow are still faintly visible.

century, Imperial Tobacco issued dozens of collectible cards bearing the pictures of players from the elite lacrosse teams, and greeting cards and postcards showed lacrosse games in action, at least one with the caption "Canada's National Game."

The Canadian team won a gold medal at the 1904 Olympics and silver in 1908, but by 1914, lacrosse's popularity was on the wane.[12] Rowdy fans, gambling, and wrangling over amateur and professional status meant that the sport was losing its respectability. It was not being taken up by schools or youth organizations, and thus lacked a critical mass of young players. It remained popular in smaller centres in southern Ontario and British Columbia, but these places lacked audiences large enough to sustain clubs. And because lacrosse was no longer played exclusively by Canadians—there were now clubs in the United States, England, Ireland, and Australia—it was also losing its potency as a national signifier that could distinguish Canadians from other nationalities. After the Great War, baseball, America's "national pastime," became the dominant summer sport in Canada, while the symbolic centre of lacrosse moved south to the United States.

During the interwar years, lacrosse was played in elite schools and colleges in the United States on a strictly amateur basis, but in Canada a new form of lacrosse developed. Box lacrosse, or "boxla" for short, emerged as a way for the owners of hockey arenas to sell tickets over the summer. This new form adopted some of the elements of ice hockey: the enclosed rink, seven players rather than ten, substitution of players during play, three twenty-minute periods, and some tolerance for rough play and fighting. This made for a faster-paced game that was frequently criticized for being too commercial and too violent, but it was very popular in Canada and largely replaced the field game in the 1930s. However, boxla didn't have enough mass support or geographic spread to warrant the old claim of Canada's national

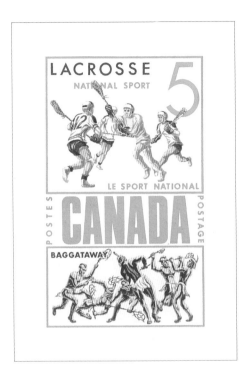

Canadian centenary postage designs:
Top left: Lacrosse the National Sport, 1967;
top right: La Crosse, 1968; bottom: Lacrosse
National Game of Canada, First day cover.
All three stamps acknowledge the Indigenous
roots of lacrosse, but represent white players
as having taken over the modern game.

game, and competition for an audience from television, baseball, and the Canadian Football League meant that its popularity waned after the Second World War.

In 1965, a private members' bill to have lacrosse officially named as Canada's national game provoked criticism that the game was not played widely enough, either in terms of its geographic reach or the number of its adherents, to merit such a designation. The bill died without a vote, but stamps designed for Canada's centennial in 1967 show that the game's old claim still had resonance, and the design for a commemorative coin issued for the 1976 Olympic Games in Montreal also used lacrosse as a symbol of Canada—even though lacrosse was no longer an Olympic sport. A bill to designate Canada's national game was tabled again in 1994, but this time its intended recipient was hockey. However, an amendment to name hockey as Canada's national winter game and lacrosse as the national summer game was accepted, and the bill passed with little dispute.

In recent decades, the sport has made a strong comeback, with the formation of a successful professional box lacrosse league, a semi-professional field lacrosse league, and amateur leagues for men and women. Canadian teams and players rank highly against their international competitors, even though the game is much bigger in the United States. Many of the best players are of First Nations origin and, as has been the case since Beers's time, their presence attracts an audience.

Indeed, while the white game was having mixed success in the United States and Canada in the twentieth century, the Indigenous game grew in strength.[13] A network of clubs emerged in First Nations communities, where games played an important role as social occasions and in cementing Indigenous networks. The game spread across the country as a result of being imposed on First Nations youth in residential schools as a "civilizing" or assimilating activity. In a nice turnaround, lacrosse was subsequently reclaimed by Indigenous players for their own purposes. Although Indigenous players recruited for boxla teams, and Indigenous teams competing with non-Indigenous ones, played the modern, competitive version, the sacred and healing aspects of "the Creator's Game" were still remembered. Playing on an Indigenous team was a source of income and pride for young First Nations men, and lacrosse became part of the Indigenous cultural revitalization and sovereignty movement in the late decades of the twentieth century.

In 1983, the Iroquois Nationals were formed as a field lacrosse team with the objective of competing in the World Lacrosse Championship.[14] As usual, organizers anticipated that an Indigenous team would attract spectators and gain worldwide attention, but the Nationals had other objectives: they were determined to travel abroad on their Haudenosaunee passports as a way to assert their own national identity, separate from Canada and the United States. However, political opposition proved too strong for the championship organizers, and the Nationals were refused entry. Their entry into international play was blocked again in 1986 when the International Lacrosse Federation Championships were held in Toronto. This time they were refused on the flimsy pretext that their inclusion would cause too much logistical inconvenience. However, they were eventually permitted to compete in the ILF World Games in Australia in 1990. Most significantly, the Nationals travelled on their Haudenosaunee passports, and they competed under their own flag and anthem. They continue to assert this right, albeit with mixed success.[15]

The game's symbolic meaning has therefore come full circle: before 1914, lacrosse was a potent national symbol for the new Dominion of Canada, and the appropriation of an Indigenous game legitimized British colonists' claim to be "native" in their new land. As the white game's popularity waned in the twentieth century, so did its strength as a patriotic symbol. But, today, lacrosse has been reclaimed by its originators and is played as a symbol of Indigenous, rather than Canadian, national identity.

NOTES

1   An engaging account of the Indigenous game is Thomas Vennum, Jr., *American Indian Lacrosse: Little Brother of War* (Washington, DC: Smithsonian Institute Press, 1994).

2   Haudenosaunee is the name the "People of the Longhouse" call themselves, but they were called Iroquois by the French and Five (later Six) Nations by the British.

3   For the early history of modern lacrosse see: Alan Metcalfe, *Canada Learns to Play: The Emergence of Organized Sport, 1807–1914* (Toronto: McClelland and Stewart, 1987), ch. 6.

4   An authoritative summary of the growth and evolution of lacrosse is given by Don Morrow and Kevin B. Wamsley, *Sport in Canada, a History*, 3rd ed. (Don Mills, ON: Oxford University Press, 2013), 78–92.

5   W. George Beers, "Canadian Sports," *Century Magazine* 14 (May-Oct 1877), 125.

6   Lacrosse and Canadian nationalism is discussed in detail in Gillian Poulter, *Becoming Native in a Foreign Land: Sport, Visual Culture, and Identity in Montreal, 1840–85* (Vancouver: UBC Press, 2009), ch. 3.

7   Beers, *Lacrosse: The National Game of Canada* (Montreal, 1869), 59.

8   Don Morrow, "Lacrosse as the National Game," in Morrow et al., eds., *A Concise History of Sport in Canada* (Toronto: Oxford University Press, 1989), 61. For discussion of the tours, see also: Morrow, "The Canadian Image Abroad: The Great Lacrosse Tours of 1876 and 1883," in *Proceedings of the Fifth Canadian Symposium on the History of Sport and Physical Education* (Toronto: University of Toronto Press, 1982), 11–23, and Kevin B. Wamsley, "Nineteenth Century Sports Tours, State Formation, and Canadian Foreign Policy," *Sporting Traditions* 13, no. 2 (May 1997): 73–89.

9   North American Indian Travelling College, *Tewaarathon (Lacrosse): Akwesasne's story of our national game* (Cornwall Island, ON: The College, 1978), 48–50.

10 Donald Guay, *La Conquête du sport: Le sport et la société québecoise au XIXè siècle* (Montreal: Lanctot, 1997), ch.5.

11 Library and Archives Canada, Montreal Amateur Athletic Association fonds, MG28 I351, vol. 16, Scrapbook 1, 116.

12 For the history of lacrosse in Canada and the United States in the twentieth century see: Donald M. Fisher, *Lacrosse: A History of the Game* (Baltimore, MD: Johns Hopkins University Press, 2002), and "'Splendid but Undesirable Isolation': Recasting Canada's National Game as Box Lacrosse, 1931–1932," *Sport History Review* 36 (2005): 115–29.

13 For the history of the modern Indigenous game see: Allan Downey, *The Creator's Game: Lacrosse, Identity, and Indigenous Nationhood* (Vancouver: UBC Press, 2018).

14 The Nationals' story is told by Allan Downey in "Engendering Nationality: Haudenosaunee Tradition, Sport, and the Lines of Gender," *Journal of the Canadian Historical Association* 23, no.1 (2012): 319–54.

15 See, for instance, their experience in 2010: Lena Camara, "A History of Iroquois Nationals Lacrosse" available online at iroquoisnationals.org/the-iroquois/a-history-of-iroquois-nationals-lacrosse/.

An outdoor hockey rink, 1956.

HOCKEY

Kristi A. Allain

"This is the story of a love affair between a country and a game. It's simple really: for many of us it's a sense of belonging." So begins a commercial for the popular television program *Hockey Night in Canada*. Many viewers would agree with this message. Indeed, a recent poll revealed that 80 percent of Canadians believe that "hockey is a key part of what it means to be Canadian."[1] What explains such devotion to a game that, at first glance, can appear to be nothing more than a frenzy of reckless abandon and violent collisions? For some, it is the skill and agility of the players, who seem to defy the laws of physics on a frozen surface. For others, it is the strategy and teamwork required for these players to successfully deposit the puck in their opponents' net. Still others celebrate the determination and reflexes of the hockey goaltender who must contend with rubber discs flying through the air at remarkable speed. The nation's bookshelves seem to confirm Canadians' love affair with this sport, boasting hockey-related titles such as *The Sport That Defines a Country*, *The Game of Our Lives*, and *Hockey Dreams,* while musical celebrations of Canada's official winter sport include Stompin' Tom Connors's "The Hockey Song" and Tom

The back of a $5 Canadian banknote, part of the Canadian Journey series, first circulated in 2002. A Roch Carrier quote from *The Hockey Sweater* included on the bill reads: "Les hivers de mon enfance étaient des saisons longues, longues. Nous vivions en trois lieux: l'école, l'église et la patinoire; mais la vraie vie était sur la patinoire.

The winters of my childhood were long, long seasons. We lived in three places—the school, the church and the skating rink—but our real life was on the skating rink."

Cochrane's "Big League." If you factor in the never-ending stream of hockey-themed Tim Hortons commercials, it is clear that culture makers and corporations circulate a relentless stream of romantic hockey imagery that informs, and is informed by, popular understandings of Canadian identity.

Yet in spite of the prevalence of this imagery—which frequently draws on hockey's link to small-town, northern settings—hockey's presence in Canadian life is complex, contested, and exclusive. The most public and celebrated version of the game is professional men's hockey (i.e., the National Hockey League), whose audiences watch primarily white, ostensibly straight, young, and able-bodied male players. It is this form of hockey that most profoundly shapes Canadians' understandings of the sport's symbolic importance. In many ways, this status is most clearly visible at critical moments when the connection between hockey and national identity is in crisis, for these moments reveal cracks in the armour of an all-too-comfortable story of Canada's relationship with hockey.

As a populist expression of Canadian identity, hockey occupies a key place in the country's political culture. Examples of national politicians using this symbol of "ordinary" Canadian identity for political gain include former prime minister Stephen Harper's much-publicized decision to write *A Great Game*, a history of the Toronto Maple Leafs. Hockey's symbolism works to secure a politician's own "ordinary" Canadianness, especially for one whose urban and/or privileged upbringing might mark them as out of touch with everyday people.[2] Indeed, the link between Canadian politics and hockey has a long history. In the mid- to late nineteenth century, Canadian nationalists developed hockey and lacrosse as distinctly Canadian sports in order to secure a unique sense of self in the British Empire that was also distinct from the United States. Canadian settlers understood that a particularly violent and hockey-centric identity, one that differed from the gentlemanly masculinity of the British, would aid in the development of a distinctly Canadian sense of self. Hockey's more relaxed rules about amateurism, relative to the sport of lacrosse, meant that it became more popular and more iconically Canadian. Canadian men's hockey's track record in beating American teams (which it did regularly in Olympic play from the 1920s until the early 1950s) worked to instill a superior sense of national identity.[3]

Beginning with its entry into the Olympic Games in 1956, the Soviet Union challenged Canada's position as the pre-eminent hockey nation. During the Cold War, Canadian politicians mobilized "hockey diplomacy" as a tool to engage the Soviet Union in political discussion, and, perhaps even more importantly, to assert Canadian "hockey authority" and the perceived supremacy of capitalism over Soviet-style communism.[4] In 1972, the Canadian and Soviet governments decided to pit their nations' best male hockey players against one another in a hockey tournament—something that had never been done because of rules forbidding professional competitors in the Olympic Games.[5] This contest, and Paul Henderson's series-winning goal, remain nationally significant markers of Canadian hockey success. As the Tragically Hip song goes: "If there's a goal that everyone remembers / it was back in ol' 72." But popular myth tends to forget that the Soviet team's remarkable play, and the series' close outcome, precipitated discussion of a national hockey "crisis." For example, after Team Canada lost the first game of the tournament, the headline of one major newspaper proclaimed that "Canada Mourns Hockey Myth," while another emphatically exclaimed, "WE LOST."[6]

While some hockey crises address ideological issues related to national identity, others are much more personal. For example, sex abuse charges levelled in the 1990s disrupted hockey's imagined innocence. The revelation that older men in powerful positions sexually abused many young (and often marginalized) Toronto boys, luring them with hockey equipment and access to an important hockey shrine, Toronto's Maple Leaf Gardens, deeply concerned the public and captivated the media.[7] Likewise, news reports of Graham James's sexual assaults on prominent Canadian junior hockey players revealed a hockey culture in which young men were often vulnerable to sex abuse. The Canadian Hockey League (CHL) responded to the controversy with a

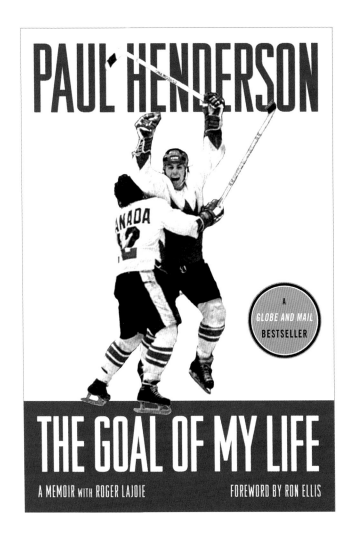

Published forty years after Team Canada beat the USSR in the 1972 Summit Series, Paul Henderson's memoir is emblazoned with the iconic image of Henderson celebrating his series-winning goal.

policy called "Players First," which attempted to provide players with adequate resources to address issues of sexual predation in the league; nonetheless, hazing and players' assaults on women continued through the nineties.[8] Young men's violence against young women did not warrant a CHL report, nor did it generate the same level of public outcry as the Graham James affair. Today, the rate of chronic traumatic brain encephalopathy caused by fighting and body checking in the men's professional game marks a new hockey crisis.

Other hockey crises have frequently involved concerns about American encroachment into Canadian cultural practice, thereby flagging anxiety about Canada's cultural autonomy. For example, Canadians widely rejected the American technological innovation of the FoxTrax puck, which glowed on the television screen to help inexperienced viewers follow the game. As the Toronto-born former ABC World News anchor Peter Jennings summed up the issue: "Canadians will hate the innovation but American fans will love it."[9] The 1988 trade (or sale) of Wayne Gretzky from the Edmonton Oilers to the Los Angeles Kings also perpetuated a crisis of Canadian cultural autonomy. In the wake of free trade talks with the United States, Canadians argued that they should not have to bear another significant cultural loss.[10] They directed their venom toward Oilers' owner Peter Pocklington for selling a national treasure to the Americans.

As various Canadians link hockey to a sense of ordinary Canadianness, others, including many French Canadians, Indigenous peoples, and women, have found that hockey perpetuates both alternative meanings and sometimes marginalization. For example, Canadian women have played hockey since the nineteenth century, with their participation increasing dramatically in the 1970s.[11] Women's hockey became an Olympic sport in 1998, and it has enjoyed television success during the Games with a level of coverage that is almost equal to that enjoyed by the men's game.[12] After a gritty overtime win by the Canadian women's team in the gold medal match at the 2014 Sochi Games, many media outlets asked the Canadian men's team to "play like girls" in their own upcoming gold medal game.[13] Yet such exalted status is inevitably short-lived. Women's hockey receives less money, ice time, media coverage, and prestige than the men's program.[14] Indeed, many people often overlook women's hockey (and women in general) when they present Canada as a nation of hockey and hockey players.

Likewise, popular conceptions of hockey frequently erase people of colour from the sport's identity.[15] While popular culture occasionally represents hockey as a way to bring outsiders into the dominant Canadian fold, it frequently shies away from recognizing the sport's exclusionary history and problematic present. Past celebrations of Canadian hockey players from immigrant families, including Wayne Gretzky and Stan Mikita, highlight the sport's capacity to facilitate upward social mobility. Similarly, the fact that *Hockey Night in Canada* broadcasts today in Punjabi attests to hockey's growing following among ethnic minorities. Not surprisingly, advertisers use these understandings of the game as a way to link their product to leading national ideals. A recent Kentucky Fried Chicken commercial depicts a young immigrant boy finding his place on a new hockey team through the sharing of camaraderie and fried chicken with his teammates, local (and mostly white) boys.[16]

Nonetheless, Canadians' track record of recognizing hockey's history of racism, and the game's ongoing examples of ethnic discrimination, leave much to be desired. Although some public spaces, such as the Willie O'Ree Place in Fredericton, New Brunswick, or the Herb Carnegie Centennial Arena in North York, Ontario, are named after significant black hockey players, the National Library of Canada's recent tribute to the game contains no texts or images depicting people of colour or

Canadian players grimly accept their silver medals after losing to the United States at the 2016 International Ice Hockey Federation Women's World Championships in Kamloops, BC.

The Canadian men jubilantly celebrate their gold medal at the 2016 International Ice Hockey Federation World Championships, held in Moscow and St. Petersburg, Russia.

Indigenous people.[17] Such omissions help to explain why the public has paid little attention to the ways that racism limits some players' access to the NHL, or the ways that racism shapes the experiences of persons of colour in the game. As one South Asian–Canadian player recalled, "I've totally been called the 'N' word on the ice. Like a lot actually."[18] After being targeted in a banana-throwing incident at an NHL exhibition game in London, Ontario, Wayne Simmonds, a black Canadian player competing with the Philadelphia Flyers, noted that he "experienced racism throughout his life."[19] Hockey's link to racism, however, is more systemic than incidents of bad behaviour in hockey arenas. A simple examination of both the men's and women's national team members over the past several years (almost all of whom, save for a few notable exceptions, appear white) tells a powerful story about hockey's link to white people, in spite of (widely celebrated) growing national racial and ethnic diversity.

Public debates about the origins of Canadian hockey often erase the significance of Indigenous peoples in the sport's development. Today, various communities, including Kingston, Ontario and Windsor, Nova Scotia, argue that they are the birthplace of the sport.[20] Deline, a community in the Northwest Territories, also stakes a claim to this title based on Sir John Franklin's 1825 diary entry, which recounts the men of his northern expedition playing a hockey-type game there.[21] Yet these debates obscure the far more likely possibility that a hockey-like game developed simultaneously in several North American places long before European contact, and evolved over time and as a result of contact between settlers and Indigenous peoples. First Nations games similar to hockey precede modern ice hockey, including *alchamadijk,* which the Mi'kmaq played with Irish settlers on a frozen pond with a curved stick and ball.[22]

Hockey's link to whiteness and white people is connected to early colonial myths that frequently attempted to erase Indigenous peoples from the story of settlement, refashioning the Canadian landscape as a place devoid of people. In the words of Canadian humourist Stephen Leacock, "Hockey captures the essence of Canadian experience in the New World." Canadians widely conceptualize hockey as emerging naturally out of Canada's northern landscape, despite the fact that the majority of Canadians live within 160 kilometres of the country's southern border.[23]

This kind of understanding is deeply connected to a European, masculine sense of national identity. Within this national vision, Canada is a land of hockey pioneers or, according to the rant of Molson mascot Joe Canadian, Canada is "the first nation of hockey." In this envisioning, only those (men) who can withstand the brutal punishment associated with settling the North, or succeeding on the hockey rink, are able to maintain an acceptable measure of appropriate Canadian masculinity. Although this metaphor explains the unique and often violent version of the game celebrated by many Canadians, one that differs from its European iteration, it is problematic in that it links Canadian national identity to the activities of young, supposedly straight, and often white able-bodied men and their use of physical violence to dominate apparently less masculine foes. Such an emphasis leaves little room for men who express a style of masculinity not linked to violence and aggression, along with racialized people, Indigenous peoples, and women and girls.[24]

Popular understandings of hockey as a unifying force nevertheless acknowledge the ways hockey cannot overcome other competing national tensions, particularly those between English and French Canada. For example, in Roch Carrier's autobiographical *The Hockey Sweater/Le chandail de hockey*, set in the small-town Quebec of the late 1940s, he recounts a childhood story about receiving a Toronto Maple Leafs jersey (a symbol of English Canada) instead of the jersey of his beloved Montreal

The cover of Roch Carrier's *The Hockey Sweater* (*Le chandail de hockey*). Based on Carrier's childhood, the deceptively simple story about the rivalry between the Toronto Maple Leafs and the Montreal Canadiens addresses very real tensions between Quebec and English Canada after the Second World War.

Canadiens, causing no end of pain and jeers. Francophone-anglophone hockey tensions played out more violently in 1955, when many French-speaking Quebecers took to the streets of Montreal and rioted after the NHL suspended their hero, Maurice Richard.[25] Many Quebec francophones understood Richard, and his ferocity on the ice, as both a literal and a metaphoric challenge to Anglo-Canadian dominance.[26] Some observers argue that the Richard Riot was the symbolic beginning of the Quiet Revolution, a political movement that sought to wrest economic control of the province from an anglophone elite.[27] Hockey, then, has proven a potent symbol not just for Canadian identity, but for Québécois national identity as well.

At times these competing national conceptions of hockey are stoked by incendiary expressions of anglophone hockey masculinity. The country's most recognized proponent of such views is Don Cherry, a former NHL coach who serves as a commentator on *Hockey Night in Canada*'s Saturday night broadcasts.[28] CBC Television viewers once voted Cherry as the seventh-greatest

Canadian of all time. In doing so they placed him ahead of numerous prime ministers, Leonard Cohen, Lieutenant-General Roméo Dallaire, and wheelchair athlete and fundraiser Rick Hansen. From Cherry's perspective, "real" Canadian identity connects to a sense of masculinity located in the bodies of mostly white, English-speaking, working-class men and their on-ice aggression. He has frequently made disparaging remarks about the masculine expression of French and European players. For example, in early 2004, Cherry embroiled himself in controversy when he argued that visor-wearing players were wimpy, and that "Most of the guys that wear [visors] are Europeans or French guys." His comments pushed the CBC to implement sensitivity training on language issues for new staff and to subject Cherry to a seven-second time delay on his broadcasts. These actions produced a media debate about freedom of speech that reached the Canadian and Ontario Parliaments.[29]

Hockey works surprisingly well when it comes to telling a particular story of Canada. The public romanticization of Canadian life as tied to a violent sport developed in the land of ice and snow perpetuates the settler colonialism, racism, and gender exclusion on display in Canada's past and present. Because of this, different social groups within Canada have taken up hockey in contradictory and less celebrated ways. For example, European, French, and Indigenous players often play less violent versions of the game, while women embrace a game devoid of body checking altogether.[30] For other French and English Canadians, Indigenous peoples, people of colour, and ethnic minorities, their relationship to hockey is one of ambivalence or indifference.[31] While many Canadians treasure hockey's symbolism as the game for everyone, closer inspection reveals a more complex story about competing national and international tensions, erasures, crises, and the privileging of some social positions over others. That this is the case is not surprising. Like other national symbols, hockey's

Titled *La Soirée du hockey/Live From the Forum*, this 1999 stamp commemorates *Hockey Night in Canada*'s French-language equivalent and its Québécois announcer René Lecavalier, whose thirty-year career included calling Paul Henderson's 1972 series-winning goal: "Cournoyer qui s'avance. Oh, Henderson a perdu la passe! Il a fait une chute. Et devant le but. ET LE BUT DE HENDERSON! Avec 34 secondes encore!"

utility as a vehicle for commonsense public expressions of identity depends upon evasion, selectivity, and erasure—or, in the common parlance of the sport itself, some fancy stickhandling.

The author would like to sincerely thank Stephanie Dotto for her important contributions to this chapter, and the Canadian Symbols workshop participants and editors for their invaluable guidance.

NOTES

1 Environics Institute, "Hockey in Canada–2012 Public Opinion Survey: Final Report," May 31, 2012, environicsinstitute.org/docs/default-source/project-documents/canadians-on-hockey-2012/final-report.pdf?sfvrsn=7e7e87e1_2.

2 Jay Scherer and Lisa McDermott, "Playing Promotional Politics: Mythologizing Hockey and Manufacturing 'Ordinary' Canadians," *International Journal of Canadian Studies* 43 (2011): 107–34.

3 Michael Robidoux, "Imagining a Canadian Identity Through Sport: A Historical Interpretation of Lacrosse and Hockey," *Journal of American Folklore* 115, no. 456 (2002): 209–25.

4 Donald Macintosh and Donna Greenhorn, "Hockey Diplomacy and Canadian Foreign Policy," *Journal of Canadian Studies* 28, no. 2 (1993): 96–112; Hart Cantelon, "Have Skates Will Travel: Canada, International Hockey, and the Changing Hockey Labour Market," in David Whitson and Richard Gruneau, eds., *Artificial Ice: Hockey, Culture, and Commerce* (Peterborough, ON: Broadview Press, 2006), 215–36; Jay Scherer, Gregory H. Duquette, and Daniel S. Mason, "The Cold War and the (Re)articulation of Canadian National Identity: The 1972 Canada-USSR Summit Series," in Stephen Wagg and David L. Andrews, eds., *East Plays West: Sport and the Cold War* (New York: Routledge, 2007), 163–86.

5 Cantelon, "Have Skates Will Travel."

6 "Canada Mourns Hockey Myth," *Globe and Mail* (Toronto), Sept. 4, 1972.

7 Steven Maynard, "The Maple Leaf (Gardens) Forever: Sex, Canadian Historians and National History," *Journal of Canadian Studies* 36, no. 2 (2001): 70–104.

8 Sub-Committee on the Study of Sport in Canada of the Standing Committee on Canadian Heritage (Nov. 5, 1998), ourcommons.ca/DocumentViewer/en/36-1/SINS/meeting-25/evidence; Laura Robinson, *Crossing the Line: Violence and Sexual Assault in Canada's National Sport* (Toronto: McClelland & Stewart, 1998).

9 Daniel S. Mason, "'Get the Puck Out of Here': Media Transnationalism and Canadian Identity," *Journal of Sport and Social Issues* 26, no. 2 (2002): 140–67;

Aaron Gordon, "Lame Puck," *Slate*, Jan. 28, 2014, slate.com/articles/sports/sports_nut/2014/01/foxtrax_glowing_puck_was_it_the_worst_blunder_in_tv_sports_history_or_was.html.

10 Steven J. Jackson, "Gretzky, Crisis, and Canadian Identity in 1988: Rearticulating the Americanization of Culture Debate," *Sociology of Sport Journal* 11 (1994): 428–46.

11 Julie Stevens, "Women's Hockey in Canada: After the 'Gold Rush,'" in Whitson and Gruneau, *Artificial Ice*, 85–100.

12 Kelly Poniatowski and Marie Hardin, "'The More Things Change, the More They . . . ': Commentary During Women's Ice Hockey at the 2010 Olympic Games," *Mass Communication and Society* 15 (2012): 622–41.

13 Gary Clement, "Gary Clement on Canadian Men's Hockey Coaching Strategy," *National Post* (Toronto), Feb. 20, 2006.

14 Mary Louise Adams, "The Game of Whose Lives? Gender, Race, and Entitlement in Canada's National Game," in Whitson and Gruneau, *Artificial Ice*, 71–84.

15 Robert Pitter, "Racialization and Hockey in Canada: From Personal Troubles to a Canadian Challenge," in Whitson and Gruneau, *Artificial Ice*, 123–39.

16 "KFC Stories: New Kid," Adland video, posted by "kidsleepy," adland.tv/commercials/kfc-best-shot-2016-200-usa.

17 Pitter, "Racialization and Hockey."

18 Courtney Szto, "South Asian Experiences in Hockey: 'One' Narrative," *Hockey in Society*, May 28, 2017, hockeyinsociety.com/2017/05/28/south-asian-experiences-in-hockey-one-narrative/.

19 "Banana Thrown at Flyers' Simmonds During NHL Exhibition Game in London," *NHL.com*, Sept. 23, 2011, nhl.com/news/banana-thrown-at-flyers-simmonds-during-nhl-exhibition-game-in-london/c-589488.

20 "Kingston, Ont., and Windsor, N.S., Battle to Be Hockey's Birthplace," *CBC News*, Jan. 6, 2016, cbc.ca/news/canada/ottawa/kingston-windsor-hockey-birthplace-1.3392158.

21 "Mounties Play Hockey in the Birthplace of Hockey: Deline, N.W.T.," *CBC News*, Nov. 19, 2015, cbc.ca/news/canada/north/mounties-play-hockey-deline-great-bear-lake-1.3325912.

22 Bruce Dowbiggin quoted in Paul W. Bennett, "A Family Squabble: What's Behind the Quest for Genesis in the Canadian Hockey World?" in Lori Dithurbide and Colin Howell, eds., *Constructing the Hockey Family: Home, Community, Bureaucracy and Marketplace* (Halifax, NS: Gorsebrook Research Institute, 2012), 23.

23 Jonathan Bordo, "Jack Pine: Wilderness Sublime or the Erasure of the Aboriginal Presence from the Landscape," *Journal of Canadian Studies* 72, no. 4 (1992): 98–128; "Stephen Leacock," *Wikipedia*, en.wikipedia.org/wiki/Stephen_Leacock; "By the Numbers," *CBC News*, May 12, 2009, cbc.ca/news/canada/by-the-numbers-1.801937.

24 Sherrill E. Grace, "Gendering Northern Narrative," in John Moss, ed., *Echoing Silence: Essays on Arctic Narrative* (Ottawa: University of Ottawa Press, 1997), 163–82; Tobias Stark, "The Pioneer, the Poet, and the Pal: Masculinities and National Identities in Canadian, Swedish, and Soviet-Russian Ice Hockey During the Cold War," in Colin Howell, ed., *Putting it on Ice*, vol. 2, *Internationalizing "Canada's Game"* (Halifax, NS: Grosebrook Research Institute, 2001), 39–43; "I Am Canadian," YouTube video, May 22, 2006, youtube.com/watch?v=BRI-A3vakVg; Adams, "The Game of Whose Lives?"; Pitter, "Racialization and Hockey"; Kristi A. Allain, "'Real Fast and Tough': The Construction of Canadian Hockey Masculinity," *Sociology of Sport Journal* 25, no. 4 (2008): 462–81.

25 Amy Ransom, *Hockey, PQ: Canada's Game in Quebec's Popular Culture* (Toronto: University of Toronto Press, 2014).

26 Ibid.; Jean Harvey, "Whose Sweater is This? The Changing Meanings of Hockey in Quebec," in Whitson and Gruneau, *Artificial Ice*, 29–52.

27 Harvey, "Whose Sweater is This?"

28 Adams, "The Game of Whose Lives?"; Allain, "Real Fast and Tough."

29 James Gillet, Phil White, and Kevin Young, "The Prime Minister of Saturday Night: Don Cherry, the CBC, and the Cultural Production of Intolerance," in Helen Holmes and David Taras, eds., *Seeing Ourselves: Media Power and Policy in Canada*, 2nd ed. (Toronto: Harcourt Brace Canada, 1996), 59–72; Chris Zelkovich, "Cherry's Visor Tirade is Very Short-Sighted," *Toronto Star*, Jan. 26, 2004; Michael Friscolanti and Joe Paraskevas, "CBC Accused of 'Censoring' Cherry," *National Post* (Toronto), Feb. 7, 2004; Norma Greenaway, "Cherry Rant Spurs Call for Sensitivity Training," *Ottawa Citizen*, July 1, 2004; Kaela Jubas and Karla Jubas, "Theorizing Gender in Contemporary Canadian Citizenship: Lessons from the CBC's Greatest Canadian Contest," *Canadian Journal of Education* 29, no. 2 (2006): 563–83.

30 Allain, "Real Fast and Tough"; Michael Robidoux, *Stickhandling Through the Margins: First Nations Hockey in Canada* (Toronto: University of Toronto Press, 2012).

31 Harvey, "Whose Sweater is This?"; Robidoux, *Stickhandling Through the Margins.*

Mark Donnelly performs "O Canada" during the
2011 Stanley Cup finals in Vancouver.

NATIONAL ANTHEM

Michael Dawson and Catherine Gidney

On July 1, 1967, some thirty-two thousand spectators gathered at Vancouver's Empire Stadium to celebrate Canada's one hundredth birthday. They were soon shocked into silence. Included among the dignitaries addressing the audience that day was Chief Dan George of the local Tsleil-Waututh Nation. He pulled no punches.

"How long have I known you, Oh Canada?" he asked. "Yes, a hundred years.... And today, when you celebrate your hundred years, Oh Canada, I am sad for all the Indian people throughout the land." "In the long hundred years since the white man came," he explained, "I have seen my freedom disappear like the salmon going mysteriously out to sea." "Oh Canada, how can I celebrate with you this Centenary, this hundred years?" he asked. "Shall I thank you for the reserves that are left to me of my beautiful forests? For the canned fish of my rivers? For the loss of my pride and authority, even among my own people?"[1]

In highlighting colonialism's impact on First Nations peoples, Chief Dan George challenged the legitimacy of the 1967 Centennial celebrations, and indeed the existence of Canada itself. It was surely no coincidence that George's speech repeatedly incorporated the title of Canada's then unofficial national anthem. By the 1960s "O Canada" was widely performed at public events, though it would not become the official anthem until 1980—some 113 years after the country was founded. The leisurely pace of its adoption parallels the country's gradual acquisition of the trappings routinely associated with a modern nation state—control over its foreign policy (1931), for example, or the power to amend its own constitution (1982).

Canada's slow embrace of an official national anthem reflected its political leaders' concerns not with Indigenous peoples but with competing Euro-Canadian interests—and the challenges of adopting an anthem acceptable to both English and French Canadians. Today "O Canada" is perhaps most commonly associated with the boisterous preambles to professional and international sporting events, especially hockey games. But it is also the subject of repeated calls for revision and reflection. In many ways, then, Canada's national anthem serves as both a rallying point for popular conceptions of Canadian identity *and* as a symbol of unreconciled political tensions.

Anthems, of course, are supposed to promote unity—though always by defining group membership in ways that differentiate "us" from "them." If "we" are the "true north strong and free," others are not. In Canada, this role has been complicated by tensions and mistrust between the country's two most populous linguistic groups. Indeed, "O Canada" does not exist as a single anthem, but rather boasts a French version, an English version, and a bilingual version. The story of how those versions came to be offers a window onto the complicated and contested nature of national identity in Canada.

On Christmas Day 1916, at the height of the Great War, Anglican archdeacon Henry J. Cody addressed the members of the Empire Club in Toronto. His topic, he noted, was a "timely" one: "The History and Present Significance of our National Anthem."

To encourage loyalty and assimilation, "God Save the Queen" was translated into Indigenous languages. This translation was produced in Lytton, BC in 1876 to encourage pro-British sentiment among the Nlaka'pamux Nation.

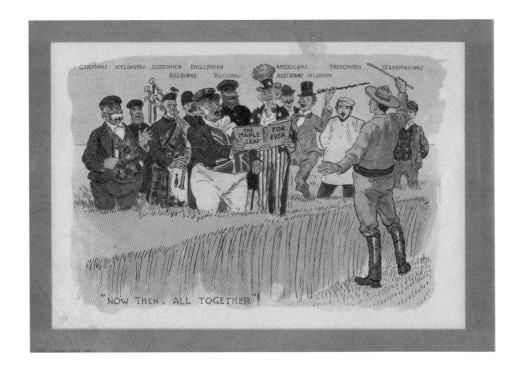

The Canadian government included this optimistic image in an early twentieth-century publication titled *Canada: the Granary of the World*. While the image emphasized ethnic unity and Canadian patriotism, the lyrics of the song celebrated British triumphs over American and French military forces.

The singing of the anthem, he explained, was among the most important "factors in developing and enriching our patriotism." But the focus of Cody's address was not "O Canada"; it was "God Save the King." And the patriotism that he championed was not distinctly Canadian but imperial and Protestant. It was also, in Cody's mind, racial. This "hymn of our race," he explained, represented the "truest expression of the fundamental patriotic sentiments of the British people" and helped to promote "a great bond of imperial unity." While Cody professed a fondness for "our stirring Canadian patriotic songs," including the "somewhat dirge-like music of 'Oh, Canada'," he dismissed the latter as "only a beautiful Provincial chanson." "There is only one National Anthem throughout the British Empire," Cody maintained as he implored his audience to sing "God Save the King" while standing at attention.[2]

For Cody and a great many English Canadians of his time, imperial and national identity were one and the same—an outlook that left little room for French Canadians in their conception of Canada's future. Indeed, the most popular "patriotic song" in English Canada at the time underscored the exclusionary nature of English-Canadian identity. "The Maple Leaf Forever," penned by Alexander Muir in 1867, was essentially a celebration of British military endeavours. Its opening verse was particularly problematic for French Canadians given its glorification of the conquest of Quebec in 1759 by British forces. (Its second verse celebrated British triumphs over the Americans in the War of

1812.) Similarly blunt was the "Dominion Hymn," a poem written by Canada's governor general, the Marquis of Lorne, in 1880 (with music from no less a figure than the English composer Arthur Sullivan): "For God, for home, our legions / Shall win, or Fighting die! ... Defend our people's union, / God save our Empire's Queen!"[3]

English Canadians should not have been surprised, then, to discover that the patriotic song gathering support in Quebec in the late nineteenth century spoke to a French-Canadian, rather than a pan-Canadian, worldview. "O Canada," penned by Sir Adolphe-Basile Routhier and set to music by composer Calixa Lavallée, celebrated the survival of the French-Canadian "race" in North America. Steeped in Catholic imagery, the song encouraged participants to "wield the sword" and "carry the cross" while wearing "the fiery halo" on their brow. "Among foreign races / Faith is our guide / Let us learn to be a nation of brothers, / Under the yoke of law."[4]

Commissioned for, and first performed publicly at, the 1880 Saint-Jean-Baptiste Day celebrations in Quebec City, an annual gathering celebrating the *survivance* of French culture, the song's popularity grew throughout Quebec. In 1901, when the Duke and Duchess of York visited Quebec City, three thousand school children greeted them with a performance. On that same tour, while inspecting Canadian troops in Toronto, the Duke was similarly serenaded with "O Canada"—this time by a marching band—in one of the earliest performances of the song outside of Quebec.[5]

By all accounts, the music itself suggested that the song could become a truly national anthem. But the lack of an English translation and the lyrics' focus on French-Canadian survival formed obvious barriers. Undaunted, and perhaps energized by the challenge before them, Canadians offered no shortage of suggestions for alternative English lyrics. A 1908 competition launched by *Collier's Weekly* solicited well over three hundred responses, though the winning entry, submitted by Mercy E. Powell McCulloch, failed to gain much traction with the public.[6] While McCulloch's submission was infused with Christian rhetoric that had the potential to assuage both English Protestants and French Catholics—"Lord God of Hosts! We now implore / Bless our dear land this day and evermore"—other suggestions retained the pro-British orientation of "The Maple Leaf Forever." One version of "O Canada," penned by a Vancouver bank manager, proved popular in British Columbia and offered a particularly enthusiastic endorsement of British imperialism: "At Britain's side, whate'er betide / Unflinchingly we'll stand."[7]

But it was Robert Stanley Weir's version of "O Canada" that gained the widest following. Written for the three hundredth anniversary of the founding of Quebec, held in 1908, Weir's poem drew upon images and phrases popular in English-Canadian patriotic poetry of the time—hence its references to our "native land" and "true patriot love" in the opening stanza:

> O Canada! Our home and native land!
> True patriot love thou dost in us command.
> We see thee rising fair, dear land,
> The True North, strong and free;
> And Stand on guard, O Canada,
> We stand on guard for thee.[8]

Weir's original lyrics were revised repeatedly in the lead-up to, and during, the Great War. In 1913, for example, the phrase "in all thy sons command" replaced "though dost in us command"—an alteration likely informed by a desire to highlight young men's current and forthcoming military duties.[9] Minor lyrical amendments continued even after the song had become widely disseminated in the 1920s.[10] At one point, some forty-five

OH CANADA! MY CANADA!

My Canada! My father's, my mother's, my children's Canada! My throat is a little full tonight—and my eyes are a bit wet, as I look out over the nearby hills and the barn oaks and the green pine that are my little piece of Canada. What a brave, fine house blows through these trees. How indomitable they stand.

God grant that nothing may happen to this Canada of ours. Grant that we may have the strength to keep her!

Make us willing and glad to make what sacrifices we must that all that Canada means, shall not perish from the earth!

GET READY TO BUY THE NEW VICTORY BONDS

By the 1940s, the popularity of "O Canada" convinced the federal government to allude to the song in its Victory Bond drive—with messages tailored for French- and English-Canadian audiences.

competing versions of the song were in circulation. In the 1950s, the Association of Canadian Clubs attempted to address one longstanding complaint—the repetitive use of "stand on guard" throughout Weir's version—by organizing a national competition for replacement verses. Alas, one official later admitted, "The submissions were so awful that we abandoned the competition about half-way through."[11]

Such initiatives spoke to the growing importance of "O Canada" in public life. But the song still lacked status as a national anthem, despite its official publication as part of Canada's 1927 Diamond Jubilee celebrations and its increasing presence in schools. Canada, many observers argued, *needed* an official national anthem—one that spoke to both English *and* French Canadians, and one that was politically in tune with the times.

Yet the adoption of "O Canada" was certainly not a forgone conclusion. In 1963, the Canadian Authors Association offered a thousand dollars to anyone who could successfully rehabilitate the lyrics to "The Maple Leaf Forever." In doing so, the association encouraged applicants to purge the song of its anti-French and anti-American sentiments and to recognize that the very reference to the maple leaf itself was discriminatory, as it excluded Canadians living in regions where maple trees did not grow.[12] Bemused by this campaign for inoffensive lyrics, one respondent championed the dandelion as the song's central motif on the grounds that it flourishes in every province and, after all, was derived from the French term "dent-de-lion."[13]

The thousand-dollar reward failed to halt the declining fortunes of "The Maple Leaf Forever"—in part because the federal

Montreal Gazette cartoonist Aislin offers his assessment of baseball fans who objected to a bilingual version of O Canada in 1978.

lyrics remained problematic, in part because multiple versions continued to circulate and because some observers found fault with key phrases in Weir's popular version. "Our home and native land," some argued, threatened to exclude those not born on Canadian soil. The phrase "We stand on guard for thee"—appearing five times in nine lines—was needlessly repetitive, argued others.[14]

Asked for their input, Canadians responded with over a thousand submissions. The committee quickly set aside those it deemed "inconsequential, obscene and vituperative," including some that were off-colour, anti-American, or that embraced the exercise as an opportunity to lyrically attack Prime Minister Pearson.[15] Committee members wrestled with the idea of a bilingual anthem—the brainchild of Jo Ouellet, a Quebec City writer eager to see the country's new anthem build bridges between French and English Canadians. Impressed by the high school choir that performed Ouellet's original lyrics, the committee nonetheless determined that a potential English-Canadian backlash rendered bilingual lyrics untenable, as did the complications involved in translating a bilingual anthem into the languages of the country's various ethnic minorities.[16]

In the end, the matter proved too controversial for the government to move forward and Canada remained, at least officially, anthem-less. Hence, debates about what form an anthem ought to take continued for the next fifteen years. With the separatist Parti Québécois forming a government after the provincial elections of 1976, these exchanges moved increasingly into the public realm. Sporting events, in particular, proved popular venues for English Canadians to express their views—especially opposition to bilingual renditions of "O Canada." In 1978, for example, irate Toronto Blue Jays fans repeatedly heckled an anthem singer who had the audacity to sing in English *and* French during a baseball series against the New York Yankees. "If they're going to sing it

government was determined to make "O Canada" the country's official anthem through a process that would also involve public input. In 1964, Prime Minister Lester Pearson tasked a parliamentary committee with the job. It quickly reached a consensus on two matters: Lavallée's music would be preserved, as would Routhier's original French lyrics. But the issue of the English

here, they should sing it our way," opined one fan. "Let them sing French in Montreal," argued another.[17]

Finally, in 1980, the Canadian Parliament reached an agreement on revising Weir's lyrics—one that decreased the number of references to standing "on guard."[18] Since that year, an updated version of Weir's original English-language poem and Routhier's unaltered French wording have shared pride of place as the official lyrics of a Canadian national anthem. An official bilingual version with alternating phrases from the Weir and Routhier versions, is now frequently sung in schools. Like so much of Canada's history, then, the production of its national anthem was anything but a straightforward process. Its development was shaped by competing national identities, diverging suggestions for improvement, and no shortage of government committees cautiously shepherding the initiative forward.

The stamp issued in 1980 to mark the hundredth anniversary of "O Canada" and its adoption as the country's official national anthem.

But the complex history of Canada's national anthem did not end in 1980. Indeed, the symbolic power of anthems is determined not only by how they are established, but also by how, when, and why they are performed. In 2016, for example, twelve people in the Indian city of Trivandrum were arrested at a local cinema for failing to stand during the playing of "Jana Gana Mana"—the Indian anthem that ostensibly champions pluralism. That same year, National Football League quarterback Colin Kaepernick made headlines (and more than a few enemies) across the United States when he decided to kneel during the "Star Spangled Banner" to protest the plight of African Americans. ("O Canada" itself was briefly pulled into that controversy when Remigio Pereira of The Tenors unilaterally altered the anthem's lyrics at the 2016 Major League Baseball All-Star Game to declare that "All Lives Matter."[19]) As such events make clear, anthems are often treated as highly charged political issues because citizens are encouraged to invest something of their own identity in the practice of publicly reciting them. Two recent incidents, each shaped by Canadian military missions, demonstrate both the fact that some Canadians embrace "O Canada" as a sincere representation of their patriotism, and the extent to which the anthem has become a lightning rod for identity politics.

In 1991, with Canadian troops participating in the Gulf War, a small-town-Ontario disc jockey named Ron Carlin decided to show his support for their endeavours by playing "O Canada" on the air every day. The problem? Carlin could not locate a suitable recording. Undeterred, he played a British record featuring a regimental band. The response was overwhelming. Supportive phone calls flooded the station. Aware that their local DJ was not satisfied with the available recordings, local schools recorded their own versions and sent them in to Carlin's show. Troops departing for the Persian Gulf from a nearby military base thanked him profusely for his public support.

Carlin placed an advertisement in a music industry magazine seeking assistance in securing an acceptable recording. The request caught the attention of industry insiders, who combined their resources to assist with the production of not only a new instrumental version, but a "modernized variation" that, they hoped, would appeal to young people. With the assistance of a local member of Parliament, the non-profit O Canada Foundation was born. With support from corporate sponsors, the foundation succeeded in securing the services of several notable Canadian musicians, including Randy Bachman, Alannah Myles, Murray McLauchlan, Maestro Fresh-Wes, and Michael Burgess. The end result of their efforts? Free copies of three recordings (two instrumental and one more "popular") distributed to the country's fourteen thousand schools.[20]

Stencil spray paint in London, Ontario in 2008 challenged pedestrians to consider the lyrics of the national anthem—and their country's colonial origins.

It may well have been one of those recordings that served as context for a nasty battle in a small New Brunswick community in 2009. With Canadian soldiers again serving overseas, this time in Afghanistan, a dispute over the playing of the anthem in an elementary school produced a firestorm of debate across the country. In response to the principal's decision to accommodate religious minorities by playing "O Canada" less frequently, a parent took her case to the local member of Parliament and the media. In light of the sacrifices of Canadian military personnel overseas, she argued, the principal's decision was highly problematic. Despite the fact that his actions did not contravene school regulations, the principal quickly came under attack amidst nationalist flourishes in the House of Commons and a flurry of radio, online, and old-fashioned newspaper editorial vitriol. Roundly denounced as disloyal and unpatriotic, the principal was effectively forced to resign. His supporters, in the words of the *Calgary Herald*, were told to "pack their bags for elsewhere."[21]

Today, "O Canada" remains a contested Canadian symbol. For the most part, disputes about Canada's anthem focus not on how or when it is played, but on its wording. It took at least twelve attempts between 1980 and 2018 for federal politicians to successfully introduce legislation to replace the phrase "in all thy sons command" on the grounds that it excluded more than half of the population.[22] The French lyrics generally receive less attention but they, too, have been singled out as problematic for their overt references to Christianity.[23] Indigenous rights campaigners have pointedly and publicly rephrased the anthem's second line to read, "Our home *on* native land."

Some object to proposed revisions on the grounds that they are awkward or grammatically incorrect. Many others conveniently overlook the anthem's long history of competing versions and revisions by claiming that to alter it (again) would be to turn one's back on tradition. In fact, "O Canada" is very much a living document. Derived from multiple sources, it has been subject to near constant revision and debate. The passion with which Canadians have expressed their views on the subject sits uneasily with the popular notion that they are, unlike their neighbours to the south, ambivalent about public displays of patriotism. "We are, as every Canadian with ears knows, the only country in the world that mumbles its national anthem," says journalist Roy MacGregor.[24] Maybe. But the history of the anthem and its symbolic resonance suggest that while some people have failed to master the words, others have mastered their patriotic outrage. Recognizing and addressing this fact is a necessary step on the country's journey toward inclusion and reconciliation.

NOTES

1   "This day in history: July 1, 1967," *Vancouver Sun*, July 2, 2015.
2   Ven. Archdeacon Cody, "The History and Significance of The National Anthem," speech given to the Empire Club of Canada, Toronto, ON, Dec. 21, 1916. Text available online at speeches.empireclub.org/62030/data?n=2.
3   "Dominion Hymn," Gilbert and Sullivan Archive, gsarchive.net/sullivan/hymns/dominion.htm.
4   Canada, *National Anthem* (Ottawa: Canadian Heritage, 2001), 14.
5   Peter Kuitenbrouwer, *Our Song: The Story of O Canada*, ill. Ashley Spires (Montreal: Lobster Press, 2004), 12–13.
6   Eugenia Powers, "O Canada: shan't be chant," *Performing Arts & Entertainment in Canada* 28, no. 2 (Summer 1993): 8; Kari K. Veblen, "'We Stand on Guard for Thee': National Identity in Canadian Music Education," in David G. Hebert and Alexandra Kertz-Welzel, eds., *Patriotism and Nationalism in Music Education* (London: Routledge 2010), 146; Helmut Kalmun, "national anthem," in Gerald Hallowell, ed., *The Oxford Companion to Canadian History* (Toronto: Oxford University Press, 2004).
7   Canada, *National Anthem* (Ottawa: Canadian Heritage, 2001), 2.
8   For the original Weir lyrics, see "O Canada," *The Canadian Encyclopedia* (online), thecanadianencyclopedia.com/en/article/o-canada/. Both highlighted phrases appear in Helen M. Johnson's poem "Our Native Land," written in the 1860s. See the Canadian Poetry Audio Archives at lac-bac.gc.ca/databases/poetry/001066-119.01-e.php?&main_id_nbr=335&&PHPSESSID=990fpolhh4vo82akujevcoa2g2.
9   "O Canada," *The Canadian Encyclopedia*, thecanadianencyclopedia.ca/en/article/o-canada/.
10 Ibid.
11 Gregory Stevens, "We stand on guard, etc." *Globe and Mail* (Toronto), Oct. 5, 1974.
12 "Wanted Now: An Anthem Without Antagonism," *Globe and Mail* (Toronto), Dec. 4, 1963.
13 "The Dandelion Our Symbol?" *Globe and Mail* (Toronto), Dec. 7, 1963.
14 "O Canada music wins favor, more study urged on lyrics," *Globe and Mail* (Toronto), Mar. 16, 1967.
15 "Facing the music," *Globe and Mail* (Toronto), June 9, 1967.
16 "Panel hears school choir sing bilingual version by Quebecker," *Globe and Mail* (Toronto), Dec. 1, 1967; "Senators, MPs clip the standing-on-guard from O Canada," *Globe and Mail* (Toronto), Feb. 17, 1968.
17 "A bilingual O Canada draws boos once more," *Globe and Mail* (Toronto), May 23, 1973.
18 "Anthem's English lyrics revised by Parliament," *Globe and Mail* (Toronto), June 28, 1980.
19 Alexis Allison, "The Tenors blame 'lone wolf' for changing O Canada lyrics to 'all lives matter' at all-star game," *CBC Sports*, July 13, 2016, cbc.ca/sports/baseball/mlb/canadian-national-anthem-all-lives-matter-change-1.3676477.
20 "O Canada," *Maclean's* 105, no. 25 (June 22, 1992), S1.
21 Editorial, "Oh, Canada! True North strong and politically correct," *Calgary Herald*, Feb. 2, 2009. On the broader dispute, see Michael Dawson and Catherine Gidney, "'There is nothing more inclusive than "O Canada"': New Brunswick's Elementary School Anthem Debate and the Shadow of Afghanistan," in L. Campbell, M. Dawson and C. Gidney, eds., *Worth Fighting For: War Resistance in Canada from the War of 1812 to the War on Terror* (Toronto: Between The Lines, 2015), 229–41.
22 "English lyrics of anthem reflect sexism, senator says," *Globe and Mail* (Toronto), June 29, 2001; John Paul Tasker, "Senators oppose 'clunky, pedestrian' gender-neutral changes to O Canada," *CBC News*, Apr. 4, 2017, cbc.ca/news/politics/senate-opposed-changes-o-canada-1.4053013.
23 Elizabeth Mandel: Canadian bilingualism stops at the national anthem," *National Post* (Toronto), Mar. 15, 2012, news.nationalpost.com/full-comment/elizabeth-mandel-canadian-bilingualism-stops-at-the-national-anthem.
24 Roy MacGregor, "Blame O Canada: The anthem is mumbled by all, its lyrics decried from far and wide," *Globe and Mail* (Toronto), May 8, 2003.

In a display of national pride, and to distinguish themselves from Americans, Canadian travellers will sew a Canadian flag to their backpacks. Taking advantage of the Maple Leaf's brand recognition, and of Canada's reputation for niceness, some American travellers will sew a Canadian flag to their backpacks too.

FLAG

Donald Wright

Calling it a "flag war" and a "flag flap," the national media converged on St. John's, Newfoundland in December 2004 when Premier Danny Williams ordered the Canadian flag removed from all provincial buildings. Negotiations over offshore oil revenues and federal transfer payments from Ottawa to Newfoundland had gone south, and a frustrated Williams wanted to make a point. Although he stopped short of calling it a foreign flag, he did call it "that flag" and "their flag." For his part, Prime Minister Paul Martin was not amused, describing the "disrespectful" actions of Premier Williams as an insult to "our most treasured national symbol."[1]

Both men were right: Williams was drawing on a long history of Newfoundland nationalism when he referred to the Canadian flag as "their flag" while Martin was drawing on a common-sense understanding of flags in general when he referred to the Maple Leaf as "our most treasured national symbol." Symbolizing "us," flags summon a shared understanding of history. But not all of "us" share the same understanding of history, turning flags into flashpoints.

Born at a difficult moment in Canadian history—the rise of Quebec separatism in the early 1960s, the decline of a British national identity in English Canada, and a crisis of national

Prime Minister Lester B. Pearson is connected to a number of Canadian symbols: the peacekeeper, health care, and, of course, the flag. In this 1957 photograph, he is wearing his trademark, if idiosyncratic, bow tie.

The Red Ensign was never Canada's official flag, but to many English Canadians it was still Canada's flag, making the 1964 flag debate a contest between two Canadian flags: the Maple Leaf and the Red Ensign. One group distributed pamphlets with an image of the Red Ensign and the caption: "This *Is* Canada's Flag. Keep It Flying!"

unity—the Maple Leaf was part of a larger effort by the Liberal Party to meet these challenges. Actually, Lester Pearson had decided that Canada needed what he called "a distinctive national flag" even earlier because the Red Ensign—which featured the Union Jack and the Canadian coat of arms but which had "never been given formal sanction by Parliament"—was so similar to the flag of the United Kingdom merchant marine that the two could be "mistaken for each other."[2]

The Red Ensign was also unpalatable to many French Canadians, a lesson Prime Minister Mackenzie King had learned in 1946. When he proposed a new flag that retained the Union Jack but replaced the coat of arms with a single golden maple leaf, some of his Quebec colleagues promised stiff resistance: the Union Jack was a colonial symbol. Meanwhile, his Ontario colleagues promised equally stiff resistance to any flag that didn't include the Union Jack, to them a national symbol. Although

King couldn't understand the opposition of his Quebec MPs, he let sleeping bears lie.

Pearson, however, entered the den of identity politics in 1963, promising that "a new Liberal government will submit to Parliament a design for a flag which cannot be mistaken for the emblem of any other country."[3] At least initially, he didn't favour one design over another, but in early 1964 he embraced what journalists dubbed the "Pearson pennant," three red maple leaves on a white field with two blue side bars, a visual representation of Canada's motto, *a Mari usque ad Mare* (From Sea to Sea).

Although never an official symbol, the maple leaf was an historic symbol in both French and English Canada. The Société Saint-Jean-Baptiste, founded in 1834 in a garden decorated with garlands of maple leaves, dedicated itself to the survival of French Canada. Two years later, its president explained its emblem when he referred to the maple tree—which grows in "our valleys" and "clings to our rocks"—as "young and beaten by the storm," but which, over time, "soars," becoming "tall and strong," finally triumphing over "the north wind": "The maple is the king of our forests," he said; "it is the symbol of the [French] Canadian people," themselves once defeated, but now tall and strong.[4] *Le Canadien*, a newspaper equally committed to French Canada's survival, included both the maple leaf and the beaver in its banner in 1836, for reasons, the editor said, that "hardly need" to be explained: "as everyone knows," the maple leaf was "adopted as the symbol of Lower Canada," like the English rose, the Scottish thistle, and the Irish clover.[5] In the Rebellion of 1837, *les patriotes*, the French-Canadian rebels, carried several different flags, each asserting "the ideal of national independence." One "wholly original design" featured a muskellunge, a pine bough, and a branch of maple leaves. But not one featured the Union Jack, "and the message of that negation could not have been clearer."[6] French Canadians continued to draw on the symbolic power of the maple leaf across the nineteenth century and into the early twentieth. For example, in 1848 and in 1896, two short-lived literary magazines were called *La Feuille d'Érable*, (or in English, *The Maple Leaf*). And the 1920 monument in Montreal's Parc Lafontaine to the French-Canadian martyr and ostensible saviour of New France, Dollard des Ormeaux, included a long string of maple leaves.

But British North Americans, and later English Canadians, also turned to the maple leaf, making it a symbol not just of French Canada, but of Canada writ large. In 1852, Susanna Moodie shouted, "Hail to the pride of the forest—hail / To the

The Pearson pennant was an early favourite to become Canada's new flag. Seeing a marketing opportunity, a costume jeweller made lapel pins and sold them at Eaton's, Simpson's, and Birks.

Designed by Sir Norman Hartnell, dressmaker by royal appointment to the Queen, the Maple Leaf of Canada evening dress now belongs to the Canadian Museum of History. Hartnell also designed the Queen's 1953 coronation dress, into which he embroidered national and Commonwealth floral and botanical emblems, including the Welsh leek, the Australian wattle, and the Canadian maple leaf.

maple, tall and green"; in 1860, "native Canadians," meaning men born in British North America, were urged to wear a maple leaf as "an emblem of the land of their birth" in a procession marking the visit of the Prince of Wales to Toronto; in 1867, Alexander Muir penned "The Maple Leaf Forever," a patriotic song to "our emblem dear"; and in 1880, poet Charles G. D. Roberts wrote that he most loved the maple and "its towers of flames."[7] By 1889, writer William Douw Lighthall could refer to Canada as the "Colony of the Maple Leaf" and his readers across Canada and the British Empire would know what he meant.[8]

The maple leaf appeared just about everywhere: in the Canadian, Ontario, and Quebec coats of arms; in the regimental badges of the Queen's Own Rifles and the Fort Garry Horse; and in the badges of the North-West Mounted Police and, after 1920, the Royal Canadian Mounted Police. It was used in recruiting posters during the First and Second World Wars, and it appeared on the uniforms of athletes competing at international events after 1900, including Tom Longboat, the great Indigenous distance runner from Six Nations on the Grand River. The maple leaf made a cameo in an early version of Robert Stanley Weir's "O Canada," and it inspired place names, literally from one end of the country to the other, from Maple Brook, Nova Scotia to Maple Mountain, British Columbia. Even Queen Elizabeth II gave a symbolic shout out to the maple leaf when she wore a dress featuring a garland of green velvet maple leaves to a 1957 state banquet at Rideau Hall in Ottawa.

Pearson was right when he said the maple leaf is "in our history and in our traditions."[9] But when he agreed to submit the question of a new flag to an all-party committee, he knew that the Pearson pennant wouldn't be selected: the Tories, led by the mercurial John Diefenbaker, would never give him his precious pennant. Making its way through nearly six thousand designs, the committee considered several different Canadian symbols,

The flag committee considered thousands of designs, including this one from St. Catharines, Ontario: a maple leaf, a beaver, and a sheaf of wheat centred between two blue bars, the Atlantic and the Pacific.

An early gesture of reconciliation, this design featured two igloos and a teepee.

Drawing on Lester Pearson's fondness for bow ties, one Canadian cut to the chase: the Pearson pennant was for the birds. Other Canadians likened it to a soup label and a beer label.

including the beaver, the grizzly bear, the Canada goose, the Rockies, the Prairies, and the boreal forest. Several designs, in a spirit of compromise, featured both the Union Jack and the *fleur-de-lys*. A handful of designs included Indigenous symbols. Writing to the *Vancouver Sun*, a group of First Nations students suggested either a raven, a thunderbird, or a totem pole: "Too long have we been ignored, for Canada is our land more than anybody else's."[10]

The committee also heard from expert witnesses, including Queen's University historian Arthur Lower, who insisted that now was the time for Canada to abandon its colonial symbols. Later, he would describe the adoption of the Maple Leaf as the "crowning step" in Canada's journey from colony to nation.[11] His University of Toronto counterpart couldn't have disagreed more.

In fact, Donald Creighton declined the committee's invitation to appear before it. He hated Pearson—he once called him a "giggling bow-tied bastard"—and he didn't want to be part of the de-dominionization of Canada, a process that, in his opinion, had severed Canada's ties to Great Britain, robbed the country of its historic word, "Dominion," and now proposed to rob the country of its flag, the Red Ensign. The whole thing "disgusted" him.[12]

Actually, it disgusted a lot of people: the flag debate was never a debate between a British flag and a Canadian flag; it was, rather, a debate between two Canadian flags. Fearing that Canadians had been "brainwashed into the false belief that Canada has no flag and that the flag which flies over the Parliament Buildings in Ottawa belongs to a foreign country," the Canadian Patriotic Association warned that there are "influences at work

If you must know ... I'm celebrating St. George's Day. Published in the *Vancouver Sun* on 23 April 1964, or St. George's Day, Len Norris's cartoon captured what many Canadians felt: the new flag was both anti-British and a sop to Quebec. One headline stuffed into the mouth of the cannon refers to a perceived sweetheart tax deal with Quebec; another refers to the Quebec Pension Plan which became the model for the Canada Pension Plan.

which appear determined to break every tie that binds our Commonwealth."[13] The Imperial Order Daughters of the Empire, which had lobbied for years to make the Red Ensign Canada's official flag, now pressed the prime minister to hold a national plebiscite.[14] So, too, did the Royal Canadian Legion, a veterans' organization founded after the First World War. But Pearson, fearing perhaps that he might lose, refused: at the Legion's national convention in May 1964, hecklers told him to "drop dead" and accused him of "selling Canada to the peasoupers," a derogatory term for French Canadians. A few months later, a poll showed that less than a third of English-speaking Canadians supported the adoption of the Maple Leaf.[15]

Working quickly, the flag committee selected a design that had been suggested by another historian, George F. G. Stanley,

then teaching at the Royal Military College in Kingston. He described the single maple leaf on a white field flanked by two red bars as a "rallying symbol" and "unifying force" that was both "clean cut" and uncluttered.[16] After a long, painful, and emotional debate, an exhausted House of Commons voted in favour of the committee's recommendation at two o'clock in the morning on December 15, 1964. Afterwards, some MPs pushed and shoved each other while others booed the singing of "O Canada."[17] "You thought the national flag was about a leaf, didn't you? Look harder," Margaret Atwood once said. "It's where someone got axed in the snow."[18] A lot of Canadians got symbolically axed that night, possibly the majority.

Two months later, on February 15, 1965, the Red Ensign was lowered and the Maple Leaf was raised in a ceremony on

Parliament Hill. Relegated to the dustbin of history, almost no one today remembers the Red Ensign, but the Maple Leaf didn't unite the country either. As Pierre Trudeau said in 1964, Quebecers "do not give a tinker's damn about the flag."[19] After all, Quebec had its own flag, the Fleurdelisé, adopted unanimously by the Legislative Assembly in 1948. In effect, then, if not in law, Canada has two national flags, one for Canada, the other for Quebec. Canada has two national anthems as well. For the most part, this works. But occasionally it doesn't.

In the lead up to Quebec's 1995 referendum on independence, which was too close to call, the Liberal government of Jean Chrétien wrapped itself in the Maple Leaf.[20] Conveniently, 1995 also marked the flag's thirtieth anniversary, giving the government a million-dollar opportunity, literally and figuratively, to celebrate a national milestone. It also gave MPs the opportunity to make earnest speeches, each more patriotic than the last. The Maple Leaf, said one MP, "stands for peace, harmony, and freedom"; another said that it "represents a wealthy and tolerant country that is open to others"; and yet another said that it symbolizes "compassion, sharing, and equity." One MP even told the House of Commons, without a hint of irony, that it "unites us from coast to coast," forgetting for a moment that Her Majesty's Loyal Opposition was the Bloc Québécois, a separatist party.[21] Indeed, a Bloc MP questioned why the government had spent $1 million to celebrate the flag "in this era of budget cuts" and accused the government of launching "a vast federal propaganda campaign" in Quebec. A disingenuous heritage minister responded that he was doing no such thing, adding that "some people have a very narrow mind on these issues, so narrow that their ears are stuck together from the inside." The Speaker wisely ended the back-and-forth: "Sometimes these exchanges give me such a headache."[22]

A near-death experience, the October 1995 referendum led the government to redouble its use of the Maple Leaf: Prime Minister Jean Chrétien proclaimed February 15 National Flag of Canada Day, or Flag Day for short; Heritage Minister Sheila Copps launched One In A Million, a campaign to give away one million flags in one year; and a Liberal MP tried, on two occasions, to get a private member's bill passed that would establish an oath of allegiance to the flag. One Bloc MP compared the government's use of the Maple Leaf to Joseph Goebbels' use of the swastika in Nazi Germany. It was a stupid thing to say, but another Bloc MP reminded the House that "our country is Quebec and two, three, or even four million flags cannot change the fact that Quebec will always be our country."[23] Undeterred, the Chrétien government pimped the flag when it initiated a sponsorship program to promote Canada in Quebec: wherever Quebecers went and wherever they gathered, the Maple Leaf would be there. Unaccountable from the start, the sponsorship program ended in accusations of corruption, a commission of inquiry, and criminal charges against the key players. No politicians were ever charged and an unrepentant Chrétien shrugged the whole thing off, saying "there's nothing wrong with showing the flag."[24]

The Conservative Party came to power on the heels of the sponsorship scandal, but it wasn't above flag politics. Refusing to concede patriotism in general, and the flag in particular, to the Liberals, Prime Minister Stephen Harper embraced Flag Day and, on the eve of the 2010 Winter Olympics in Vancouver, urged Canadians to fly the flag.[25] A year later, one of his backbenchers went further. Worried that the Maple Leaf couldn't defend itself, John Carmichael introduced a private member's bill making it a crime, punishable by up to two years in prison, for a person to prevent another person from displaying the Canadian flag. As he told the House, this bill "represents an opportunity for us to stand behind those who wish to display our most important national symbol" but who are prevented from doing so by condominium boards, homeowner associations, and landlords.[26]

White Flag, 2015, by Emma Hassencahl-Perley, compels us to see and read the Canadian flag through the lens of colonialism.

An incredulous NDP MP from Quebec observed that the proposed *National Flag of Canada Act* was "eerily similar" to the 2006 *Freedom to Display the American Flag Act*, the brainchild of Roscoe Bartlett, then a Republican congressman, member of the Tea Party Caucus, and survivalist. Besides, the NDP member asked, is it "really necessary to turn a hapless caretaker, following through on a condo bylaw on behalf of a condo board, into a criminal?" The "last thing we want is the flag police," a Liberal MP added.[27] Agreeing to remove the threat of prison, Carmichael insisted that it was "fundamentally wrong that people could intimidate, bully, or otherwise restrict Canadians from flying our flag."[28] Supported by the Conservatives and the Liberals, but opposed by the New Democrats, over one-half of whom were from Quebec, Carmichael's bill became law in 2012. Because it only encourages, and does not compel, apartment buildings, co-ops, condominiums, and gated communities to allow the Canadian flag to be displayed, the *National Flag of Canada Act* is purely symbolic—like the flag itself.

To mark the flag's fiftieth anniversary in 2015, Senator James Cowan told his colleagues that although Lester Pearson "gave us" the Maple Leaf, it "goes beyond any government or leader"; it goes "beyond politics or policies"; indeed, it goes "beyond even history."[29] Of course, flags are never outside of policies, politics, or history, something Emma Hassencahl-Perley understands. A Wolastoqiyik (Maliseet) visual artist from Tobique First Nation in New Brunswick, she covered the Maple Leaf with thin shreds of the *Indian Act*, transforming what former prime minister Paul Martin called "our most treasured national symbol" into a symbol of colonization and assimilation. Visible between pieces of the *Indian Act* is the colour red, the colour of Indigenous peoples, making *White Flag* a symbol of resistance and renewal as well: despite your best efforts, Canada, we are still here.

NOTES

1 See "Williams declares flag war over equalization payments," *Globe and Mail* (Toronto), Dec. 24, 2004; "Nfld. premier fights for 'fiscal survival' in flag flap," *CBC News*, Jan. 4, 2005, cbc.ca/news/canada/nfld-premier-fights-for-fiscal-survival-in-flag-flap-1.543059; "Canadian flag ordered down: Williams," *CBC News*, Dec. 23, 2004, cbc.ca/news/canada/newfoundland-labrador/canadian-flags-ordered-down-williams-1.505946.

2 Lester Pearson, *Mike: The Memoirs of the Rt. Hon. Lester B. Pearson,* vol. 3 (Toronto: University of Toronto Press, 1975), 270.

3 "Liberal Platform of 1963," in D. Owen Carrigan, ed., *Canadian Party Platforms, 1867–1968* (Toronto: Copp Clark, 1968), 295.

4 "La Saint-Jean-Baptiste," *La Minerve* (Montreal), June 27, 1836.

5 *Le Canadien* (Quebec City), Nov. 14, 1836.

6 Allan Greer, *The Patriots and the People: The Rebellions of 1837 in Rural Lower Canada* (Toronto: University of Toronto Press, 1993), 197.

7 Susanna Moodie, *Roughing It In The Bush* (London: Virago Press, 1986), 516; "Native Canadians," *Globe* (Toronto), Aug. 22, 1860; "The Maple Leaf Forever," in Helmut Kallmann et al., eds., *Encyclopedia of Music in Canada* (Toronto: University of Toronto Press, 1981), 593; Charles G. D. Roberts, *Orion and Other Poems* (Philadelphia, 1880), 103.

8 W. D. Lighthall, *Songs of the Great Dominion* (London, 1889), xxii.

9 Lester B. Pearson, House of Commons, June 15, 1964.

10 Bertha Garner et al., *Vancouver Sun,* c. 1964. Copy in University of Saskatchewan Archives and Special Collections, J. G. Diefenbaker fonds, Series IX/C, box 114, file 268.2 - Flag, nd.

11 Arthur Lower, "Centennial Ends: Centennial Begins," *Queen's Quarterly* 74, no. 2 (Summer 1967): 237.

12 Quotations in Donald Wright, *Donald Creighton: A Life in History* (Toronto: University of Toronto Press, 2015), 260, 263.

13 Canadian Patriotic Association, Toronto, c. 1964. Pamphlet in Public Archives of New Brunswick, Malabeam Chapter IODE (Hartland) fonds, MC2218, MS10 D-K.

14 Lorraine Coops, "'One Flag, One Throne, One Empire': The IODE, the Great Flag Debate, and the End of Empire," in Phillip Buckner, ed., *Canada and the End of Empire* (Vancouver: UBC Press, 2005), 255.

15 "Pearson Booed, Hissed Over Maple Leaf Flag," *Globe and Mail* (Toronto), May 18, 1964.

16 Quotation in Rick Archbold, *I Stand For Canada* (Toronto: MacFarlane Walter & Ross, 2002), 95.

17 "Chretien remembers fight over Canadian flag design as he marks fiftieth anniversary with Trudeau," *National Post* (Toronto), Feb. 15, 2015.

18 Margaret Atwood, *Strange Things: The Malevolent North in Canadian Literature* (Oxford: Clarendon Press, 1995), 12.

19 Quotation in C. P. Champion, "A Very British Coup: Canadianism, Quebec, and Ethnicity in the Flag Debate, 1964–1965," *Journal of Canadian Studies* 30, no. 3 (Fall 2006): 79.

20 Lester Pearson, "The Symbols of Canada Have Changed," *Globe and Mail* (Toronto), May 18, 1964.

21 Jess Flis, Feb. 13, 1995, House of Commons; Ron Duhamel, Feb. 14, 1995, House of Commons; Andrew Telegdi, Feb. 15, 1995, House of Commons; Harbance Singh (Herb) Dhaliwal, Feb. 16, 1995, House of Commons.

22 Monique Guay, Michel Dupuy, Gilbert Parent, Feb. 15, 1995, House of Commons.

23 Paul Mercier, Jean-Guy Chrétien, Feb. 17, 1997, House of Commons.

24 Jean Chrétien, *My Years As Prime Minister* (Toronto: Vintage, 2007), 159.

25 See also Richard Nimijean and E. Pauline Rankin, "Marketing the Maple Leaf: The Curious Case of National Flag of Canada Day," in Matthew Hayday and Raymond Blake, eds., *Celebrating Canada*, vol. 1, *Holidays, National Days, and the Crafting of Identities* (Toronto: University of Toronto Press, 2016).

26 John Carmichael, Nov. 18, 2011, House of Commons.

27 Tyrone Benskin, Joyce Murray, Nov. 18, 2011, House of Commons.

28 John Carmichael, Feb. 2, 2012, Standing Committee on Canadian Heritage, House of Commons.

29 James Cowan, Feb. 17, 2015, Senate.

A *fleur-de-lys*-themed hot air balloon participating in the International Balloon Festival of Saint-Jean-sur-Richelieu.

FLEUR-DE-LYS

Alan Gordon

"Vive le Québec libre!" These words, spoken by General Charles de Gaulle, the president of France, in July 1967, are what most people remember of his famous Canadian visit. But his entire trip, which culminated in his use of a slogan employed by Quebec's independence movement, was a symbolic gesture, from his arrival by ship at Quebec City to his motorcade's drive to Montreal along Quebec's Chemin du Roy highway. Newly christened to invoke memories of French control of Canada, portions of the "King's Road," as it is known in English, were painted with *fleurs-de-lys*. A reminder of Quebec's connection to France, the *fleur-de-lys* symbolizes a memory of sovereignty and of glory.

Widely recognized as a symbol of Canada's French heritage, the *fleur-de-lys* has never been a uniquely Canadian symbol. Certainly, it figures on the flag of Quebec, and it appears on both the Quebec and Canadian coats of arms. But it is also a widely used decorative feature on buildings, railings, and ephemera around the Western world. It figures on the royal banner of Scotland, the Lion Rampant, and on the coat of arms of Florence, Italy. It has been used as one of the symbols of the international boy scouts

Quebec's official flag played an important role in establishing the *fleur-de-lys* as a national symbol.

movement. Yet, despite its wide range of uses, it remains closely tied to French identity. The story of this symbol tells of a voyage from royal emblem to abandonment, and ultimately rediscovery and re-embrace with the development of the Fleurdelisé, the flag of Quebec. Indeed, the Quebec flag played a prominent role in stabilizing and promoting the use of the *fleur-de-lys* as a symbol in Canada.

As a symbol, the *fleur-de-lys* has a long history. Its origins are lost to memory, yet it is clearly tied to European cultural traditions. In medieval Europe, it appeared on the dynastic coats of arms of numerous kingdoms and principalities. In France, its use dates from the reign of Clovis I, first king of the Franks, who wore a robe bedecked with the image at the baptism that marked his conversion to Christianity in the late fifth century. Some have speculated that the flower's three petals may represent the Holy Trinity or the three estates of medieval France: the commoners,

the nobility, and the clergy.[1] And indeed, it is with France—and especially the House of Bourbon—that the symbol is most commonly associated. Although abolished during the French Revolution as a sign of the monarchy, and never again adopted by the French government, the *fleur-de-lys* is often held up as a symbol of French ethnicity. In North America, it is widely seen as a symbol of francophone culture, and it has been featured not only on the Quebec flag, but on the flags of a number of other French-speaking communities in Canada and the United States.

The *fleur-de-lys* was introduced to Canada by the earliest French explorers and colonists. Its first recorded appearance in North America came on July 24, 1534, when, at the end of his first voyage of exploration, Jacques Cartier raised a thirty-foot wooden cross emblazoned with the motto "vive le roi de France" and three *fleurs-de-lys*. Although Samuel de Champlain did not make use of the *fleur-de-lys*, subsequent governors of New France did. Louis de Buade de Frontenac even created a coat of arms for Quebec City comprised of a beaver, a moose, and the *fleur-de-lys*. During the French colonial period, it symbolized the legitimacy and power of the monarchy. As such, it was used to make claims of possession. For instance, in 1671 a cross bearing the king's arms was raised at Sault-Ste-Marie to stake a claim of possession of the interior of North America.

Under the reign of Louis XIV, prisoners were sometimes branded with the *fleur-de-lys* to mark them as guilty. Known as a "prisoner's brand," in 1681 this penalty was inflicted on *coureurs de bois* who engaged in the illegal fur trade. Those convicted of more serious crimes, such as theft, murder, or rape, were branded with a *fleur-de-lys* before their execution. The brand signified the king's sanction for their punishment and thus affirmed his sovereignty.

When France ceded Canada to Britain at the end of the Seven Years' War in 1763, this symbol of French sovereignty was

Charles Walter Simpson, *Jacques Cartier at Gaspé, 1534.* Cartier's men are depicted raising a cross adorned with three *fleurs-de-lys* at Gaspé in 1534. This was the first recorded appearance of the *fleur-de-lys* in Canada.

abandoned and new symbols emerged to represent the French-Canadian people. The political leaders of patriotic French Canada selected the maple leaf as their emblem, and they designed a red, white, and green tricolour flag as their banner. Even after the armed insurrection known as the Rebellions of 1837–38 failed, the old symbols of the maple leaf and the beaver continued to be employed as emblems of the people. As French-Canadian society became more religious, these symbols were joined by the figure of John the Baptist, the people's unofficial patron saint. Through the nineteenth century, the publicization of Saint-Jean-Baptiste Day events in newspapers were routinely accompanied by decorative maple garlands, while the triumphal arches that adorned parade routes were often constructed from leafy maple boughs.

At about the same time, the *fleur-de-lys* began its slow return to the symbolic landscape. It was in the 1840s that one of the founders of the patriotic Saint-Jean-Baptiste Association of Quebec City, Louis de Gonzague Baillairgé, became interested in recovering lost relics of New France. One of the relics Baillairgé located was a flag flown by French troops who, under the command of Louis de Montcalm, had defeated a superior British Army at the Battle of Carillon in 1758. Popularly believed to have been carried into battle by French-Canadian militia troops, according to legend this flag was brought home to Quebec City with the message of victory by the chaplain of the French Army and preserved in a church in the city. Although no one has questioned the age of the flag, some have doubted its connection to the famous battle.[2] Nevertheless, the flag, now known as the Carillon flag, came to be associated with religious nationalism among French Canadians. Greatly faded when discovered in the 1840s, Baillairgé could make out a coat of arms and *fleurs-de-lys* pointing diagonally from the corners to the centre of the banner.

Baillairgé was also involved in the discovery of the remains of French soldiers killed in the Battle of Sainte-Foy in 1760, and the effort to construct a monument to their memory. When the remains of these soldiers were reinterred on the Plains of Abraham in 1854, the Carillon flag, enclosed in a protective case, preceded the ceremonial procession.[3]

Alongside renewed pride in the preservation of French culture, this event was the impetus for the creation of new symbols of French heritage in the Americas. In 1855, for example, in an event that foreshadowed de Gaulle's visit over a century later, the French warship *La Capricieuse* paid a visit to Canada on a trade and good will mission. This, the first official French visit to Canada since the fall of New France in the 1760s, was widely hailed as the "return of the *fleur-de-lys*." The event inspired Octave Crémazie to compose one of his more famous poems, "Le Drapeau de Carillon: légende Canadien," a thirty-two-stanza verse commemorating the battle. However, most nationalists continued to favour the maple leaf as their symbol.

The Carillon flag was later adopted by Papal Zouaves, civilian volunteers who undertook the military defence of the papacy in the 1860s. Upon their return to Canada, the Zouave volunteers carried Baillairgé's banner at the head of their parades, rolled up and stored in a cloth case. The symbol's connection to sacrifice and faith was cemented. In 1868, Quebec's official coat of arms, approved by Queen Victoria, displayed two *fleurs-de-lys* above a lion and maple leaves. However, as English Canadians began adopting the maple leaf as their emblem following Confederation, French Canadians sought a symbol that would distinguish their unique collective identity, and over the course of the next century, the *fleur-de-lys* replaced the maple leaf as the prime symbol of French-Canadian identity.

In September 1902, a *fleur-de-lys* flag, designed by Father Elphège Filiatrault, flew over a church in Saint-Hyacinthe. Filiatrault championed the creation of a new flag for a new nationality, and he borrowed his design from the Carillon banner to produce a white cross on a blue field with gold *fleurs-de-lys* pointing diagonally from the corners to the centre of the cross. Others joined the search for a symbol of French-Canadian nationality. Flag committees were struck in Montreal and Quebec City, each proposing a variation on the Carillon banner, but they also urged that a Sacred Heart be added at the centre, surrounded by maple leaves and bearing the provincial motto, "Je me souviens." This design, known as the Carillon-Sacré-Coeur, was shared widely through the sales of postcards, buttons, badges, brochures, and over seventy-five thousand flags of various sizes. But Filiatrault himself opposed the effort to combine the emblems of religion (the Sacred Heart) with those of French-Canadian heritage (through the *fleur-de-lys* and maple leaves); the flag, he insisted, should not combine nationality with the faith.[4] Nevertheless, the Carillon-Sacré-Coeur became popular with Catholic nationalists in Quebec and elsewhere in French Canada.

Not all uses of the *fleur-de-lys* were religiously tinged. The earlier connection to military service—reinforced through the connection to the Battle of Carillon and the Zouaves—continued to play a role. During the First World War, French-Canadian regiments adopted many symbols, including the maple leaf, the beaver, and, increasingly, the *fleur-de-lys*. The 178th Battalion adopted as its banner a modified Carillon-Sacré-Coeur, with a beaver replacing the Sacred Heart. The celebrated Royal 22ᵉ Régiment—the Van Doos—incorporated Quebec's coat of arms, with its two *fleurs-de-lys*, into its badge. The Voltigeurs de Québec chose the Cross of St. Louis as their emblem. This most coveted of medals and symbols of Old Regime France included four images of the *fleur-de-lys* in its design.

By the middle of the twentieth century, the *fleur-de-lys* was well on its way to supplanting the maple leaf and beaver in French Canada. René Chaloult, a lawyer and member of the Quebec legislature in the 1930s and 1940s, led the fight to establish

This postcard was used to promote the adoption of the Carillon-Sacré-Coeur flag in the first decades of the twentieth century.

an official Quebec flag. A fierce nationalist, Chaloult saw in a national flag a way to cement Québécois unity. Chaloult moved that the provincial legislature adopt the Carillon-Sacré-Coeur as an official flag in 1946. He intensified his efforts over the course of 1947. Finally, on the afternoon of January 21, 1948, Quebec premier Maurice Duplessis announced that a new flag had that very day been raised to replace the Union Jack that had flown atop the Quebec Parliament Building. Duplessis had been skeptical of the flag issue, but he consented, under pressure from Chaloult and his own cabinet, to an order-in-council establishing the new flag. The approved design was a variant of Filiatrault's flag without the Sacred Heart and with the four *fleurs-de-lys* oriented vertically in accordance with the rules of heraldry. But it was the older Filiatrault design that flew that day, as no versions of the chosen design existed.[5]

Combining symbols: youth groups held annual rallies to promote patriotism in front of Montreal's Dollard des Ormeaux monument. By the 1940s, the *fleur-de-lys* flag figured prominently at these rallies, such as this one held in 1944.

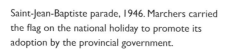

Saint-Jean-Baptiste parade, 1946. Marchers carried the flag on the national holiday to promote its adoption by the provincial government.

Duplessis's announcement was greeted in the legislature by thunderous applause and a unanimous endorsement. Thus, what was vaguely described as "the Fleur de Lis of Old France" returned to official use along the St. Lawrence River. Not one anglophone member of the provincial legislature spoke in the chamber, and outside Quebec the news was greeted with mild concern. Chaloult, however, pointed out that Nova Scotia had years earlier adopted a distinct provincial flag. And excitement quickly spread through the province.[6] The new flag signaled that Quebec had its own interests, its own traditions, and its own identity. Although Duplessis was initially skeptical, he quickly embraced the popular *fleur-de-lys*. The flag appeared on every page of the five-volume Tremblay Report defending Quebec's constitutional autonomy in 1956.[7]

Although it had lost the Sacred Heart, the Fleurdelisé was not entirely stripped of its religious imagery: it retained the white cross on a blue field, a standard symbol of European Christianity. However, with the coming of the Quiet Revolution, the rapid modernization and secularization of the Quebec state beginning in 1960, the symbol was quickly secularized. The turbulent 1960s saw English Canadians continue to elevate the maple leaf as a national symbol, most prominently in 1965 when the Canadian flag was adopted. Even as they celebrated the unveiling of a Canadian flag shorn of British symbolism, the maple leaf could no longer represent French Canada's distinct national identity, much less a uniquely Québécois one. The *fleur-de-lys*, emblazoned on the provincial flag, therefore began to take a more central symbolic role.

Duplessis had added the *fleur-de-lys* to the province's licence plates in 1950, but as the Quebec government expanded its activities in the 1960s, the symbol's visibility increased. It appeared on government reports, on government signage, and was embossed on government cheques. It thus came to represent the provincial state. Moreover, in the ethnic and linguistic politics that erupted during and immediately after the Quiet Revolution, the provincial state became more and more closely identified with francophone Quebec. Thus, the use of the Quebec flag, emblazoned with the *fleur-de-lys*, also came to be closely associated with the political ambitions of francophone Quebecers and their status as a distinctly French people.

Through the 1970s, political parties of all stripes in Quebec adopted the *fleur-de-lys* to symbolize their provincial loyalties. During the first referendum on independence in 1980, both the Yes and the No sides used the *fleur-de-lys*, and afterwards the federalist Liberal Party of Quebec incorporated it into its official logo. The *fleur-de-lys* had become a powerful symbol. Indeed, when in 1989 a group of anti-bilingualism demonstrators desecrated a Quebec flag in Brockville, Ontario to protest French-language services in their province, the image seemed to confirm stereotypes of anti-French bigotry. The incident incensed both federalists and sovereigntists in Quebec. It also increased tensions in the lead up to the failure of the Meech Lake Accord in 1990, a constitutional agreement that, among other things, would have recognized Quebec as a distinct society. The *fleur-de-lys* was also used in the 1995 sovereignty referendum, increasingly contrasted with the Canadian Maple Leaf flag.

Outside of formal politics, the symbol also figured in popular culture. In 1973, singer Diane Dufresne appeared on an album cover wearing *fleur-de-lys* body paint, a political statement combining her feminism and nationalism. However, the stylized flower also appeared in comic books, popular art, and advertising. It adorned the uniforms of the Quebec Nordiques professional hockey team from its founding in 1972 to its relocation to Denver in 1995. The team's jerseys were popularly referred to as the *fleurdelisé*. A few years earlier, in 1992, faced with declining attendance, the Montreal Expos baseball team changed its

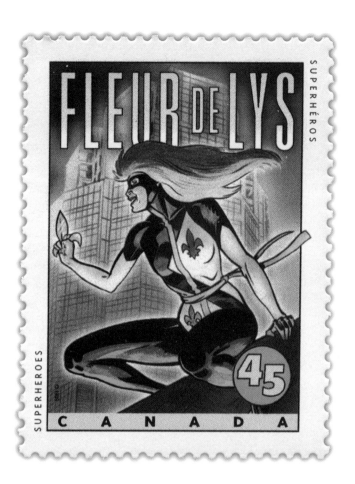

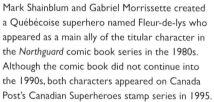

Mark Shainblum and Gabriel Morrissette created a Québécoise superhero named Fleur-de-lys who appeared as a main ally of the titular character in the *Northguard* comic book series in the 1980s. Although the comic book did not continue into the 1990s, both characters appeared on Canada Post's Canadian Superheroes stamp series in 1995.

Three flags in Montreal, 2017. The flags of Montreal (top), Canada (middle), and Quebec (bottom). The *fleur-de-lys* on the Montreal flag is joined by the thistle, rose, and shamrock to represent the city's European settler populations.

uniforms to reconnect with fans. Significantly, the club added a *fleur-de-lys* to its uniforms, forming the acute accent above the "e" in the French rendering of "Montréal." In more recent years, the Montreal Impact—the city's professional soccer team—placed a prominent *fleur-de-lys* on its crest, signifying the club as a team for all Quebec, not just Montreal.

Outside of Quebec, as the Brockville incident suggests, the symbol is closely connected to French heritage. In the United States, the National Football League's New Orleans Saints adopted a *fleur-de-lys* as the team's logo in 1966, alluding to Louisiana's French past. Similarly, the minor league St. Louis F. C. soccer club crest shows a *fleur-de-lys* alongside the year 1764, in memory of St. Louis, Missouri's founding by French fur traders.

Other francophone communities in Canada also turned to the *fleur-de-lys*. In the 1960s, an early proposal for a Franco-Ontarian flag adopted the Carillon flag's layout but replaced the Sacred Heart with a stylized trillium, Ontario's provincial flower. Later, in 1975, Gaétan Gervais and Michel Dupuis, a professor and student, respectively, at Laurentian University, designed a green and white flag pairing Ontario's trillium with a *fleur-de-lys*. This flag was adopted by the Association des Canadiens français de l'Ontario in 1977 and eventually (in 2001) given official sanction by the provincial government as the flag of Franco-Ontarians.[8]

Of course, not all francophone communities adopted the symbol as their own. Most famously, the Acadian people placed the star of the Blessed Virgin of the Assumption on a French *tricolore* to create their national flag. However, other *fleur-de-lys*-based flags were designed in Saskatchewan in 1976, in Alberta in 1982, and in the Northwest Territories in 1992. In each case, the symbol invoked the memory of a long-standing francophone presence in Western Canada.

Indeed, memory is a crucial element of the *fleur-de-lys*'s symbolism. It harkens back to the time when French kings reigned in northern North America, as the response to the visits of both *La Capricieuse* and de Gaulle hinted. However, the central feature in the story of the symbol's prominence was the struggle to create a distinct French-Canadian (later Quebec) flag in the first half of the twentieth century. By placing the *fleur-de-lys* on the flag, the Quebec government connected it to the aspirations and identity of a province and a people. Through these flags, the *fleur-de-lys* became a symbol that linked francophone communities in Canada. In this way, an old symbol from the days of colonial New France was recovered, revived, and transformed into a cherished symbol not only of modern Quebec but of modern Canada as well.

NOTES

1   H-A Bizier and Claude Paulette, *Fleur de lys: D'hier à aujourd'hui.* (Montreal: Art global, 1997), 36

2   Bizier and Paulette, *Fleur de lys*, 113.

3   Jean-Marie Lebel, "Baillairgé, Louis de Gonzague," in *Dictionary of Canadian Biography,* vol. 12, University of Toronto/Université Laval, 2003, biographi.ca/en/bio/baillairge_louis_de_gonzague_12E.html.

4   Michèle Jean, "Un anniversaire, une découverte: les 50 ans du fleurdelisé," *Cap-aux-Diamants* 54 (Spring 1998): 52–3.

5   Luc Bouvier, "Du tricolore canadien au fleurdelisé québécois: Vers le fleurdelisé," *Action nationale* 10 (Dec. 1996): 99–111.

6   See "Le fleurdelisé, emblème de la province de Québec," *Le Devoir* (Montreal), Jan. 22, 1948; «Quebec Flies Own Flag While Assembly Cheers,» *Globe and Mail* (Toronto), Jan. 22, 1948.

7   Susan Mann Trofimenkoff, *The Dream of Nation: A Social and Intellectual History of Quebec* (Montreal and Kingston: McGill-Queen's University Press, 2002), 267, 274.

8   François-Olivier Dorais, "Gaétan Gervais: témoin et agent d'une mutation référentielle en Ontario français." *Mens: revue d'histoire intellectuelle et culturelle* 13, no. 2 (2013): 59–99.

Maple syrup production on display at a *cabane à sucre* in Quebec.

MAPLE SYRUP

Elizabeth L. Jewett

Maple syrup is one of Canada's most recogniz-
able commodities. Indeed, visitors and Canadians alike are
hard pressed to avoid the multitude of treats made from maple
syrup or maple sugar artfully displayed in souvenir shops and
airport terminals, as well as the country's maple-infused recipes
and menus. From literary giant Alice Munro's recipe for maple
mousse (available in Margaret Atwood's *Canlit Foodbook*) to a
Toronto burger joint's determination to celebrate Canada's one
hundred and fiftieth anniversary with a syrup-laden maple
bacon cheeseburger, maple-flavoured foods abound.[1]

Even those not inclined to imbibe maple-flavoured bacon,
marshmallows, coffee, cola, or beer are reminded daily of the
maple tree's symbolic connection to Canada. The country boasts
no less than nine communities named Maple Grove, ten Maple
Ridges, eight Maple Creeks, and countless Maple Streets. In
2012, journalists provided in-depth coverage of the "Great Canadian Maple Syrup Heist," which saw millions of dollars worth
of syrup stolen from reserves in Quebec and smuggled into
other provinces and the United States—a high-profile gambit
that only served to reinforce the mystique surrounding the

From "Maple Popcorn" to "Maple Ice Wine" cookies, Canada produces a seemingly limitless variety of maple-syrup-themed foods.

Left: sugar maples, among other trees, changing colour in the Eastern Townships of Quebec. Right: a sugar maple in front of the reconstructed Turtle Clan long house at Crawford Lake Conservation Area, Ontario, 2017.

sweetener's connection to Canada.[2] When the Canada 150 celebrations declared March "maple" month, news articles eagerly documented the industry's historical continuity and links to Canadian-ness.

Though other trees produce edible syrups, no other tree (or sweetener) is as emblematic of the land that we call Canada, as evidenced in song, in military insignia, on flags, and in descriptions of the country's vibrant fall foliage. Indeed, the long saga of the saccharine elixir predates the existence of Canada itself, and this history is central to a national narrative that recalls and celebrates lived experiences connected to a rural Canadian heritage of food, family, community, and nature. Sugaring

traditions (methods for boiling down sap to desired consistencies) continue today in producers' camps and sugar bushes, but also in expeditions to operational sugar bushes and sugarhouses or sugar shacks, where participants can observe the process and share in a customary meal.

The dominant narrative associated with maple syrup's status as a Canadian national symbol has changed little over the years. This account is visible in the textual and visual imagery of the sugaring experience, which freezes and idealizes the history of sugaring to focus on early to mid-twentieth-century experiences. It provides an aesthetically pleasing depiction of a peaceful rural nature, of a quaint sugarhouse, and "traditional" technologies of

Maple sugar and syrup production offered labour activities for all members of a farming family. The harvesting and processing of maple products also provided space for community-building and the development of local cultural practices.

Indigenous maple syrup production provided the basis for early Euro-Canadian settlers' introduction to, subsequent experimentation with, and adaptation of maple sugaring methods and products.

buckets and human power that centres on white settlers' adoption and integration of sugaring practices built upon knowledge shared by Indigenous peoples.[3]

The emphasis on the sharing of sugaring knowledge between Indigenous and non-Indigenous peoples was evident in popular renderings of maple syrup's customs, which by the nineteenth century included a growing travel literature about Canada that often involved abbreviated explanations of the sugaring process. Similar themes inform more recent media histories, such as Historica Canada's 1997 maple syrup Heritage Minute featuring an Indigenous family generously introducing their European counterparts to maple sugar production.[4] But while there is

verity and value in these constructions, they also obscure the complex and at times contested nature of this product.

For it is not all "Love and Maple Syrup"—to borrow the title of folk singer Gordon Lightfoot's 1971 ballad—when it comes to the Canadian sweetener. Maple syrup's symbolism is not singular. Dominant understandings obscure, among other things, Indigenous relationships with the production of maple syrup, as well as the importance of technology and regulation in the industry. Its histories, vocabulary, and euphemisms reveal strong local and provincial connections, not just national ones. Its economic value has ebbed and flowed. Moreover, maple syrup's valued status within the country is highly constructed—its rise to multi-million-dollar commodity and cultural prominence required a concerted effort to secure its culinary significance. Its history and importance, then, is intimately connected to layers of family or local traditions, provincial identities, and a national heritage.

To begin, an essential factor in maple syrup's symbolism is that it is made in Canada. While the northeastern United States also boasts a long history of maple syrup production, Canada is the world's maple syrup powerhouse, producing about 80 percent of the global stock. However, as a consequence of political boundaries, physiography, climate, and the need for ample stands of sap-producing maple trees, preferably the sugar maple (*acer saccharum*), maple syrup is only produced in substantial quantities in part of the country—from Ontario through Quebec, New Brunswick, and Nova Scotia. Quebec produces on average 90 percent of the nation's maple syrup and sugar; the other three provinces make up the remaining 10 percent.[5] But even within these provinces, not all regions produce the same quality or quantity. Thus, while maple syrup is associated with all of Canada, large-scale production is a regional practice with deep economic and cultural roots tied to specific places.

Yet as the national flag attests, the regional reality of maple syrup production does not hinder its endurance as a national symbol. In terms of Canadian cuisines, many foods or dishes with a regional claim form part of a national Canadian creole.[6] In menus across Canada, this sweetener is one of, if not, the most common "Canadian" ingredients. Its use reinforces particular themes in Canadian eating that emphasize wild, fresh, and seasonal foods.[7] As such, maple syrup consumption strengthens a connection with a very particular vision of Canadian nature, and culinary rituals enhance its association with a deep history of place and national development.

Maple syrup's long-established presence in Indigenous and settler histories and seasonal traditions is also a central factor in its status as Canadian symbol. Cold nights and warmer days characterized Indigenous and settler sugaring times, and these coincided with the rather quiet seasonal farm cycle anywhere from late February through March and April. Syrup and sugar could be made in the camp or on the farm with minimal equipment, on-site fuels, and pertinent local knowledge of environmental conditions and processing techniques. Sugaring, moreover, provided a distinct outdoor workspace for both men and women in Indigenous and non-Indigenous settings.

Knowledge about maple sap and sugaring practices is rooted in dynamic Indigenous traditions and cultures. The most common Canadian maple syrup tales, however, often fail to address the depth and diversity of Indigenous maple syrup histories, and they ignore how these Indigenous practices were altered because of settlers' government policies. For instance, as a consequence of policies like the *Indian Act* and the establishment of the reserve system, Indigenous peoples lost access to traditional lands, were restricted in their ability to gather resources and perform ceremonies, and were confronted with patriarchal family models and land ownership systems that lessened Indigenous women's access to traditional knowledge and territories.[8] These colonial realities made it difficult, if not impossible, for Indigenous peoples to pursue the cultural and economic benefits of collecting, producing, and selling maple products.[9]

Today, many Indigenous individuals and communities are reclaiming their connections to maple syrup and their sugaring stories and experiences. For example, Leanne Betasamosake Simpson notes that her retelling of the creation story of maple sap, and her learning how to boil it, is contextualized by her clan affiliation, contemporary life, and interpretation of Nishnaabeg thought.[10] Similarly, Waaseyaa'sin Christine Sy explores her personal experiences at "the boiling place" and examines the extent to which her knowledge comes through male teachers as

The product of an alliance between Indigenous and non-Indigenous artists, the Oh Oh Canada Maple Candy Project employs symbols such as the bison, the noose that hanged Louis Riel, and the tongue—which represents the rupture of Indigenous languages and the resurgence of women's voices—to highlight Canada's history of settler colonialism and to encourage frank discussions about Canada's future.

a result of historical disruptions between Anishinaabe women and the sugar bush caused by colonial governance and gender constructs.[11] These are but two examples of how mainstream narratives of maple syrup and the realities of its production are slowly changing within the country.

What bears remembering, then, is that white-settler knowledge of sugaring originated from Indigenous practices. In turn, settler technologies, coupled with trial and error, were used to develop these practices into a form of maple production that became an important part of the farm cycle. Though labour-intensive, maple sugar offered a cheaper alternative to refined sugar from the West Indies until the 1880s—with some observers advocating that every farm should produce maple sugar to remain free from the burdens of foreign goods.[12] It even became a rallying cry for abolitionists seeking alternatives to cane sugars produced through slave labour.[13] Since before the mid-nineteenth century, popular narratives about the sweetener associated it with Canadian men's and women's lives. An 1831 account suggested that "maple sugar will nevertheless ever continue [as] a favourite luxury, if not a necessity, with the Canadian peasant, who has ... been considered as having for it the same natural predilection that an Englishman has for his beer, [and] a Scotchman for his scones."[14]

Consequently, maple syrup production sites became places where gender, family, and community norms were encountered and reinforced. Making maple syrup was a family affair, with all members helping to collect and then boil down the sap. Neighbours and community members were often hired on to lend a hand, and these moments of community togetherness helped perpetuate a particularly local rural identity. In time, sugaring became a cultural event that involved meeting at sugaring camps and sugarhouses and that took the form of sugar bees and sugaring-off parties. These gatherings created spaces for social interaction and for new family networks to develop. As one 1864 observer stated, "sugar making partakes more of the character of amusement than work, and generally a good deal of flirtation goes on at the camp fire in the woods."[15]

Cooking with maple products also became part of these rural family and community traditions. Already by 1842, the skills of a good Canadian wife were said to include the art of manufacturing maple sugar.[16] Cookbooks teemed with family maple recipes, and these were shared locally. As time went on, sugar makers' primary occupation shifted away from agriculture, and many continued to participate in the industry for cultural and economic reasons; these were often tied to a sense of history and tradition linked to specific places and to a mainstream narrative of maple syrup that involved a sense of community.[17]

As local practices produced surplus goods, maple sugar and syrup became representations or markers of Canadiana at international events and exhibitions where, between the 1850s and the mid-twentieth century, maple sugar and syrup were commonly showcased at Canadian stands and pavilions. In 1928, a Scottish report commented favourably on Canada's "growing importance and prestige as a food-producing country" by mentioning "its celebrated maple syrup."[18] New contests emerged in Canada to promote maple products and to encourage higher-quality production. News articles circulating during both

By the First World War, maple sugar and syrup were staples of Canadian life and culture on the international stage. Here, Canadian soldiers enjoy maple sugar treats.

This rendering of the 540 ml maple syrup can epitomizes the industry's continued idealization of a certain rural scenery that places the sugaring experience "out of time" and infuses it with qualities that emphasize peaceful, harmonious interactions with nature and a sense of quaint, community-centred country life. Importantly, the fact that the can's label reads "Product of Quebec" emphasizes the strong regional identity and industry guidelines that characterize maple production within different parts of the country.

World Wars spoke of sending maple syrup to soldiers overseas.[19] Indeed, "Jam for Britain" campaigns in the Second World War involved substantial donations of maple syrup, especially from Quebec.[20] This period also witnessed federal and provincial demands for the increase of maple production, even on Crown lands, to make Canada a sugar-producing region for the world and to address a global sugar shortage.[21] In 1958, Prime Minister John Diefenbaker included maple syrup as a suitably Canadian gift for world leaders on his multi-country tour.[22] In the 1960s, members of the federal Ministry of Agriculture actively encouraged the year-round marketing of maple products at home and abroad.[23] Such activities were not just aimed at selling a product, but at selling participation in a particular Canadian experience and identity as well.

However, for many the narrative of maple syrup's long history remains tied to a regional or provincial identity. This is especially true in Quebec, which retains a resilient connection to its particular history of *sirop d'érable*. Considering the geography and scale of sugar production, it is not surprising that early travel literature and accounts of sugaring come mostly from Quebec, where official state celebrations often involved the natural sweetener. For instance, in 1910 the government of Quebec proclaimed July 1 as the "Jour de sucre d'érable," and it gave out samples and brochures to railways and shipping companies for international distribution, and by mid-century, there were plans to link Saint-Jean-Baptiste Day with maple-infused foods.[24] Sugaring and using maple syrup are part of French-Canadian identity, and partaking in these traditions has linked local communities to broader stories about culture and the reimagination of tradition. For example, Martin Picard's Cabane à Sucre Au Pied de Couchon offers an exclusive dining experience near Montreal with maple cuisine made with syrup produced by the chef. Picard advocates creativity with the product, yet ties it to a traditional French-Canadian or Québécois identity. He suggests that maple syrup has its own "designations of origin taken as seriously as those for wine."[25]

Yet maple syrup and the sugaring experience can also make visible certain tensions within society. The long histories of sugaring-off parties or visits to the *cabane à sucre* (sugar shack) have been a way to bring people together. These spaces and activities are entry points into Canadian and local culture for many newcomers. But they can also be sites of controversy. In 2007, for example, tensions arose when several sugarhouses accommodated Muslim visitors with space for prayer and dietary options that did not include ham (the traditional pea soup and beans served at sugarhouses includes pork). Reaction was swift, with some suggesting these changes threatened traditional Québécois culture.[26] This culinary artifact thus acts as both a symbol of inclusion and exclusion.

To truly understand maple syrup's complex history, though, it is important to recognize that its development into a tasty and exclusive luxury good required technological advances, regulatory intervention, and strategic marketing initiatives. Evolving scientific and technological discoveries helped maximize quantity while reducing the time and labour required to produce maple syrup. Such technologies included equipment for tapping trees, collecting and boiling sap, and storing syrup. For instance, Grimm Brothers, initially based in Waterloo, Quebec, developed maple syrup cans that significantly shifted the industry's focus from sugar to syrup. The syrup can or tin was not only practical but also a material artifact, one that was able to transmit cultural meaning through the artistic representations of sugaring depicted on the can. The focus on marketing a more nostalgic vision of maple syrup and sugaring is also connected to the touring of operational sugar bushes and the eating of traditional meals as opportunities to immerse oneself in history. However, connections to place and history were only part of the symbolism and marketing schemes designed to promote the sweet stuff.

The quest to promote maple syrup at home and abroad led to industry regulation, and regulation entailed educating audiences to distinguish the best product.[27] The Department of Agriculture and industry leaders defined a maple syrup's quality by its purity and according to a hierarchy of colour and taste, all of which were cultural constructions that became enduring components of the commodity's status. By 1910, the Canadian *Adulteration Act* included maple products, while newly formed organizations such as the Pure Maple Sugar and Syrup Co-operative Agricultural Association brought together producers from the four sugar- and syrup-producing provinces to promote pure products of good quality to an international clientele.[28] By 1930, the *Maple Sugar Industry Act* further clarified standards of adulteration, types of labels, grading, and sanitation. Since then, governments and business associations have regulated maple products with an emphasis on strict grading and labeling guidelines.

No organization more clearly illustrates the role of these associations than the Fédération des producteurs acéricoles du Québec (FPAQ). Formed in 1966 to protect producers' rights and establish a collective agreement on marketing, production quotas, and quality standards in Quebec, the FPAQ ultimately created a stockpile of syrup in a "strategic reserve" within the province—the site of the 2012 heist mentioned above—and it continues to sell its wares in bulk. Most importantly, the FPAQ requires its members to advertise their goods as both a "product of Quebec" and "made in Canada." This labeling guideline is one more example of the mix of identities linked to maple syrup. At times, this reinforces a national narrative, but it also reinforces other connections to place and cultures.

There is clearly no single maple syrup narrative for Canada. The country makes the majority of the maple products in the world and for over a century its governments and private organizations have worked to refine the sweetener's quality and boost its international renown as a Canadian luxury or niche culinary good. Maple sugar and syrup have deep roots that predate the existence of Canada itself, and this long history ties these commodities to many local traditions. Clichéd as the phrase may be, observers attempting to understand maple syrup's status as a Canadian symbol face a sticky situation. Just as people's personal palates differ when it comes to maple syrup, so, too, do their cultural connections to it.

NOTES

1 Margaret Atwood, *Canlit Foodbook: From Pen to Palate—A Collection of Tasty Literary Fare* (Toronto: Totem Books, 1987); Harmeet Singh, "Foodora's secret celebration," stimulantonline.ca/2017/05/15/foodoras-secret-celebration/.

2 Brenden Borell, "The Great Canadian Maple Syrup Heist," *Bloomberg*, Jan. 3, 2013, bloomberg.com/news/articles/2013-01-02/the-great-canadian-maple-syrup-heist; Rich Cohen, "Inside Quebec's Great, Multi-Million-Dollar Maple-Syrup Heist," *Vanity Fair*, Dec. 5, 2016, vanityfair.com/news/2016/12/maple-syrup-heist; "Ringleader in maple syrup heist gets 8 Years in prison, $9.4M fine," *CBC News*, Apr. 28, 2017, accessed May 6, 2017, cbc.ca/news/canada/montreal/richard-vallieres-sentencing-1.4090811.

3 See, for example, Quebec Standard Products: Maple Syrup and Maple Sugar. (Quebec?: s.n., 192?).

4 Historica Canada, "Heritage Minute: Syrup," 1997, historicacanada.ca/content/heritage-minutes/syrup.

5 Agriculture and Agri-Food Canada, "Statistical Overview of the Canadian Maple Industry, 2015," Sept. 2016, agr.gc.ca/eng/industry-markets-and-trade/statistics-and-market-information/by-product-sector/horticulture-industry/horticulture-sector-reports/statistical-overview-of-the-canadian-maple-industry-2015/?id=1475692913659.

6 Lenore Newman, *Speaking in Cod Tongues: A Canadian Culinary Journey* (Regina: University of Regina Press, 2017), 70–90.

7 Newman, *Speaking in Cod Tongues*, 92.

8 Waaseyaa'sin Christine Sy, "At the Boiling Place: Reading Sap for Future Anishinaabeg Sugar bush (Re)Matriation," *GUTS*, May 25, 2016, gutsmagazine.ca/boiling-place/.

9 Hayley Moody, "Indigenous Knowledge and Maple Syrup: A Case Study of the Effects of Colonization in Ontario" (MA thesis, Wilfrid Laurier

University, 2014), 51–5, scholars.wlu.ca/cgi/viewcontent.cgi?article= 1000&context=sjce_mrp.

10 Leanne Betasamosake Simpson," Ninaatigoog," in *Dancing on our Turtle's Back: Stories of Nishnaabeg Re-Creation, Resurgence, and a New Emergence* (Winnipeg: Arbeiter Ring, 2011), 83. See also, "Plight" in *This Accident of Being Lost: Songs and Stories* (Toronto: House of Anansi, 2017), 5–8.

11 See Waaseyaa'sin Christine Sy, "ishkigamizigan: the sugarbush," *InTensions: The Resurgence of Indigenous Women's Knowledge and Resistance in Relation to Land and Territoriality* 6.0 (Fall/Winter 2012), yorku.ca/intent/issue6/ poems/waaseyaasinchristinesy.php.

12 Moody, "Indigenous Knowledge and Maple Syrup," 91.

13 Catherine Parr Traill, "Maple Sugar," in Cynthia Sugars and Laura Moss, eds., *Canadian Literature in English: Texts and Contexts*, vol. 1 (Toronto: Pearson/Longman, 2009), 206.

14 Joseph Bouchette, *The British Dominions of North America* (London, 1831), 372.

15 "Wayside Jottings of a Ramble in Canada—Maple Sugar Making, Canadian Pastimes," *Paisley Herald and Renfrewshire Advertiser* (Paisley, UK), May 20, 1865.

16 Births, Deaths, Marriages and Obituaries. *The Leicester Chronicle: or, Commercial and Agricultural Advertiser* (Leicester, UK), Nov. 12, 1842.

17 C. Clare Hinrichs, "Off the Treadmill? Technology and Tourism in the North American Maple Syrup Industry," *Agriculture and Human Values* 12, no. 1 (1995): 39–47, and "Sideline and Lifeline: The Cultural Economy of Maple Syrup Production," *Rural Sociology* 63, no. 4 (1998): 507–32.

18 "Attractive Grocery Exhibition in Aberdeen," *Aberdeen Press and Journal* (Aberdeen, UK), Oct. 3, 1928.

19 For example, "Maple Sugar and Jam for Wounded Soldiers" *The Globe* May 13, 1915, pg. 8

20 Ian Mosby, *Food Will Win the War: The Politics, Culture, and Science of Food on Canada's Home Front* (Vancouver: UBC Press, 2014): 122–3.

21 For example, "Tap Every Maple Tree—Enough Maple Sugar Could be Produced to Meet Canada's Total Needs," *Globe* (Toronto), Mar. 6, 1918.

22 Donald Wright, *Donald Creighton: A Life in History* (Toronto: University of Toronto Press, 2015), 289.

23 "Have Special Booklet On Syrup Recipes," *Globe* (Toronto), Apr. 18, 1962.

24 For more examples, see J. C. Dupont, *Le temps des sucres* (Sainte-Foy, QC: Les editions GID, 2004).

25 Newman, *Speaking in Cod Tongues*, 122.

26 Gérard Bouchard and Charles Taylor, "Building the Future: a Time for Reconciliation," 2008, 53, 57, mce.gouv.qc.ca/publications/CCPARDC/ rapport-final-integral-en.pdf.

27 J. B. Spencer, "The Maple Sugar Industry in Canada," Department of Agriculture, *Bulletin* No. 2B (1913), 46–7, 57.

28 Spencer, "The Maple Sugar Industry in Canada," 52–4.

A Canadian Pacific Railway locomotive in the mountains
of British Columbia, 1889.

CANADIAN PACIFIC RAILWAY

Bill Waiser

It is one of the most iconic photographs in Can-adian history: the driving of the last spike of the Canadian Pacific Railway in Craigellachie, British Columbia, on November 7, 1885. The event had been delayed several days because of inclement weather, but a break in the rain allowed the white-bearded Donald A. Smith, a member of the CPR Syndicate, to drive home the last spike that fog-shrouded morning. Other prominent railway men, surrounded by a sea of navvies, solemnly looked on, seemingly in relief that the project—a fixture in Canadian politics for over fifteen years—had finally been completed. Reflecting on the picture, one author claimed that the "moment had arrived which so many Canadians had believed would never come."[1] Much of the credit for completing the line has fallen to CPR general manager William Cornelius Van Horne. But Van Horne believed that the real force behind the project was Conservative prime minister John A. Macdonald. No sooner was the ceremony over than he wired Ottawa, thanking Macdonald for his "far-seeing policy and undying support ... the Canadian Pacific Railway is completed ... this (Saturday) morning at 9:22."[2] Van Horne's congratulatory note was understandable. During Macdonald's

Donald A. Smith drove the last spike of the CPR at Craigellachie,
British Columbia on November 7, 1885

Once the last spike had been driven,
CPR general manager William Cornelius
Van Horne sent a telegram to John A.
Macdonald, thanking the prime minister
for his support of the project.

tenure as prime minister, he had made the building of the railroad an absolute necessity if the young country was to achieve its destiny as a transcontinental nation. Little wonder, then, that the CPR is sometimes called the "national dream." But once the railway began operating in the Prairie West, farmers complained vociferously that the private company and its monopoly position worked against their interests. The railway that had made western settlement possible was looked upon as a regional nightmare.

The idea of a transcontinental railroad was intertwined with the Confederation movement. In the mid-nineteenth century, Canadian expansionists championed the great plains of the North-West Territories as an agricultural Eden that would provide the means to empire for the young Dominion. There were also practical territorial reasons for expanding Confederation to the Pacific Coast. Since the United States was transcontinental, Canada had to be transcontinental too in order to avoid being absorbed by the ambitious republic to the south. The vehicle to bring about economic integration, settle the great northern plains, and help maintain Canadian sovereignty over the northern half of the continent was a transcontinental railroad. Victorian Canadians had a great faith in the new railroad technology of the mid-nineteenth century—and a great faith in that technology's ability to overcome the twin challenges of distance and isolation. The steam engine promised to shrink the vast geography of Canada and tame the intervening wilderness. The new railroad technology would also have a civilizing effect on the western plains by displacing Indigenous peoples and ensuring that the best features of Anglo-Canadian civilization flourished there.

The steam locomotive represented modernity and would help Canada take its rightful place on the world stage.

Building the transcontinental railroad became a federal responsibility in 1871. During negotiations to bring the colony of British Columbia into Confederation, Canada promised to complete a transcontinental line to the Pacific Coast within ten years. Prime Minister Macdonald believed that Canada's connection with British Columbia "would have been merely a connection on paper" without a transcontinental railway.[3] But the first attempt to issue a charter foundered when it was discovered that one of the bidders for the railway contract had materially assisted the

The CPR was expected to have a civilizing influence on Western Canada by removing Indigenous peoples from the land.

WHAT IT MUST COME TO
(With the Encroachment of Civilization)
OFFICER: [Sir John A. Macdonald]: Here, you copper colored gentlemen, no loafing allowed, you must either work or jump.

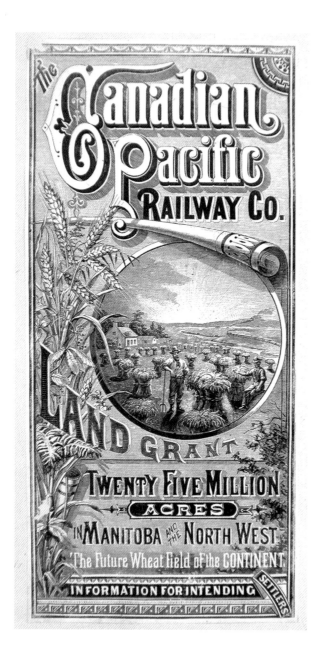

A CPR poster advertising its newly acquired
25-million-acre land grant.

Conservatives in Quebec in the 1872 general election. The "Pacific Scandal" brought down the Macdonald government in November 1873, and with it, the CPR project. It was an ignominious defeat. Macdonald reportedly told his wife after his government's resignation, "It's a relief to be out of it."[4] But writers have tended to link Macdonald's setback—and that of the Pacific railway—with the larger struggles of the young Dominion. Indeed, the railway became a symbol of Canadian tenacity in carving out a separate destiny in North America.

Because a stubborn recession gripped Canada in the mid-1870s, the Liberal government of Alexander Mackenzie turned the railway into a public works initiative. It also considered making the project a series of water and rail links. Mackenzie is generally portrayed as a dour stonemason, lacking in imagination, who would never fulfill the BC promise. That certainly was the message of the Macdonald Conservatives, who romped back into office in 1878, intent on completing the transcontinental railway. Taking advantage of the return of prosperity, the Macdonald government offered an unprecedented hundred-million-acre land grant to any company that would assume responsibility for the Canadian Pacific Railway project. No one took up the challenge. Ottawa redoubled its efforts in 1880 and deliberately courted the business community by offering cash, land, and other incentives open to negotiation. This time, a deal was concluded with a consortium headed by George Stephen, president of the Bank of Montreal.

The terms of the 1880 CPR contract were determined by the requirements of the Canadian government and the "disadvantages" that these requirements created for the CPR Syndicate. The Macdonald government insisted that the Canadian Pacific Railway go through the shield country north of the Great Lakes and through the Rocky Mountains to the Pacific Coast. It also expected the Syndicate to operate the railway in the long term.

These demands resulted in generous terms. In return for completing the transcontinental line within ten years, the Canadian government would hand over to the CPR any sections of the line already built or under construction; provide a cash subsidy of $25 million and a land grant of 25 million acres (to be land "fairly fit for settlement"); provide tax exemptions on CPR lands and property; allow construction materials to be imported duty free; and forbid the construction of any line south of the main line for twenty years. None of the contract terms was more controversial than clause 15, otherwise known as the monopoly clause, which effectively turned the North-West into the CPR's exclusive domain. George Stephen insisted that such protection was necessary to prevent a rival line from siphoning off CPR traffic on the Prairies—especially a rival railway that did not have the disadvantage of constructing and maintaining a line north of Lake Superior.

During the parliamentary debate on the CPR contract, the Conservatives expected pushback, but were surprised by the bitterness of the Opposition's attack and the lengths to which it would go—including reciting poetry—to drag the matter out. These critiques were no match for Prime Minister Macdonald's spirited linking of the CPR with Canadian nationhood. Without an all-Canadian transcontinental railway, Macdonald insisted, Canada would be reduced to "a bundle of sticks ... without a binding cord." The railway, he continued, would "give us a great and united, a rich and improving, developing Canada."[5]

Macdonald's identification of the railroad with Canadian economic nationalism has been echoed over the succeeding decades, and it has gone a long way in establishing the CPR's symbolic importance to Canada. "The prime purpose of Canada was to achieve a separate political existence on the North American continent," reasoned Macdonald's biographer, Donald Creighton. "The prime function of the Canadian Pacific Railway

The CPR wanted to generate traffic, and it consequently did its part to promote and assist Western settlement.

was to assist in this effort."[6] Author Pierre Berton went even further in singing the praises of the project in a sub-chapter entitled, "The dawn of a new Canada." He called the contract "the most important Canadian document since the British North America Act.... The tight little Canada of Confederation was already obsolete; the new Canada of the railway was about to be born."[7] Even veteran journalist Richard Gwyn, in his recent biography of Macdonald, singled out the railway as "that most un-Canadian of events—the taking of a great dare.... Macdonald had set in motion the creation of a new Canada."[8]

Construction of the Canadian Pacific Railway began in earnest in the late spring of 1881. The Prairie section was completed with amazing speed; by 1883, the line had reached beyond Calgary and into the foothills of the Rocky Mountains. The difficult shield and mountain sections took more time and money, but here again the story is one of the railway builders defying formidable construction challenges. Even the use of "coolie" labour has been given a positive spin in a sixty-second Canadian Heritage Minute. In an episode titled, "Nitro," a young Chinese worker is asked to lay an explosive charge in a tunnel under construction and miraculously survives the blast.

To help meet spiralling construction costs, the CPR builders had to ask twice for additional government funding. Prime Minister Macdonald was open to these requests on the grounds that the CPR's "interests and those of the Dominion are identical."[9] That seemed to be the case in the spring of 1885, when the still-incomplete CPR line brought Canadian troops west during the North-West Rebellion and helped put down an Indigenous resistance, effectively clearing the way for white newcomers.

ONE BY ONE HE IS BREAKING HIS BONDS

The CPR was often portrayed as one of the monopolies that held the Western farmer down.

Months later, when Donald Smith drove the last spike, the CPR cemented its role as a builder of Canada.

This lauding of the CPR project tends to obscure another side to the CPR story, one that contrasts sharply with the railroad's image as a fulfilment of a "national dream." The coming of the CPR was highly anticipated in Western Canada. It had been widely believed throughout the 1870s that settlement and development of the region had been delayed because of the lack of a railway, and that the North-West's future—much like that of Canada as a whole—now depended on the railroad. What the Prairie West got instead was a privately owned railway that was meant to benefit the businessmen in the Last Spike photograph and other capitalists who had invested in the project. "The Canadian Pacific

Railway was built for the purpose of making money for the share-holders," General Manager Van Horne grumbled, "and for no other purpose under the sun."[10] He could have added that the railroad was a classic Canadian example of corporate welfare—a corporation that was endowed with an incredible land base in Western Canada.

One of the first acts of the CPR Syndicate in the spring of 1881 was to reroute the main line directly west from Winnipeg across the southern Prairies. This decision profoundly altered the regional map by shifting the axis of western settlement and development away from established communities in the North Saskatchewan country. Westerners also objected to the incredible amount of power concentrated in the company. The contract gave the CPR twenty-five million acres that not only had to be "fairly fit for settlement," but could be selected anywhere in the territories at the expense of settlers waiting to get on the land. Then there was the controversial and much-criticized twenty-year monopoly over western traffic. To compensate for those sections of the line that ran through regions where there was little traffic and other regions where there was stiff competition from cheaper water transport, the CPR set dizzying freight rates for Prairie traffic that put many pioneer farms in jeopardy.[11] The Manitoba government tried repeatedly to charter other railways to secure competitive rates, but each time the legislation was struck down by Ottawa—three times in 1882 alone! Charles Tupper, the minister of railways, did not mince his words in defending federal action: "Are the interests of Manitoba and the North-West to be sacrificed to the policy of Canada? I say, if it is necessary—yes."[12] Western settlers consequently looked upon the CPR as nothing more than an instrument of Eastern exploitation. Charles Mair, a one-time Canadian expansionist who settled in Prince Albert, even spoke of "CPR extortion."[13]

These conflicting images of the CPR—as both a "national dream" and an "obstacle to western aspirations"[14]—were reinforced in the late nineteenth and early twentieth centuries. From the beginning of its operations, the CPR portrayed itself as a builder of Canada. In the summer of 1886, for example, it put a private "Jamaica" railway car at the disposal of Sir John and his wife Agnes for a much-celebrated train trip to the Pacific Coast. Agnes later recounted in *Murray's Magazine* that the cross-country tour was "the realization of the darling dream of [her husband's] heart—a railway from ocean to ocean ... and the birth of a new nation."[15] It was the CPR that helped settle the West by carrying prospective setters in "colonist cars." And it was the CPR that brought unemployed labourers to the region on "harvest excursions" and thereby helped get the wheat crop to market. The company logo also featured a beaver atop the CPR crest; the idea may have originated with CPR engineer-in-chief

A CPR company logo featuring both the maple leaf and the beaver.

A 1920s gold scorecard advertising the CPR's Banff Springs Hotel.

Sandford Fleming, who chose the beaver for his design of Canada's first postage stamp in 1851. Perhaps the CPR's greatest promotional activity was the building of luxury hotels, such as the Banff Springs, and then selling Canada as a world-class tourist destination. The mountain scenery in company advertisements offered an unspoiled imagining of Canada—one that still resonates today with many people, both in Canada and abroad.

Canadian authors and artists have simply reinforced the CPR popular image. Before the term was attributed to the Canadian military victory at Vimy Ridge, R. G. MacBeth argued in his 1924 book *The Romance of the Canadian Pacific Railway* that the Last Spike photograph represented "the birth of a nation."[16] Then there was E. J. Pratt, who proclaimed that "Union required the Line" in his 1952 Governor General's Literary Award–winning poem, "Towards the Last Spike."[17] Fifteen years later, folk singer Gordon Lightfoot released the evocative "Canadian Railroad Trilogy" for Canada's Centennial Year. The lyrics rhapsodized the CPR's role in the building of the Canadian nation: "Oh the song of the future has been sung / All the battles have been won / O'er the mountain tops we stand / All the world at our command." The CPR's biggest cheerleader, though, was Pierre Berton, who spoke glowingly of "a nation created through the construction of a railway"[18] in a popular 1970s television miniseries based on his two-volume history.

But the flip side of the story is one of anger and alienation in Western Canada during the era of settlement. It has even been suggested that successful occupation of the land in the late nineteenth century was delayed, in part, because of CPR practices. An August 1887 editorial in the *Manitoba Free Press* derided "the hideous robbery to which the people are subjected by the extortionate [CPR] railway rates."[19] And even when pioneer farms finally produced record crops, the CPR's inability to handle the volume of grain in 1901 resulted in half the harvest being lost to spoilage. The grain blockade, as it was called, prompted farmers to form co-operative associations to improve grain handling and marketing. For agrarian leader E. A. Partridge, the CPR was just another big monopoly that placed profit over service and had to be challenged by the collective voice of Prairie producers. This enmity towards the CPR was best captured by a popular tale, which held that whenever hail wiped out a grain crop, Prairie farmers would shake their fist at the heavens and defiantly shout, "Goddamn the CPR." It was also no coincidence that hundreds of unemployed men boarded CPR boxcars in Vancouver in June 1935 to ride across the country to Ottawa to protest the federal government's handling of the Great Depression. The On-to-Ottawa Trek would be stopped in Regina on the grounds that the men were "trespassing."

Little had changed by the late twentieth century. In October 1989, Ottawa announced the cancellation of VIA Rail's passenger service along the CPR transcontinental line. The decision elicited howls of national protest—even though passenger numbers had declined steeply and service had slipped; all the critics could understand was that the Canadian government was shutting down a historic route that had been in operation for more than a century. Contrast that with the company's adoption (in use from 1993 until 1996) of a new symbol to reflect its acquisition of several rail lines, ironically south of the border. The logo for the new CP Rail System, as it was called, featured stylized sections of both the American and Canadian flags—something that would have been anathema to mid-nineteenth-century Canadian politicians. Today, the company simply brands itself as the "CP." And its past role as a Canadian symbol is less important than its market performance to stockholders.

These tensions between these differing views of the CPR's symbolic role were foretold at the November 7, 1885 ceremony. Even though the last spike had been carefully set in place before the event, Donald Smith's first swing of the hammer delivered a glancing blow. The bent spike was hurriedly pulled out, tossed to the side, and replaced with the one that Smith drove into history. That twisted spike was a harbinger of the CPR's complicated history as a Canadian symbol.

NOTES

1   Pierre Berton, *The Last Spike: The Great Railway 1881–85* (Toronto: McClelland and Stewart, 1971), 414.

2   Quoted in Donald Creighton, *John A. Macdonald: The Old Chieftain* (Toronto: Macmillan, 1955), 436.

3   Quoted in Andy A. den Otter, *The Philosophy of Railways: The Transcontinental Railway Idea in British North America* (Toronto: University of Toronto Press, 1997), 204.

4   Quoted in Pierre Berton, *The National Dream: The Great Railway 1871–1881* (Toronto: McClelland and Stewart, 1970), 142.

5   Canada, House of Commons Debates, Jan. 17, 1881, p. 492.

6   Creighton, *The Old Chieftain*, 301.

7   Berton, *The Last Spike*, 355, 382, 388.

8   Richard Gwyn, *Nation Maker: John A Macdonald, His Life, Our Times*, vol. 2, *1867–1891* (Toronto: Random House, 2011), 337, 340.

9   Quoted in Gerald Friesen, *The Canadian Prairies: A History* (Toronto: University of Toronto Press, 1984), 177.

10 Quoted in Daniel Francis, *National Dreams: Myth, Memory, and Canadian History* (Vancouver: Arsenal Pulp Press, 1997), 20.

11 The 1883 Prairie schedule charged 30.6 cents to carry a bushel of wheat from Moose Jaw to Thunder Bay. That was almost half the price of a bushel of wheat at the time. Frost-damaged wheat fetched much less—about 40 cents per bushel.

12 House of Commons Debates, May 4, 1883.

13 Quoted in Douglas Owram, *Promise of Eden: The Canadian Expansionist Movement and the Idea of the West, 1856–1900* (Toronto: University of Toronto Press 1980), 183.

14 Quoted in Ibid.

15 Quoted in Gwyn, *Nation Maker*, 501.

16 Robert G. MacBeth, *The Romance of the Canadian Pacific Railway* (Toronto: Ryerson Press, 1924), 172.

17 Edward J. Pratt, "The Last Spike" in S. Djwa and R. G. Moyles, eds., *E.J. Pratt: Complete Poems, Part II* (Toronto: University of Toronto Press, 1989), 202.

18 Berton, *The National Dream*, 11.

19 Quoted in Gwyn, *Nation Maker*, 542.

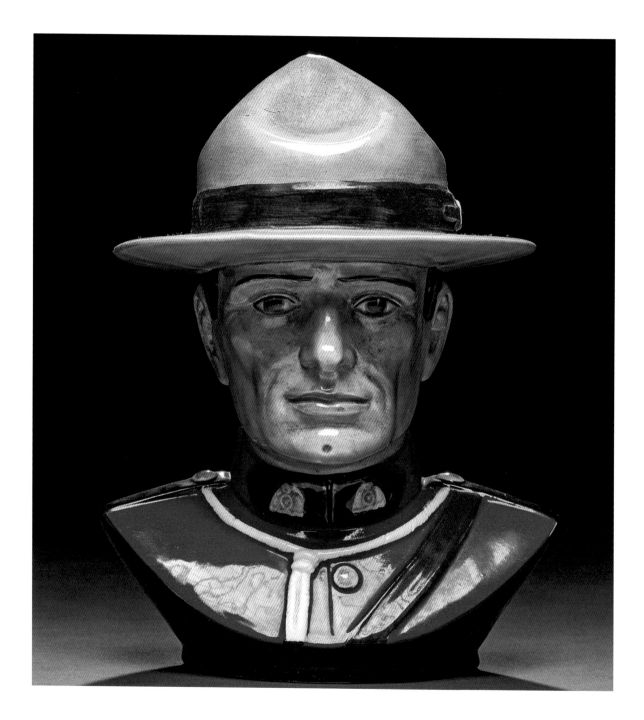

A Royal Doulton Mountie bust commemorating the hundredth anniversary of the Royal Canadian Mounted Police in 1973.

MOUNTIE

Michael Dawson

On special occasions they can be found patrol-ling Parliament Hill on horseback. For key sporting contests they stand at attention during the national anthem for all to see. During the 1970s and 1980s, they were featured on Canada's fifty-dollar bill. They lend their image to postcards and tourist memorabilia ranging from key chains to stuffed animals. But it's not just tourists that seem keen to purchase a piece of Canada's commodified police force. Indeed, the Mountie Shop, the official retailer of the Royal Canadian Mounted Police, offers internet shoppers a range of Mountie-related paraphernalia, from baby bibs and blankets to men's pajamas to "home décor" items like statues, shot glasses, and framed prints featuring the scarlet-clad hero. What explains this ongoing fascination with Canada's national police force? In part, it is the tangible product of individual achievements and the force's central role in the expansion of Canada's western and northern frontiers. But it is also very much a story of selective amnesia and successful public relations.

As Canada's national police force, the Royal Canadian Mounted Police, in addition to its federal responsibilities, provides services to eight of the country's ten provinces, the three

The connection between modern policing and the RCMP's celebrated history is maintained, in part, through formal appearances on Parliament Hill and the famous Musical Ride.

territories, some one hundred and fifty municipalities and over six hundred Indigenous communities.[1] Today's RCMP is a direct descendent of the North-West Mounted Police, which was created in 1873 in order to promote the efficient colonization of Canada's newly acquired western territories. In the late nineteenth century, the NWMP patrolled the Prairies in an effort to maintain law and order, protect Canadian sovereignty, and ensure that Indigenous peoples did not prevent the orderly settlement of the West as successive governments opened the country up to large-scale immigration. In the twentieth century,

the police force patrolled Canada's Arctic and played a key role in the government's campaign to forcibly relocate Inuit communities. Within a context that celebrated individual achievement and British racial superiority, the exploits of Mounties such as James F. Macleod on the Prairies or Sam Steele in the Yukon were woven into the tapestry of Canadian history.

While today's officers' duties bear little resemblance to those of the frontier police force, the RCMP's popular image remains firmly connected to that bygone era. In part, this is the product of the sheer power of mass culture. The achievements of early NWMP members on the Prairies and, later on, in Canada's northern climes, struck a chord with authors and movie producers. Hundreds of novels, popular histories, and films embraced these tales of courage and determination, and in so doing reached audiences around

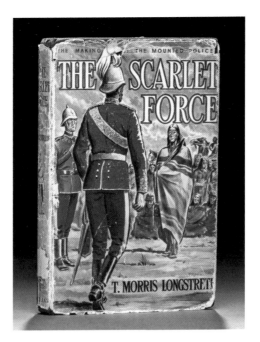

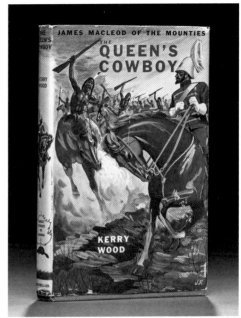

Popular histories such as *The Scarlet Force* (1958) and *The Queen's Cowboy* (1960) frequently celebrated the Mounties' role in the resettlement of Canada's Western territories.

the world. This played a key role in enhancing and disseminating a popular mythology that celebrated individual achievement, mastery over nature, self-sacrifice, duty, honour, and heroism.

Adventure novels by authors such as Ralph Connor and James Oliver Curwood featured young Mounties battling both criminals and Canada's harsh environment to ensure that the rule of law was upheld. Popular histories, penned by the likes of T. Morris Longstreth and Richard L. Neuberger, further enhanced the Mountie mythology through glorified accounts of the NWMP's achievements. Hollywood drew on both literary traditions to establish the Mountie as a recognizable symbol of Canada. Some films, such as *North West Mounted Police* (1940) starring Gary Cooper, were (very) loosely based on historical events. Others, including all three versions of the musical *Rose*

Marie, simply drew upon the established tropes of the early novels to entertain audiences.[2]

To bring the Mountie's enviable characteristics into sharp relief, the protagonist in these stories usually required a human adversary. Hence, whether on paper or on the silver screen, Indigenous peoples, French Canadians, Eastern European immigrants, and, occasionally, Americans occupied the role of villain. Female characters appeared frequently as both love interests and damsels in distress. These were the "Other" against which the mythic Mountie was measured—and celebrated. Hence, in *North West Mounted Police*, Mountie Jim Brett teams up with Texas Ranger Dusty Rivers to triumph over the Catholic, French-speaking leader of the Métis, Louis Riel, and an invented character named Jacques Corbeau. During the Cold War, Dale of the Mounted had

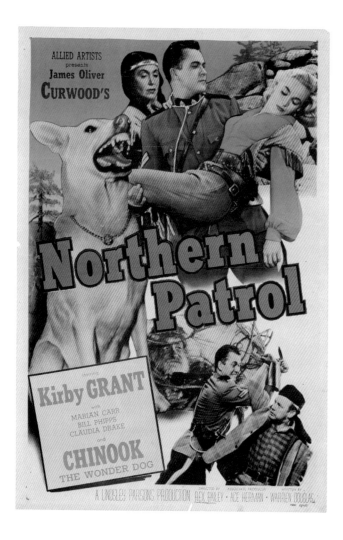

ALLIED ARTISTS
presents

James Oliver
CURWOOD'S

Northern Patrol

Kirby GRANT

with
MARIAN CARR
BILL PHIPPS
CLAUDIA DRAKE
and

CHINOOK
THE WONDER DOG

A LINDSLEY PARSONS PRODUCTION ALEX GAILEY · ACE HERMAN · WARREN DOUGLAS

Films such as *Northern Patrol* (1953) offered colourful, if simplistic, tales of Mountie heroism.

to contend with Karl Reiger, Giorgy Kovass, Polish spies, and a plethora of other threats to the Canadian nation. Other Mountie antagonists included "Chink" Wooley, Pete Gonzales, "Kid" Canceolinni, and Joseph Lipinski.[3]

The Mountie's popularity in books and on the silver screen convinced Canadian tourism promoters to incorporate his image into their campaigns to attract visitors (especially Americans) to the country. And the police force itself quickly recognized that it could use such positive symbolism to its advantage—though, at times, it found the expectation that its officers appear on duty in scarlet tunics to be wearisome.[4] While the origins of Mountie mythology were firmly rooted in late-nineteenth-century concerns about the quickening pace of modern life, fears of social change, and a critique of materialism, by the middle of the twentieth century the symbol of the Mountie had been fully enmeshed in North America's growing culture of consumption.

Like all national heroes, then, the Mountie was made, not born. But the story of Canada's police force illustrates that such mythic symbols sometimes need to be remade as well. The prevalence and continued popularity of Mountie imagery in Canada today renders this point difficult to see, but in fact, while a popular image of the Mountie has existed almost since the founding of the NWMP in 1873, it has undergone a dramatic transformation. This reinvention has kept the Mountie relevant and largely in step with English-Canadian political culture. (French-Canadian affection for the force was hindered by the organization's role in a number of divisive campaigns, including the colonization of the West, which was seen largely as an English-Canadian endeavour, the suppression of the North-West Rebellion and the execution of Louis Riel in 1885, and the enforcement of military conscription during the Second World War.)

From the 1880s to the 1950s, the image disseminated through popular fiction, popular histories, films, and television

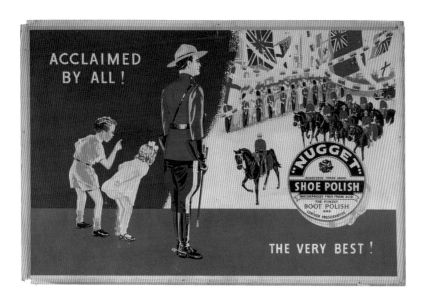

Companies have been eager to incorporate Mountie imagery into their efforts to sell a wide variety of items—even shoe polish.

celebrated ideals that were under attack as Canadian society was transformed by urbanization, large-scale immigration, industrialization, and secularization. The Mountie personified Christianity, Britishness, and individuality, and he had been celebrated for his ability to subdue Indigenous peoples, immigrants, and French Canadians. By the 1950s and 1960s, however, these sorts of ideals were increasingly out of step with a political culture that was being reshaped by, for example, support for bilingualism, second-wave feminism, decolonization, and the welfare state.

This cultural shift was particularly apparent on television. By the early 1960s, that medium boasted a cartoon send-up of Mountie mythology, *Dudley Do-Right*, which featured an inept Mountie who didn't save the damsel in distress—she saved him. Viewers were also introduced to Monty Python's "Lumberjack sketch," which featured a choir of uptight Mounties looking increasingly uncomfortable singing in support of a cross-dressing lumberjack.[5] These anti-establishment representations coincided with a series of news reports that raised questions about the actions and motivations of the modern RCMP. Police violence on Aboriginal reserves, questionable arrests of Québécois nationalists, and a first-hand report by a former Mountie documenting perjury, forgery, and a dysfunctional organizational structure, made headlines across the country.[6]

Faced with this cultural shift, the RCMP did not sit idly by. Instead, it hired public relations consultants to reshape its image, which, RCMP leaders decided, needed to be less Victorian, less racist, and more about community membership than individual achievement. In short, the aim was to reinvent the mythic Mountie so that it fit more comfortably with a political culture that had been transformed by the civil rights movement of the 1960s and was in the process of embracing bilingualism and multiculturalism. The force's first and best opportunity to perform this renovation occurred in 1973, when it was called upon to publicly celebrate its hundredth anniversary.

These celebrations provided both opportunity and danger— for in a politically charged environment, the RCMP was aware that it needed to proceed cautiously. In consultation with its hired public relations experts, the force settled on a strategy that would employ a highly selective approach to history, one that would emphasize (and at times simply invent) elements of its

By the 1990s, souvenir manufacturers had embraced a multicultural interpretation of RCMP history that obscured the force's role in colonial expansion. Hence this Indigenous Mountie doll.

past that were likely to win over an increasingly sceptical public, such as ethnic harmony and a positive relationship with Indigenous peoples.

How keen was the police force to publicly embrace Canada's new multicultural orientation? Very. The 1973 centennial celebrations included a re-enactment of the NWMP's original (1874) westward march to the Prairies. In assigning parts for the officers to play no detail was overlooked. Each officer received a short character sketch to follow. One was told to emulate a "Half-breed scout." Another was asked to perform as if he was a "Happy-go-lucky Irishman." Both were meant to highlight the force's attempts to emphasize inclusiveness. But neither was nearly as ambitious as a third role, which called upon the participant to portray a "Czechoslovakian immigrant trying to learn the English language." Setting aside the unlikely idea that the nineteenth-century NWMP would hire an officer without a strong command of English, it's worth noting that in 1973 police officials were so keen to embrace the rhetoric of multiculturalism that they backdated Czechoslovakia's creation by some forty years![7]

A similar determination to embrace Canada's new political culture shaped representations of the police force's relationship with Aboriginal peoples. Aware of both the ongoing criticism of RCMP activities on First Nations' reserves and the tendency of those popularizing Mountie mythology to emphasize conflict between the force and Indigenous peoples, the organizers of the RCMP centennial celebrations went out of their way to avoid repeating past tropes. Instead, they chose very selectively from the force's history to highlight moments in which Aboriginal peoples praised the NWMP's actions. At times, this strategy required explicit instructions to rely on statements and examples from some First Nations leaders while ignoring the more critical views of many others.[8]

Commercial interests moved quickly to incorporate this updated mythology into their marketing campaigns. By the 1980s, for example, it was not difficult to find postcards featuring Mounties and First Nations peoples standing together as allies rather than enemies. Some Canadians, however, remained staunch supporters of the "traditional" Mountie image. Hence, their opposition to the decisions to hire female officers in 1974 and to allow a Sikh officer, Baltej Dhillon, to wear a turban while on duty in 1990. The latter episode proved particularly vicious, with an Alberta organization calling itself the Defenders of RCMP Tradition securing some 150,000 signatures opposing the decision. The sheer cruelty of the country's anti-immigrant sentiment was perhaps best conveyed by a widely circulated poster depicting a turbaned RCMP officer with the moniker "Sgt Camel Dung."[9]

Despite these voices of dissent, and the awkward elements involved in selectively mining the past for useable historical material to update the Mountie image, the renovation of Mountie mythology was largely successful. Perhaps the most tangible piece of evidence on this front was the decision by Walt Disney Canada to enter into a licensing agreement with the RCMP in 1995. In search of a marketable and politically correct symbol, the entertainment company was convinced that the mythic Mountie fit the bill—but only because the RCMP and its public relations allies had been hard at work editing and massaging—and even effacing—elements of the police force's history.

For much of its history the RCMP has benefitted from the popularity of its heroic image. Indeed, at times the romantic icon of the Mountie seemed to shield the force from sustained public scrutiny. The determined campaign to update the popular image in the early 1970s was certainly an attempt to maintain and perhaps enhance the efficacy of this protective imagery. But historical renovations can be expected to do only so much heavy

Minnie (Mouse) of the Mounted. Licensed by Disney and the RCMP, some of the proceeds from the sale of such toys are directed toward community policing initiatives.

lifting. And in fact, since the late 1990s, the RCMP has endured a series of self-inflicted public relations setbacks.

In particular, heavy-handed tactics and human-rights abuses have marred the police force's image in recent decades. In 2001, a $10 million public inquiry into the RCMP's actions at the 1997 Asia-Pacific Economic Cooperation summit in Vancouver found that many of the fifty-two formal complaints about the RCMP's treatment of protestors, which included instances of unnecessary pepper-spraying and inappropriate strip searches, were well founded.[10] In 2006, the RCMP commissioner was forced to issue a public apology for the role his organization played in facilitating the detention of Maher Arar by American officials. A public inquiry determined that the force had forwarded "inaccurate and misleading information" to American authorities that "very likely" led to Arar's arrest and deportation to Syria, where he was tortured and jailed for ten months.[11] The following year, Robert Dziekanski, a Polish immigrant arriving at Vancouver International Airport, was killed after being tasered five times and forcefully subdued by RCMP officers. His death resulted in yet another inquiry and a thirty-month sentence for an officer who was convicted of perjury and of colluding with his colleagues to cover up their actions.[12] As these controversies mounted, the federal government responded by appointing a civilian to head the RCMP from 2007 until 2011—an acknowledgement that the organization seemed incapable of addressing its shortcomings on its own.

Adding to this crisis in confidence in the national police force was a series of sexual discrimination complaints. By 2015, more than 350 female RCMP officers and employees were pursuing a class-action lawsuit against the force.[13] The following year, the police force set aside $100 million to compensate its former female employees for the "harassment, discrimination and sexual abuse" they suffered at the hands of male RCMP members.[14] More recently, a series of media reports have revealed a police force rife with frustration about "heavy caseloads, a toxic workplace culture, officer safety and low pay."[15] With internal and external criticism mounting, Canada's national police force appeared to be an organization in crisis.

During this sustained period of criticism, the RCMP endured two horrific events that laid bare the dangers facing its officers on a daily basis. In 2005, four RCMP officers were ambushed and killed during a raid on a marijuana grow op in Mayerthorpe, Alberta. In 2014, three RCMP officers were murdered and two others wounded as a result of a shooting rampage in Moncton, New Brunswick in which the assailant actively targeted police officers. Canadians marked these tragedies with widespread and sincere expressions of sympathy and support. Both events were the subject of lengthy reviews and investigations, but while the report on the Mayerthorpe shootings declared the incident unavoidable, examinations of the Moncton tragedy led to the successful prosecution of the RCMP for labour code violations that rendered its officers ill-equipped and vulnerable. The conviction earned the police force a $550,000 fine and thirty days' probation.[16]

As a national symbol, the mythic Mountie has undergone a pronounced transformation—from a celebratory ideal of Christian manliness and British achievement to a more inclusive and civic-based encapsulation of what it means to be Canadian. The latter version, hastily constructed in the early 1970s, successfully embraced the zeitgeist by tapping into a new English-Canadian nationalism that was increasingly comfortable with a multicultural orientation and which sought at least some measure of reconciliation with Indigenous peoples. Because of such adaptability, the mythic Mountie has remained a consistently attractive symbol for entrepreneurs and it has retained its allure for tourists—though its utility in shielding the actual police force from public criticism appears to be waning. National symbols (and national identities) are almost always presented as unchanging and traditional. In fact, as the Mountie shows us, they are often the product of awkward, creaking transitions and highly selective editing.

NOTES

1   Royal Canadian Mounted Police, "About the RCMP," 2016, rcmp-grc.gc.ca/about-ausujet/index-eng.htm.

2   Michael Dawson, "'That Nice Red Coat Goes to My Head Like Champagne': Gender, Antimodernism and the Mountie Image: 1880–1960," *Journal of Canadian Studies* 32, no. 3 (Fall 1997): 119–39.

3   Keith Walden, *Visions of Order: The Canadian Mounties in Symbol and Myth* (Toronto: Butterworths, 1982), 130.

4   Michael Dawson, *The Mountie from Dime Novel to Disney* (Toronto: Between the Lines, 1998), ch. 3.

5   Dawson, *The Mountie*, 81–4.

6   Ibid., 87–9.

7   Ibid., 134.

8   Ibid., 118.

9   "Turbans In The RCMP," *Parli: The Dictionary of Canadian Politics*, parli.ca/turbans-in-the-rcmp/.

10 "RCMP slammed in APEC report," *CBC News*, Aug. 7, 2001, cbc.ca/news/canada/rcmp-slammed-in-apec-report-1.266508.

11 "RCMP chief apologizes to Arar for 'terrible injustices'," *CBC News*, Sept. 28, 2006, cbc.ca/news/canada/rcmp-chief-apologizes-to-arar-for-terrible-injustices-1.578665.

12 "Robert Dziekanski Taser death: Kwesi Millington sentenced to 30 months for perjury," *CBC News*, June 22, 2015, cbc.ca/news/canada/british-columbia/robert-dziekanski-taser-death-kwesi-millington-sentenced-to-30-months-for-perjury-1.3122941.

13 "More than 350 female RCMP members seeking class-action suit, alleging decades of discrimination," *National Post* (Toronto), May 31, 2015.

14 "Mounties offer apology and $100M compensation for harassment, sexual abuse against female members," *CBC News*, Oct. 6, 2016, cbc.ca/news/politics/rcmp-paulson-compensation-harassment-1.3793785.

15 Alison Crawford, "Some Mounties swapping red serge for blue as they seek jobs with other forces," *CBC News*, Mar. 24, 2017, cbc.ca/news/politics/rcmp-mounties-leaving-jobs-police-1.4037752; Alison Crawford, "Thousands of Mounties sign union cards and remove the yellow stripes from their pants," *CBC News*, Apr. 10, 2017, cbc.ca/news/politics/mounties-sign-union-cards-1.4064903.

16 "RCMP deaths in Mayerthorpe unavoidable: judge," *CBC News*, Mar. 28, 2011, cbc.ca/news/canada/edmonton/rcmp-deaths-in-mayerthorpe-unavoidable-judge-1.1063248; "RCMP charged with labour code breach over deaths of three officers in Moncton shootings" *National Post* (Toronto), May 15, 2015; Kevin Bissett, "RCMP faces labour code trial for 'mistakes' in 2014 Moncton shootings," *Globe and Mail* (Toronto), Apr. 23, 2017; "RCMP must pay $550K penalty for Labour Code conviction in Moncton Mountie shootings," *CBC News*, Jan. 26, 2018, cbc.ca/news/canada/new-brunswick/moncton-mountie-shootings-rcmp-sentencing-1.4504819.

Louis-Philippe Hébert, *Dollard's Heroic Death at Long Sault*, 1895.
Appearing on the base of the monument to the founder of Montreal,
Paul Chomedey de Maisonneuve, this bas-relief is one of the most
reproduced images of the Battle of Long Sault.

DOLLARD DES ORMEAUX

Patrice Groulx

Imagine that you are a student at a French- Catholic boys' school between 1920 and 1960. You would have likely taken part, on or near May 24, in a patriotic ceremony in front of a statue, or perhaps a bust, of Dollard des Ormeaux. You might have participated in a military-style vigil, listened to speeches, acted in a play, or sung to the glory of the heroes of New France. You might have known, too, that thousands of other young people like yourself were doing the same thing. You might have identified with the seventeen valorous young Frenchmen who, at the Battle of Long Sault in May 1660, stopped what two

historians, writing in 1921, unproblematically described as the "swarming" of French settlers by "half-naked" Iroquois bent on "destroying the colony."[1] You might have asked yourself if, like them, you could have given your life for your country. Finally, your teachers, priests, and community leaders might have asked you this question: What sacrifices are you prepared to make today, Pierre, Raoul, or Georges, to prove yourself worthy of your ancestors?

What remains of this patriotic cult surrounding Adam Dollard, Sieur des Ormeaux? Frankly, not much. In Quebec, the

Fête de Dollard has been replaced by the Journée nationale des patriotes, or National Patriots' Day, while three public monuments remain the only tangible evidence of the cult's existence. The most famous is in Montreal and the most spectacular, a memorial garden, is in Argenteuil, near the site of the 1660 battle. Uncertain about the exact location of the conflict—which may well have occurred on the Ontario side of the Ottawa River—the Historic Sites and Monuments Board of Canada also put up two discreet bronze plaques, the main one in Quebec, and an "additional" one in Ontario, a model of commemorative ambivalence.[2]

Who was Adam Dollard des Ormeaux and what was the Battle of Long Sault? He was a young militia officer in Montreal in the late 1650s, when New France found itself on the brink of economic collapse: Haudenosaunee (Iroquois Confederacy) warriors had blocked the water routes into the interior of the continent, cutting off the fur trade. In the winter months, they trapped furs in the *pays d'en haut*, or upper country, and in the spring they brought them down the Ottawa River in small groups. Knowing their route, Dollard and sixteen other young men decided to launch a surprise attack in April 1660. At the same time, and with the same goal, forty Wendat (Huron) warriors, led by Annaotaha, a respected chief with experience in war, left Quebec. On the way, they were joined by several Anishinaabe (Algonquin) warriors. These sixty-odd men soon joined forces, forming a loose French-Indigenous alliance at the foot of the rapids at the Long Sault on the Ottawa River.

They didn't have to wait long before clashing with three hundred Haudenosaunee warriors, who forced them into a small abandoned fort that lacked water. Once alerted, five hundred other warriors arrived. The besieged held out for a week, their situation growing more and more desperate, "the cold, the stench, the sleeplessness, the hunger, and the thirst" breaking them "more than the enemy."[3] The Haudenosaunee launched a final assault and, in the end, the French, the Anishinabeg, and many Wendats were either killed or captured. The wounded were tortured on site, according to Haudenosaunee tradition. The rest were taken prisoner. A small number of Wendats escaped and reported to Montreal and Quebec what had happened. The Haudenosaunee returned home.

Discovering that the Haudenosaunee had intended to invade the colony, the French concluded that Dollard and his companions had saved the country. But why had the Haudenosaunee changed their plans after the initial battle? Had they suffered too many losses? Had they been surprised by the resistance they encountered? Or had they returned home in order to share their prisoners? (In effect, the capture of Wendat warriors was for them a spring highlight!) Still, in their reports to France, colonial officials used the battle at the Long Sault to press for more military aid.

Little by little, the heroes of 1660 were forgotten as other attacks poisoned life in the colony. It was not until 1845 that François-Xavier Garneau, in his book *The History of Canada*, became the first modern historian to write about the Battle of Long Sault. For Garneau, Dollard and his companions were model citizen-soldiers who inspired respect for the French-Canadian nation.[4] But he viewed the past through a secular lens. In the 1860s, the Catholic Church prescribed a religious conception of the world and, in the process, transformed the history of New France into a nursery for model Christians ready to sacrifice their life for the triumph of the faith. Abbé Faillon, in particular, identified a mortal menace (the Iroquois), a collective hero (Dollard and his companions), an approximate date (May 21, 1660), and a place (the Long Sault). In his version of events, the French took the initiative of voluntary sacrifice to save the colony. The defeat was in fact a victory because the Iroquois were terrified by the resistance mounted by such a small number of

The Dollard monument in Montreal's Parc Lafontaine at its inauguration, June 24, 1920. Artist Alfred Laliberté imagined Dollard brandishing a sword and protecting an allegorical New France.

Frenchmen.[5] Writers began to produce poems and plays on the Battle of Long Sault; the best artists of the day illustrated them with engravings, paintings, and sculptures; and all subsequent history books repeated this fabled version of the event.

Dollard's exploits crossed the linguistic divide in 1874, when the American historian Francis Parkman introduced the hero to his many readers in the United States and Canada.[6] Even if their collective memories were different,[7] both French and English writers shared a basic conviction: the colonization of North America was legitimate and European "civilization" was superior to Indigenous "barbarism." Parkman's work was the source of inspiration for one of the pageants—an outdoor historical spectacle—presented during the celebrations of Quebec's tercentenary in 1908.[8] It was also turned into a silent film shot on location in Montreal and Kahnawake and distributed by the Maple Leaf Exclusive Film Exchange in 1912.[9]

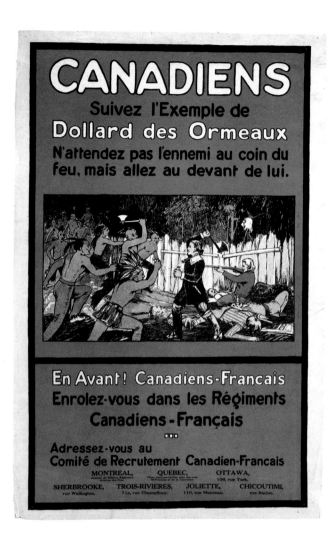

"French Canadians, follow the example of Dollard des Ormeaux," 1914–18. In order to recruit French Canadians to an unpopular war, the Canadian government hoped, without success, that Dollard's sacrifice would serve as an example.

Dollard was so well known that the *Montreal Herald,* an English-language daily, led an initiative to highlight the two hundred and fiftieth anniversary of the Battle of Long Sault in 1910, in effect launching a movement to build a monument in Montreal to Dollard and his companions.[10] However, the fundraising campaign was marked by nationalist drum beating among French-Canadian elites who wanted to recall Dollard's bravery and sacrifice. For them, Confederation had been a series of deceptions; the attacks against French-language education rights in the Maritimes and the West had in the meantime only increased; and both the federal Liberals and Conservatives had supported British imperialism in the Boer War in 1899, fueling yet more tensions between Quebec and English Canada. Quebec's anger was further fanned by a 1912 regulation banning French-language education in Ontario and, five years later, by the conscription crisis brought on by the First World War. It was in this context of competing nationalisms that French-Canadian and English-Canadian memories of the Battle of Long Sault diverged completely. The campaign to raise funds was so successful that soon there was enough money to build two monuments, not just one. Both commissions went to sculptor Alfred Laliberté, best known for his depictions of national moments and traditions in Quebec history.[11] In 1919, a large grave stone was erected at Carillon, near the Long Sault rapids on the Ottawa River. A year later, a large, majestic monument was unveiled in Montreal's Parc Lafontaine.

Meanwhile, depictions of the Haudenosaunee changed. In propaganda posters during the First World War, the Haudenosaunee were used as a metaphor for German barbarism. Later, they came to represent the cultural domination of the English language in North America. "If Dollard were alive today," wrote Abbé Lionel Groulx, Quebec's most famous historian and its leading Dollard propagandist, he would not be met "by the confused call of a race yet to be born," but rather by "the worried and gasping voice of a people dispersed to the four corners of the continent who feel surrounded by a formidable coalition of ancient barbarism."[12]

Because the Battle of Long Sault took place at the end of May, it offered an auspicious, even audacious, moment to reinvent the meaning of Victoria Day in Quebec.[13] The Association catholique de la jeunesse canadienne, the journal *Action nationale,* and the priest-historian Lionel Groulx had already seized on Dollard's religious connotations to transfigure him into a symbol of French Canada's resistance to its minority status. Now Victoria Day, which celebrated Canada's attachment to the British Empire, could be transformed in 1920 into Fête de Dollard, a day to celebrate French Canada and mobilize young people in public demonstrations of patriotism—parades, special masses, and oaths of national loyalty. Both the Scouts and the military cadets participated in this expression of national pride.[14] School children, including a young Pierre Trudeau, wrote short papers on Dollard and his companions, calling them martyrs and saints. (Trudeau's teacher wrote "Beau travail" on the future prime minister's assignment.[15]) Dollard even became a first name, as seen, for example, with Brigadier General Dollard Ménard, a Second World War hero, and the hockey player Dollard Saint-Laurent. And in the 1920s, Dollard des Ormeaux became the name of a suburb on the Island of Montreal and of a village—three thousand kilometres to the west—in Saskatchewan.[16] Looking back many years later, Abbé Groulx remembered the enthusiasm of young French-Canadian Catholics who had presented, with great pomp, busts of Dollard to the House of Commons, the Legislative Assembly, the Montreal City Council, and the University of Montreal.[17]

Yet at the same time, history, as an academic discipline, became more scientific and critical of its own nationalist excesses.

In the 1930s, researchers began to view some of the heroes associated with foundational events in Canadian history, including General Wolfe, Laura Secord, and Adam Dollard, through a more critical lens.[18] The McGill historian E. R. Adair doubted that it was ever Dollard's intention to save New France, arguing instead that the French-Indigenous expedition had intended to steal the furs of the Haudenosaunee and that Dollard was caught in a trap

Dollard, 1921, detail from a print by Jean-Baptiste Lagacé. This image was one of thirty-six colour prints depicting key moments in Quebec's history included in a school textbook and hung in classrooms.

An April 1926 advertisement in *L'Action française*, a monthly journal. The memory of the Battle of Long Sault was represented in any manner of ways—in plaster busts, on stamps and postcards, and in stories, poems, and plays. The Dollard rose, shown here, was meant to be worn on Fête de Dollard and was intended to rival the red poppy worn on Armistice Day.

of his own making. "As a saviour of his country," Adair wrote, "Adam Dollard, Sieur des Ormeaux, must be relegated to the museum of historical myths."[19]

That didn't happen, at least not right away. In order to rally support for conscription in Quebec during the Second World War—despite the solemn promise that conscription would not be instituted this time around—the Canadian Army organized its own Fête de Dollard with parades and assemblies featuring politicians who now renounced their opposition to conscription. The federal government's exploitation of Dollard, according to Abbé Groulx, discredited both him and his companions. "The imposture disgusted young people," he said. "To celebrate Dollard, dressed up as a recruiting agent for the defence of Christianity and the British Empire, was to be complicit in nonsense."[20]

Meanwhile, commemorative fatigue was setting in. Frozen in the contemplation of a sanctified past, the celebration of Dollard and its religious overtones did not reflect the spirit of protest spreading across Quebec after the war. It no longer resonated with young people and, more problematically, it degraded Indigenous people in Quebec's collective imagination. For a growing segment of the public, Dollard represented a conservative nationalism, Catholic and anti-Indigenous. In 1958, the writer and socialist Jacques Ferron proposed replacing Dollard with André Chénier, a patriot leader killed in the armed uprising of 1837 and a symbol of a revolutionary and anticolonial ideal.[21] There is not, he explained, "any glory to be found against the Iroquois, more colonized than us and representatives of the Third World."[22] Indeed, the Rebellions of 1837–38, in both Lower and Upper Canada, expressed the profound desire to reform and even abolish foreign domination.

During the tercentenary celebration of the Battle of Long Sault in 1960, Dollard was at once the object of celebration and of mockery. Abbé Groulx clung to the idea that Dollard's heroism

In this 1960 editorial cartoon, Robert La Palme of *La Presse* symbolically reverses the Dollard myth. The "good" become the "evil." Dollard is depicted as Nikita Khrushchev, leader of the Soviet Union, besieged in the company of other communist leaders, including East Germany's Walter Ulbricht, Poland's Wladyslaw Gomulka, China's Mao Zedong, and Vietnam's Ho Chi Minh. Confronting him are the leaders of the Western world, American President Dwight Eisenhower, British Prime Minister Harold Macmillan, and French President Charles de Gaulle.

was not a myth,[23] but Quebecers, when it came to their national symbols, were undertaking a massive house cleaning. Slowly but surely, Dollard faded from Quebec's collective memory. And in November 2002, the governing Parti Québécois replaced the Fête de la Reine et de Dollard with the Journée nationale des patriotes in the calendar of official holidays, recalling that "in the spring of 1837, 100 popular assemblies were held across Quebec, bringing together more than 10,000 people, in order to claim reforms and the creation of a democratic system of government."[24] Because the idea of replacing the Fête de Dollard with the Journée nationale des patriotes had achieved consensus, the new name was kept by the federalist Liberal Party when it was elected a few months later, in April 2003.

A handful of authors remain attached to Dollard and persist in nourishing his memory, because courage, especially if it is tragic, is always worthy of respect. But it is the Battle of Long Sault, because of the range of interpretative strategies that can be brought to bear on the event, that fascinates the majority of observers.[25] Studying the battle from the perspective of Indigenous peoples has opened a new avenue of research, one that

The Dollard monument in Montreal's Parc Lafontaine was vandalized in June 2016. Because monuments depict specific interpretations, or readings, of history, they are convenient targets in today's history wars. In this instance, the excessive language—a colonist-soldier, Dollard was neither a rapist nor an assassin—highlights Dollard's violence and challenges the monument's depiction of him as the protector of New France. However, we cannot know for sure what the author meant given that no one claimed responsibility.

deliberately decentres Dollard and instead focuses on Annaotaha, the Wendat chief. Only a Eurocentric interpretation of the evidence, concludes one historian, would put Dollard at the centre of events: what happened at the Long Sault was not about the French and the Haudenosaunee, it was about two historical enemies, the Haudenosaunee and the Wendat.[26] For their part, the Haudenosaunee have not preserved the memory of an event that for them had no long-term consequences.[27]

In 1920, the Battle of Long Sault was celebrated in an effort to denounce the emergence of a civilization founded on materialism, selfishness, and ignorance of the past. Produced by great artists, the various monuments to Dollard venerated the lost "heroic age" of New France, but their original meanings no longer resonate and are now opaque. In Montreal's Parc Lafontaine and in Carillon these monuments are defaced, even mutilated.[28] The large memorial garden in Argenteuil has since 2015 hosted an electronic music festival, the cries of the young combatants from 1660 replaced day and night by the rhythmic beat of synthesizers and the clamour of a largely American-inspired commercial culture.[29] If Abbé Groulx were alive today, he would see the triumph of the "barbarism" that he denounced. What are we to make of the irony of this new incarnation of Dollard as a symbol?

The author wishes to thank Donald Wright for translating this chapter from French into English.

NOTES

1 See *Tableaux d'histoire Desrosiers-Bertrand* (Montreal: Granger Frères, 1921), s.v. "Dollard."

2 Parks Canada, "Fight at the Long-Sault National Historic Event," pc.gc.ca/apps/dfhd/page_nhs_eng.aspx?id=1384&i=60945.

3 Adrien Pouliot and Silvio Dumas, eds., *L'exploit du Long-Sault: Les témoignages des contemporains* (Quebec: Société historique de Québec, 1960), 27.

4 François-Xavier Garneau, *History of Canada*, vol. 1, trans. Andrew Bell (Montreal: John Lovell, 1860), 155–6.

5 Étienne-Michel Faillon, *Histoire de la colonie française en Canada*, vol. 2 (Montreal, 1866), 395–419.

6 Francis Parkman, *The Old Régime in Canada*, vol. 1 (Boston: Little, Brown, 1906, [1874]), 127–39.

7 See Alan Gordon, *Making Public Pasts: The Contested Terrain of Montreal's Public Memories, 1891–1930* (Montreal and Kingston: McGill-Queen's University Press, 2001).

8 H. V. Nelles, *The Art of Nation Building: Pageantry and Spectacle at Quebec's Tercentenary* (Toronto: University of Toronto Press, 1999), 140–63.

9 See "Filmographie: Fiche de film," *The Battle of the Long Sault*, cri.histart.umontreal.ca/grafics/fr/filmo/viewrec.asp?lang=fr&id=257.

10 "1660–Dollard des Ormeaux–1910," *Montreal Herald*, Mar. 26, 1910.

11 Aegidius Fauteux, "Introduction," in E. Z. Massicotte, ed., *Dollard des Ormeaux: Notes et Documents* (Montreal: Le Comité du Monument, 1920), 15.

12 Lionel Groulx, *Si Dollard revenait…* (Montreal: Bibliothèque de l'Action française, 1919), 13.

13 Patrice Groulx, *Pièges de la mémoire: Dollard des Ormeaux, les Amérindiens et nous* (Hull, QC: Vents d'ouest, 1998), 206.

14 Ibid, 197–243.

15 John English, *Citizen of the World: The Life of Pierre Elliott Trudeau* (Toronto: Knopf, 2006), 26.

16 See Ville de Dollard-Des Ormeaux, "Histoire," ville.ddo.qc.ca/ma-municipalite/histoire; "Dollard," Musée virtuel francophone de la Saskatchewan, available online at musee.societehisto.com/dollard-n381-t661.html.

17 Lionel Groulx, *Mes mémoires*, vol. 2 (Montreal: Fides, 1971), 52–4.

18 See E. R. Adair, "The Military Reputation of Major-General James Wolfe," *Canadian Historical Association Annual Report* (1936); and Colin Coates and Cecilia Morgan, *Heroines and History: Representations of Madeleine de Verchères and Laura Secord* (Toronto: University of Toronto Press, 2002).

19 E. R. Adair, "A Re-interpretation of Dollard's Exploit," *Canadian Historical Review* 13, no. 2 (June 1932): 138.

20 Groulx, *Mes mémoires*, vol. 2, 58.

21 Jacques Ferron, "Sieur Dollard, trois fois morts [sic]," *Historiettes* (Montreal: Éditions du Jour, 1969), 135–44; Patrice Groulx, *Pièges de la mémoire*, 291–326.

22 Jacques Ferron, "Lionel Groulx et le nationalisme noir," *Le Jour* (Saint-Laurent, QC), Jan. 13, 1978.

23 Lionel Groulx, *Dollard est-il un mythe?* (Montreal: Fides, 1960); André Vachon, "Dollard des Ormeaux, Adam," *Dictionary of Canadian Biography*, vol. 1 (University of Toronto/Université Laval, 2003), biographi.ca/en/bio/dollard_des_ormeaux_adam_1E.html.

24 "Décret 1322-2002, 20 novembre 2002, concernant la Journée nationale des patriotes," *Gazette officielle du Québec*, Dec. 11, 2002, no. 50, 8463.

25 See Aurélien Boisvert, *Dollard, ses compagnons et ses alliés selon les textes du xviiie siècle* (Sillery, QC: Septentrion, 2005); Jean Laporte, *La vieille dame, l'archéologue et le chanoine: la saga de Dollard* (Vanier, On: Éditions l'Interligne, 1995); Terry Crowley, "Doing History," in Crowley, ed., *Clio's Craft: A Primer of Historical Methods* (Mississauga, ON: Copp Clark Pitman, 1988), 253–303.

26 John A. Dickinson, "Annaotaha et Dollard vus de l'autre côté de la palissade," *Revue d'histoire de l'Amérique française* 35, no. 2 (Sept. 1981): 163–78.

27 David Blanchard, *Seven Generations: A History of the Kanienkehaka* (Kahnawake, QC: Kahnawake Survival School, 1980).

28 Camille Dufétel, "Le monument à Dollard des Ormeaux vandalisé," *Le Journal de Montréal*, June 28, 2016; Éric-Yvan Lemay, "On a volé Dollard des Ormeaux!," *Le Journal de Montréal*, July 12, 2009.

29 See "Montreal AIM Electronic Music Festival," fr-ca.facebook.com/Montreal-AIM-Electronic-Music-Festival-513459868790359/.

The War of 1812
La guerre de 1812

Laura Secord

CANADA

2012 Laura Secord postage stamp.

LAURA SECORD

Cecilia Morgan

Despite the flurry of commemorative activity that recently surrounded the two hundredth anniversary of the War of 1812, most Canadians probably associate Laura Secord with the candy company that bears her name. Indeed, Secord's identity is so readily identified with confections that the CBC Television comedy show *This Hour Has 22 Minutes* has repeatedly incorporated this theme into its satirical sketches. In one, Secord is played by a male, mixed-race actor chased through the woods by beavers intent on stealing her chocolates; in another, played by a female comic, Secord attempts to deliver her message to British troops, who care only that she makes them chocolates (and who are killed by Americans as a result).[1]

Early twentieth-century English-Canadian nationalists and feminists—Secord's first commemorators—would not have been amused. Their depictions of Secord's famous walk were earnest to the point of piety, a quality noticed by cartoonists and satirists since the 1960s, who have mocked her walk as a means of poking fun at the seriousness of earlier forms of English-Canadian nationalism. Each of these groups related to Secord's narrative in very different ways, but they shared one quality:

IN EGYPT, CLEOPATRA IS A LOVE GODDESS. FRANCE TURNED JOAN OF ARC INTO A SAINT... CANADA PUT ME ON A CHOCOLATE BOX!

Aislin cartoon, 1998.

the Niagara River. Around 1797, Laura Ingersoll married James Secord, a young Queenston merchant whose family had been part of the influx of Loyalist refugees fleeing the American Revolution; the couple went on to have six daughters and one son.

In June 1812, the United States declared war against Britain, the culmination of tensions that had been escalating between the two countries during the Napoleonic Wars (1799–1815). The Americans then launched a series of attacks on Upper Canada beginning in August 1812; in October of that year James Secord, a member of the colony's militia, was badly wounded at the Battle of Queenston Heights. By the early summer of 1813, British and American troops were vying for control of the Niagara Peninsula. On June 21, the Secords received news of a surprise attack to be launched against British lieutenant James FitzGibbon at Beaver Dams, approximately thirty-two kilometres to the west of Queenston. With her husband unable to make the journey, Laura set out the next morning to warn FitzGibbon, tramping on foot through the rough terrain of the Niagara bush until she met an encampment of Haudenosaunee warriors. She convinced them that she needed to see FitzGibbon, and delivered her news to him. With this information, the British and Indigenous fighters were able to outwit the Americans and win the Battle of Beaver Dams. The battle did not end the war: that would not happen until the 1814 Treaty of Ghent. Nor did it end the American belligerence in the Niagara area, which came to a head with the burning of Newark (present-day Niagara-on-the-Lake) in December 1813. But the Battle of Beaver Dams has been regarded by military historians as an important moment when the Americans were prevented from dominating the region.[2]

The subsequent commemoration of Secord as a heroine of Upper Canada did not occur overnight. She went home once it was safe to travel—the details of her return are hazy, to say the least—and resumed her life with James and their children.

the desire to use Secord for their own purposes. Secord is also notable as a national symbol since, unlike the vast majority of female figures who have come to symbolize Western nations, her story centres on the exploits of an actual—not mythical or allegorical—woman.

She was born Laura Ingersoll in 1775 in Barrington, Massachusetts, and, along with her family, emigrated to Upper Canada in 1795, settling in the village of Queenston, near the mouth of

The first written accounts of her walk are to be found in various petitions, filed from the 1820s on, to the Upper Canadian government requesting either patronage appointments or a pension in recognition for her service to the Crown. Like many other Upper Canadians, the depredations of the war had left the Secords in financial distress, as James's disabilities made it very hard for him to support his family. Little came of these requests, though. It was not until 1845 that the first published account of Secord's walk appeared in the *Church*, an Anglican paper. Written by the Secords' son Charles, its purpose was not to honour his mother's loyal service, but rather to support James FitzGibbon's pension claim.[3]

During the mid-nineteenth century, Secord's narrative began to appear in a number of histories of the War of 1812, both in the United States and in Canada. By 1860, she gained recognition for her contribution to the war effort when the Prince of Wales, currently touring British North America, awarded her one hundred pounds.[4] In 1864, Ontario historian William F. Coffin wrote an account of her walk that added a cow to Secord's story, claiming that she had taken it to milk as a way of getting past American sentries. While there is no evidence of her doing so, the cow has persisted in many popular accounts and has been used to emphasize Secord as a symbol of pioneer domesticity—and thus assuage concerns about celebrating female involvement in such a pivotal military endeavour.

Laura Secord died in 1868 and thus did not live to see her story became part of the popular commemoration of the war, a process that started in the late 1880s with a campaign to put up a monument that united middle-class English-Canadian women's rights supporters, English-Canadian nationalists, and advocates of Canada's imperial ties to Britain.[5] Temperance advocate and suffragist Sarah Curzon and St. Catharines resident and suffragist Emma Currie wrote accounts of Secord's

Map of the Niagara Frontier, 1812–1815.

walk; with their contemporaries in women's groups and in the newly formed Ontario Historical Society, they were successful in their efforts to raise monuments to Secord in Niagara Falls (1901) and Queenston Heights (1910).[6] Over the course of the early twentieth century, school textbooks began to publish accounts of Secord's walk. Along with Madeleine de Verchères, the "heroine" of New France, Secord often was the only historical woman to appear in these texts.[7] In 1913, Ontario businessman (and future senator) Frank O'Connor named his candy company after Secord. According to company lore, O'Connor did so out

Mrs. James Secord, c. 1865.

of a desire to identify his products with wholesomeness, purity, domesticity, and cleanliness.

National symbols often take on different layers of meaning over time. In Secord's case, little changed as far as the basic elements of her story were concerned: her commemorators' claim that she was a loyal and patriotic heroine always rested on her walk to Beaver Dams. What did change, though, were some of the details of the story, the elaboration of certain aspects of it, and the meanings that were meant to be drawn from these embellishments. One of the most striking aspects of Secord's transformation into an English-Canadian heroine was the theme of her femininity, which rested on her domesticity, her role as a wife and mother—and thus her respectability. Her commemorators focused on the details of her appearance, such as her physical fragility, which masked a sturdiness of character and bravery. They also provided detailed descriptions of her clothing, even though historical accounts of it were scarce. Most importantly, these narratives emphasized her role as a wife and mother, stressing her devotion to her family as well as to the Crown. Some writers believed that after finding her husband wounded at Queenston Heights, Secord had protected him against brutal American soldiers.[8]

For these commemorators, Secord's walk was proof that settler women in Canada were capable of being both devoted wives and mothers and dedicated members of the nation and the British Empire. If Secord, a pioneer housewife and mother, could make such a contribution to the Dominion's well-being, then her (figurative) descendants could follow in her footsteps by winning the right to vote. Woman's suffrage, then, would not undermine their femininity and commitment to home and family. Even those Canadian nationalists who were not keen to see the franchise extended to women could see Secord as a symbol of loyalty to country and Crown. After all, she returned home once her duty

Laura Secord monument, Queenston Heights.

Secord Company candy boxes, c. 1920s.

was done and did not ask for any reward, thus representing both maternal and national self-sacrifice. Furthermore, she did not take up arms: there was, in other words, no suggestion that she had behaved in a disreputable or disorderly manner.[9]

But for her supporters, Secord was not just any woman: her whiteness was also a significant aspect of her story. Turning

Laura Secord into a symbol of white settler society was accomplished in various ways. Most importantly, over time the narratives of her walk stressed, and indeed elaborated on, her encounter with Indigenous warriors. Secord's earliest petition of 1820 did not mention this meeting and she touched upon it only briefly in her 1840 account; by 1853 she discussed it in greater detail, mentioning that she'd met "an Indian," had felt great fear, and yet had overcome it. But as her story was retold, her commemorators had much more to say about Secord's emotions on encountering the Haudenosaunee, since according to the historians their violence was memorable. In more than one textbook, the illustrations that accompanied these narratives reinforced these sentiments. While some artists presented the Haudenosaunee as dignified figures of diplomacy, others showed them as threatening, brutal, and vicious figures who were a direct danger to Secord, whose blonde hair, fair skin, and modestly clothed body contrasted with the dark-skinned, muscular, and nearly

Laura Secord Meets the Kahnawake Mohawk,
Henry Sandham, 1927.

Meeting Between Laura Secord and James FitzGibbon.
Lorne K. Smith, 1920. This painting was used in a
number of school textbooks.

nude physiques of Indigenous men.[10] And although the candy company rarely featured Secord's walk in its advertising, its portrayal of Secord became progressively youthful and evocative of upper-class white femininity, and it often employed symbols of Canada, such as maple leaves.[11] The company also advised its store managers to hire blond women, whenever possible, as salesclerks, although it is difficult to know if this policy was put into practice.[12]

In 1930, Laura Secord's story came under attack by William Stewart Wallace, a University of Toronto librarian and historian. Wallace conceded that Secord had performed her famous walk, but he argued that her historical significance was highly overrated. The story as she told it, Wallace claimed, was based on her memory and did not match the "facts" of her accounts. In short, she had not played a part in determining the battle's outcome because, according to Wallace, FitzGibbon already knew of the impending attack from Indigenous scouts.

What precipitated Wallace's desire to challenge Laura Secord's story? Many myths and half-truths had grown up around the War of 1812; Wallace could surely have chosen other events and figures. What was at stake for him, though, was not just Secord herself but the very nature of historical "truth," historical methodology, and the question of who was a "real" historian. For Wallace, historical veracity was to be found in the military and legal sources on which he based his account. He objected to both Secord's and FitzGibbon's stories because they were based on memory, which he called "treacherous and fallacious." He also attacked Secord's 1820 account because it was motivated by financial need. However, Wallace did not subject the military accounts to the same scrutiny, nor did he question their narrators' possible motives (military pensions and glory).

Overall, Wallace's target was not just Secord but also her commemorators, the most prominent having been women historians based in local and women's historical societies. In contrast, Wallace was part of a larger movement to professionalize Canadian history, one that sought greater recognition for those historians based in the country's universities. In his eyes, only those with academic training in the discipline (mostly, although not entirely, men) and whose accounts were based in the careful scrutiny of official documents should be considered historical experts, not those amateurs who believed in romantic tales and whose narratives were grounded in unverifiable reminiscences.[13]

Wallace's attack was met with great indignation by Secord's supporters, who mounted a number of public defences in her support. Some textbook writers simply ignored Wallace. Others, though, modified their accounts of Secord's walk; they claimed that even if FitzGibbon had already received the news, Secord was a very brave woman and thus an inspiration to children, especially girls.[14] Yet despite all this, Secord's appeal as a national symbol of feminine service and loyalty did not vanish. For one, the candy company's advertising kept her name in the public consciousness, particularly in the Niagara Region. In the early 1970s, the company bought and renovated the Secord home in Queenston, turning it into an interpretive site with costumed guides and a candy store next to it.[15] Moreover, even if textbook writers changed the way they treated Secord's walk, she still remained one of the very few Canadian women to be included in the teaching of Canadian history. A 1999 internet poll named Secord as one of the top ten most memorable Canadians, along with Terry Fox, Louis Riel, Tommy Douglas, Nellie McClung, and Isaac Brock.[16] On the level of popular consciousness, then, Wallace failed in his attempts to debunk Laura Secord.

It is perhaps not a surprise, since her story was always meant to inspire children as well as adults, that Secord's name lives on today in books for girls, Ontario's elementary curriculum, and on school buildings in a number of Canadian cities.[17] At the national level, the Department of Canadian Heritage declared Secord a person of national significance in 2003, and it erected a plaque commemorating her walk at the Secords' Queenston homestead. Three years later, a statue of Secord was erected as part of Ottawa's Valiants Memorial, a site that features individuals involved in wars from the period of the French Regime (1534–1763) to the Second World War. Described by the government in unabashedly nationalistic sentiments, the site honours "Canadians" known for their patriotism, heroism, and nation building.[18] During the bicentennial commemoration of the War of 1812 in 2012, Secord's image appeared on both a coin issued by the Royal Canadian Mint and a postage stamp.[19] In the latter image, a bonneted Laura Secord gazes calmly at the viewer, as if she is accepting thanks for her service—but in a modest and dignified manner.

Recent commemorations of Secord continue to treat her walk in different ways. For example, the walk is the subject of a Heritage Minute, in which Secord's meeting with the Kahnawake Mohawk is depicted as a moment of union in the struggle to save Canada. The short film played fast and loose with the historical

Laura Secord in the Angel Inn, Niagara-on-the-Lake.

give her any speaking lines at all.[21] This representation of Secord is a clear departure from other depictions. Since the late nineteenth century, feminists, nationalists, and imperialists strove to ensure that her voice was heard and incorporated into the historical record.

Commemorations of Secord that anchor her firmly to the Niagara area are, it seems, more meaningful to their creators than grandiose national narratives. The Friends of Laura Secord, a non-profit organization led by one of her descendants, has set up the Laura Secord Legacy Trail, a hiking path that reconstructs her walk from Queenston to Beaver Dams. While the Friends claim Secord as a "Canadian" heroine, they also seek to remember First Nations' and African-Canadians' contributions to the war and to encourage people to appreciate the environment and the health benefits of walking.[22] Moreover, during the 2012 commemorations, Toronto artist Barbara Klunder staged an exhibit of paper cuts and a book that tells Secord's story. Although these works honour Secord's bravery, they also incorporate the motifs of death and destruction—seen through such images as soldiers' skeletons—thereby pointing to a counternarrative of the War of 1812.[23] Klunder's work confronts the triumphalist and militaristic narratives pushed by the Conservative government, which glorified the War of 1812 as an exercise in patriotism and nation building.

And, lastly, some representations of Secord have been more irreverent and sexualized. In Jane Urquhart's 1987 novel *The Whirlpool,* the main character (himself an amateur historian) is so enamoured of Secord that he persuades his bride, in fulfillment of his sexual fantasy, to wear "a muddy calico dress"—in effect, to dress as he imagines Secord would have dressed and to appear as he imagines Secord would have appeared, wild and in disarray "after her valorous trek through the woods."[24] As well, a cheeky and sexualized image of the 1812 "heroine" hangs in

record by suggesting that Secord and the Mohawk consciously united to defeat a common enemy, the Americans. Significantly, this version downplays the racial tensions that underpinned early twentieth-century descriptions of their meeting; moreover, Secord is the central character in this drama.[20] In contrast, the federal government's 2012 video of Secord's walk does not

Niagara-on-the-Lake's Angel Inn. The candy company, it seems, does not enjoy a monopoly on the commercialization of Laura Secord's image, as she offers the inducement of the Angel Inn's beer as a reason to walk the hazardous path to Beaver Dams.

Secord's story, then, grew over the course of the nineteenth and early twentieth centuries, both in its detail and its importance. In the hands of multiple narrators, her walk to Beaver Dams was used to promote nationalism, feminism, the imperial tie to Britain, and the importance of local history. Some also used it to promote their literary careers and—not least—to boost Canadian commerce in the form of chocolate sales. In this way, the tale of Laura Secord's walk to Beaver Dams shows us how historical events and personalities can be both used and abused in the creation of a national symbol. Moreover, it suggests how an obscure figure can take on national significance. Little was known, after all, about Secord and her walk and she died long before her heyday as a national symbol. Thus her commemorators were able to create—and then recreate—a narrative for their own purposes. One wonders what Laura Secord would have made of their stories.

NOTES

1   "Secord Chocolates 1812," *This Hour Has 22 Minutes* (CBC Television, 2012), cbc.ca/22minutes/videos/clips-season-20/secord-chocolates-1812; Jane Taber, "All in a day's work: Poking fun at Laura Secord, hockey and Harper," *Globe and Mail* (Toronto), Sept. 16, 2010.

2   Ruth McKenzie, "Ingersoll, Laura (Secord)," *Dictionary of Canadian Biography*, vol. 9 (University of Toronto/Université Laval, 2003), biographi.ca/en/bio/ingersoll_laura_9E.html.

3   Colin M. Coates and Cecilia Morgan, *Heroines and History: Representations of Madeleine de Verchères and Laura Secord* (Toronto: University of Toronto Press, 2002), 122–7.

4   Ibid., 129.

5   Ibid., 149–57.

6   Ibid., 195–207.

7   Ibid., 214.

8   Ibid., 151.

9   Ibid., 153.

10 Ibid., 151–3.

11 Ibid., 215–31.

12 "Memorandum to Laura Secord Store Managers," c. 1920s, Laura Secord Company Archives.

13 Coates and Morgan, *Heroines and History*, 157–62.

14 Ibid., 162–3.

15 Ibid., 248–50.

16 Ibid., 266.

17 For example, see Connie Brummel Crook, *Laura's Choice: the Story of Laura Secord* (Winnipeg: Wildflower Communications, 1992); Susan E. Merritt, "Laura Ingersoll Secord: Heroine of the War of 1812," ch. 6 in Merritt, *Her Story: Women From Canada's Past* (St. Catharines, ON: Vanwell Publishing, 1994). See also Ontario Ministry of Education, "Social Studies Grades 1 to 6 and History and Geography Grades 7 and 8," *The Ontario Curriculum, 2013*, available online at edu.gov.on.ca/eng/curriculum/elementary/sshg18curr2013.pdf. Laura Secord schools can be found in Vancouver, St. Catharines, and Winnipeg.

18 Government of Canada, "Valiants Memorial," canada.pch.gc.ca/eng/1443025435856/1443025433752.

19 Don Fraser, "Coin and Stamp Celebrate a Canadian Heroine," *Welland Tribune*, June 21, 2013.

20 Sponsored by a non-profit organization, Heritage Minutes is a series of minute-long short films portraying significant people or events in Canada's history.

21 See Government of Canada, "Transcript of Laura Secord," canada.ca/en/canadian-heritage/services/art-monuments/monuments/valiants/video-laura-secord.html.

22 For more information, see friendsoflaurasecord.com/.

23 Barbara Klunder, "Weekly Fibre Artist Interviews," worldofthreadsfestival.com/artist_interviews/120-barbara-klunder-14.html.

24 Jane Urquhart, *The Whirlpool* (Toronto: McClelland and Stewart, 1986), 50, 53.

In 1934, the *Toronto Star* and the *Winnipeg Free Press* ran major spreads of startlingly realistic war photographs, drawing praise from veterans grateful that, after years of official censorship and saccharine romanticism, candid war images were available to the public.

VIMY RIDGE

Ian McKay and Jamie Swift

It happened at 5:30 a.m. on April 9, 1917.

For years, on the Great War's Western Front extending from the North Sea to the Alps, the British and the French had struggled to regain lands lost to the invading Germans. And for years they had confronted the great towering whaleback fortress of German-held Vimy Ridge, commanding the Douai Plain in northern France and repelling every Allied attack.

They said the Ridge could not be taken. But they forgot to explain that to the rugged, fighting Canadians under General Arthur Currie—those brave country boys fighting, according to historian Jonathan Vance, for "Canada, Western civilization, and Christianity."[1]

Amidst the snow and sleet, after months of meticulous planning, the Canadians, nearly one-hundred-thousand-strong, followed an ear-splitting barrage that shook the Ridge and its German defenders. Then, over the course of the next few days, through discipline and fortitude, they conquered them. In this "big turning point in the war," the Canadian Army did much more than seize a height of land in distant Europe. It constructed the "crucible of Canadian nationhood."[2] "We went up Vimy Ridge as

Royal Canadian Legion haberdashers flog busy-looking ball caps that feature the Vimy memorial, the Legion's poppy logo, colour bars representing four Canadian divisions and, of course, the "Birth of a Nation" claim.

Albertans and Nova Scotians," goes the saying. "We came down as Canadians."[3]

According to popular historian Pierre Berton, "Canadians could grumble that Ypres, the Somme, and Passchendaele were bungled by the British. But Vimy! That was Canada's, and nobody could take that victory away."[4] Or, as hockey commentator Don Cherry enthused, "April 9th—boy—that is when Canada … became a nation. … The French and the British tried to take it for a whole year … and General Currie said, 'No British, No French involved. I'm a Canadian general, we will take it in *two days*.'"[5]

In short, martial nationalists have attempted to turn an inconsequential tactical victory that led to the 1917 Conscription Crisis—a crisis that many thought brought French and English Canadians to the point of civil war and that embittered Quebec politics for generations—into a grand happening symbolic of Canada's maturity as a nation. One need look no further than the online shop of the Canadian Legion, Canada's pre-eminent veterans' association, where Vimy "Birth of a Nation" ball caps are on offer. Or ponder VIA Rail's distribution of the "Vimy Pin" to passengers on the occasion of the battle's centenary. Affixed to the pin was a little marketing piece declaring the slaughter

Canada's best-known war memorial contains not a jot of Vimyist martial nationalism; indeed, Toronto sculptor Walter Allward's masterpiece reflects the artist's insistence that the soaring monument was a mournful "sermon against the futility of war."

"a milestone where Canada came of age." Similarly, the Vimy Foundation pin is "to be worn by all Canadians" on the recently invented "Vimy Day."

Vimyism—the network of ideas and symbols that treat Canada's Great War experience as a national creation story, a war of independence constituting the "Birth of the Nation"—was certainly present as a sub-theme in July 1936, when Walter Allward's soaring monument was unveiled on the Ridge. (Many observers at the time, contending like Arthur Currie that the battle had been overrated, thought the honour should have gone to other, more militarily significant sites). But Allward himself

meant his statue not as the salute to Canadian nationhood it has become, but as a "sermon against the futility of war."[6] None of his allegorical statues actually depicts the nation valiantly defeating its foes (if they had, the statue would not have survived Adolf Hitler, who celebrated his later conquest of the site with a well-publicized victory lap). Yet to today's martial nationalists, the Vimy monument is all about saluting the deeds of Canada's valorous soldiers, and they imagine that the figure on top of it, "Mother Canada," to be saying something like: "What happened here was worth all the cost. Many sons may have fallen but they won the day and thus were reborn."[7] It is thus a sacred site commemorating a sacred battle—a monument to the big bang theory of Canadian history.

A closer look at Vimy and Vimyism, though, tells a different story. First, some practicalities. Instead of marking a turning point in the war, Vimy was similar—in both its cruel level of casualties and its inconclusiveness—to many other battles in the war of attrition waged on the Western Front from December 1914 to April 1918. It was fought under British leadership (unsurprisingly, since Canadian soldiers fought as part of a unified military effort under British command) with strategies strongly influenced by both the British and the French and with a force almost 50 percent of which was non-Canadian. It did not redraw the Western Front. In fact, because they were able to consolidate their position more strongly further to the east, many Germans thought the battle a tie (indeed, the German government struck a medal to honour *its* valiant Vimy soldiers). Vimyism, then, has exalted an inconclusive battle, merely one part of a doomed offensive to oust the Germans from France.

And by equating the larger battle with the conquest of the hill, it edits out earlier Canadian attempts to take the Ridge through the use of chemical weapons—whose unskilful deployment caused many Canadian soldiers to die a gruesome death, perhaps extending over an eighteen-hour period, expelling yellowish fluids from their lungs. If Don Cherry's imagined General Currie is the admirable go-getting Canuck who got things done, standing up for Canada against the less capable French and British, the real-life Currie was so subordinate to the British command that, although convinced the legendarily bloody 1917 Battle of Passchendaele (which followed closely on the heels of Vimy) was waged for worthless real estate, he was unable to shield Canadian soldiers from that fruitless slaughter. That battle's toll? 15,654 Canadians killed or wounded, many of them drowned in the mud.

The practical arguments for Vimy as the battle that won the war have always been threadbare. Most contemporary professional military historians respond to its overhyped treatment with ill-concealed exasperation. But its status as a great unifying symbol of Canadianism has long seemed equally problematic. Considering that the battle is closely associated with the 1917 Conscription Crisis (to which, in good measure, it contributed), a clash that came close to tearing the country to pieces, Vimyism was never likely to appeal to Canada's large francophone minority.

Vimyism privileges the opinions of Empire boosters while marginalizing ethnic minorities (some of whom were forced into wartime concentration camps) and oppressed races (some of whom were either denied entry to the Canadian forces or shunted into racially segregated units). It marginalizes francophone Quebec, which massively rejected military conscription, and the substantial minority of anglophone farmers, fishers, and workers who were also sceptical of it, if less vociferously so. Strikingly, it also silences many critical voices among the Canadian soldiers themselves, many of whom waxed ironic about the war when it was happening. At least nine returning veterans wrote novels after 1918, and Vimyist themes are absent from almost all of these works. The Vimyist "Myth of Canada," then, is one that excludes many Canadians, not least of whom Mackenzie King, who conspicuously did *not* serve in the war and yet who managed, again and again, to achieve top political office.

In the Vimyist framework, even Allward's towering monument at Vimy Ridge is imagined to be a war monument saluting the heroism of Canadian soldiers. Yet the sculptor considered his masterpiece a peace monument. It was unveiled in a 1936 ceremony that resounded with peace hymns and peace poems. The monument was so beloved by some interwar peace activists that they placed its image on the cover of their publications.

It is a Vimyist article of faith that almost all Canadians worth counting were Great War enthusiasts. But this is a faith founded upon partial and superficially analyzed information. In inter-war Canada, the rights and wrongs of the war were intensely discussed—in passionate debates about war commemorations and about Canada's role in the League of Nations. (One petition in favour of beefing up Canadian participation in the League's disarmament talks secured an astonishing 480,000 signatures. Pro-disarmament petitions and statements rolled into Ottawa from such seemingly unlikely peace activists as the Baptists of Owen Sound, Ontario; Kiwanis and Rotary Clubs from coast to coast; the Canadian Business and Professional Women's Club of Kitchener and Waterloo; the YWCA; and even from members of the Royal Canadian Legion.)

Many of the war's leading enthusiasts, including some of its most celebrated publicists, renounced their previous opinions. Critical appraisals of militarism proliferated, often from surprising sources. Arthur Meighen, one of the main architects of conscription in Canada, argued that war no longer "served a human purpose.... It solves no problem; it affords no security; it offers no prizes to the victor." The convictions of Robert Borden, the wartime prime minister, were quoted in a blurb for one of the many memoirs and novels critical of the Great War—a good number, as we have seen, written by veterans themselves. For Borden, the war had revealed "the crumbling of civilization's thin veneer," and the only redemption for the "broken lives, the horror, the brutality, and … the futility" would be a world at peace.[8] (Granted, both Meighen and Borden may have been playing to the gallery—but that in itself is suggestive of where public opinion was heading.) Both the *Toronto Star* and the *Winnipeg Free Press* published major spreads of startlingly graphic war photographs in 1934. These incurred some criticism from veterans who worried about reopening the wounds of war. But they drew far more praise from veterans grateful that, at last, after years of official censorship and saccharine romanticism, candid representations of the war were being made available to the general public.

There were many war sceptics and critics in post-1945 Canada, at a time when the Great War's reputation as an honourable conflict had declined in both Britain and the United States. High school history textbooks might devote just a few lines to Vimy, but they were often found amidst withering critiques of the mismanagement and mayhem of the war. Commemorative films such as Donald Brittain's *Fields of Sacrifice* (1965) and Don Shebib's *Good Times, Bad Times* (1970) lamented the cruelty and folly of war. John Diefenbaker and Lester Pearson, the country's leading federal politicians in the 1960s—and themselves both veterans of the war—denounced it as a bloodbath and holocaust.[9]

There were, however, some in that decade marking the centenary of the Dominion who were starting to see the battle as an inspirational milestone for a crisis-prone country. Some regarded it as a fine moment in which Canadians dedicated their lives to the British Empire. Others, paddling upstream against the abundant evidence of the war's divisive impact, especially in conscription-averse Quebec, saw the battle as an appropriate symbol of national unity, even going so far as to imagine that the Vimy monument itself symbolized the partnership of English and French Canadians. In 1969, writing one of the four most widely circulated Vimy books of the decade, Lieutenant-Colonel D. J. Goodspeed proclaimed: "No matter what the constitutional historians may say, it was on Easter Monday, April 9, 1917, and not on any other date, that Canada became a nation."[10] It was no accident that this early and strong affirmation of Vimyism was accompanied by a complaint about the ruminations of constitutional scholars pondering the need for a made-in-Canada constitution. Such opinions were deeply troubling to

In 2012, the government of Stephen Harper introduced a new twenty-dollar banknote, replacing the images of sculptures by Haida artist/activist Bill Reid that had featured on the previous twenty with a representation of the Vimy memorial.

those Canadians for whom the country was, and should forever remain, a British dominion.

After the 1986 publication of *Vimy* by Pierre Berton, the Vimyist trickle became a flood. As in Australia's history wars—which saw a determined right-wing push-back against Aborigines' claim to recognition and attempts by historians to rewrite the country's history in ways that included the cultures and suffering of the continent's Indigenous peoples—the 1990s witnessed a concerted effort to reassert the primacy of white male heroes. Proponents of this newly imagined history encouraged Canadians to see all the country's wars, defined broadly to include even struggles preceding the Dominion's formation, as heroic exploits—even fights for freedom.[11] By imagining the Canadian soldiers at Vimy to have been fresh-faced farm boys (although in actuality most were white- and blue-collar urban workers, a majority of whom were born in Britain), Vimyism sets them up as archetypal Canadian heroes. These lads would never rape, loot, or kill prisoners—as Canadians did in many of the major battles in which they partook, often with the surreptitious approval of their military leaders.[12] An emphasis on these men's

unblemished characters—an understandable coping strategy found in funeral orations and monument dedications in the years just after the war—has morphed into a simplistic Cult of the Soldier. Those who fought are remembered not as they were but as militarists imagine them to have been.

Once confined to a few sentences, discussion of Vimy began to loom ever larger in high school textbooks. Nowadays, it consumes dozens of pages in some texts, and students might well spend much of their history classes reconstructing trenches. Historians such as Jack Granatstein, who once spoke clinically (and accurately) of the war as a "battle of rival imperialisms" and of Ottawa as a purveyor of Quebec-enraging "broken promises," now hailed it as "the noblest example yet given of the ability of Canadians to ... accomplish great things."[13]

Under the government of Stephen Harper (2006–15), militarists sensed the wind in their sails. The state depicted the Vimy monument on the country's currency. To celebrate the bicentenary of North America's most inconclusive war, claimed as a victory by both Americans and Canadians, Parliament Hill was bedecked with War of 1812 fighting figures on the understanding that they might make the seat of power as shrine-like as Vimy Ridge. And a sustained campaign—blocked as of 2017 by environmentalists and anti-militarists—was mounted to construct in Cape Breton a giant-sized version of Allward's *Canada Bereft*, no longer a symbol lamenting the horrors of war but an emblem of the valour of Canada's heroic war dead. As the campaign's website declares, "The Never-Forgotten National Memorial will be a place for visitors to reach back through the generations and forge a very real connection with this young nation's Fallen Heroes."[14] The new official line—that the Great War was *great* again—was exalted in the citizenship guide that anyone aspiring to become a Canadian citizen is required to read and digest. And the new Canadian passport contains not only a representation of the memorial, but words from Brigadier-General A. E. Ross: "in those few minutes I witnessed the birth of a nation."[15]

Even the ascension to power of Harper's alter-ego, the ostensibly progressive Justin Trudeau, did little to disrupt this problematic and selective understanding of the country's past. "Le Canada est né ici," Trudeau told the crowd gathered at Vimy for the battle's centenary in 2017.[16] "Canada was born here": just like Australia, whose national spirit was said by some to be revealed during the ill-fated Gallipoli campaign of 1915–16, somehow the country was "born" on a continent thousands of miles away, serving in the forces of a now very distant and defunct Empire.

In the 1920s and 1930s, Canadians strenuously debated the Great War, with a large number, probably the majority, coming to query its underlying morality, deficient leadership, staggering costs, extraordinary hardships, and disappointing geopolitical outcome. Many veterans—in letters, novels, speeches, memoirs, and histories—wanted to impress upon their fellow citizens the stark realities of modern industrialized warfare.[17] But from the 1980s to the 2010s, through a well-financed official campaign involving state agencies, major financial institutions and, after 2005, a lavish Canadian War Museum, Canadians were urged not to debate, but to venerate, this war in ways that many Great War veterans would find sharply discordant with their own critically observed experiences. The War Museum does display Group of Seven member Fred Varley's stunning 1918 painting *For What?*, its unsparing depiction of the heaped bodies of Canadian soldiers awaiting burial on a blood-drenched battlefield. But the museum's curators offer a caption that openly questions the artist's first-hand impression: "Was the war pointless? If the war had been pointless, why had more than 400,000 Canadians continued to serve and fight overseas?" (By that logic, of course, all prolonged wars involving thousands of soldiers must, somehow, have a "point.") In much of the country, Remembrance Day, celebrated each year on November 11, moved from a day on which victims of all wars were remembered and mourned to one on which the patriotic cult of the soldier was the predominant theme.

Vimyism fit within a wider pattern of the militarization of North American culture—even in an epoch in which inter-state wars had been shown to be almost sure-fire disappointments for the governments launching them.[18] (And a thermonuclear war promises to be even more of a let-down.) In parts of Belgium and northern France, commemoration is most often about transcending, not solidifying, national divisions. But in Vimyist English Canada, the culture of commemoration seeks to re-enchant us with war, imagined to be the pith and substance of nationhood.

"The reason the world pays heed to Canada is because we fought like lions in the trenches of World War I, on the beaches of World War II, and in theatres and conflicts scattered around the globe," Justin Trudeau remarked in June 2016.[19] Only someone who has never served in an actual battle could say

In 2014, Ottawa inaugurated Parliament Hill's first-ever war memorial. Seven bronze Vimyist action figures were intended to evoke the memory of "heroes"; the public was assured that "sacred soil" from War of 1812 battlefields had been solemnly deposited under the new installation.

something so silly, his words a reminder of the enduring appeal of Vimyism's child-like simplicity—and of its capacity to inspire Canadians with a guilt-free, if factually challenged and deeply conservative, tale about their country. Vimyism offers a divided and confusing country an opportunity to reimagine itself as a unified people—pro-British, pro-Empire, militarily strong, and universally respected. As long as the romance of war lures the young and the foolish, it will be there to offer us a tempting entrapment in a narrowly nationalistic world of chivalrous war and swashbuckling Canadian heroes: a fairy tale that works to shield Canadians from the sterner realities of the twenty-first-century world they actually inhabit.

NOTES

1   Jonathan Vance, "Remembrance," *Canada's History*, Oct./Nov. 2014, 32.

2   The phrase "big turning point in the war" comes from the developers of a Vimy Ridge video game: see Joe Lofarno, "In the Digital Trenches: Kanata Company Developing Vimy Ridge Simular," *OurWindsor*, Nov. 10, 2015, ourwindsor.ca/news-story/6110747.

3   See canadianmilitary.page.tl/First-World-War.htm, which attributes the saying to an "unidentified veteran." The quotation has been put to work countless times in popular works, generally with such vague notions of its provenance.

4   Pierre Berton, *Vimy* (Toronto: McClelland and Stewart, 1986), 295.

5   "Coach's Corner with Don Cherry & Ron McLean," YouTube video, excerpt from *Hockey Night in Canada*, Apr. 5, 2014, youtube.com/watch?v=Gjy4cA4kOxk.

6   Cited in Jacqueline Hucker, "Vimy: A Monument for the Modern World," *Architecture Canada* 33, no. 1 (2008): 43.

7   Sandra Gwyn, *Tapestry of War: A Private View of Canadians in the Great War* (Toronto: HarperCollins, 1992), 345.

8   Arthur Meighen, "The Supremely Important Task," *Interdependence* 8, no. 1 (January 1931): 21–31; Robert Borden as quoted in an advertisement for *All Else is Folly*, in *Globe* (Toronto), Dec. 14, 1929, reproduced in Brian Busby and James Calhoun, "Introduction," in Peregrine Acland, ed., *All Else is Folly: A Tale of War and Passion* (Toronto: Dundurn, 2014), 9.

9   See Tim Cook, *Vimy: The Battle and the Legend* (Toronto: Penguin-Random House, 2017) 325, and McKay and Swift *The Vimy Trap: Or, How We Learned to Stop Worrying and Love the Great War* (Toronto: Between The Lines, 2016), 182.

10 D. J. Goodspeed, *The Road Past Vimy: The Canadian Corps 1914–1918* (Toronto: Macmillan, 1969), 93.

11 Tim Cook, *At the Sharp End: Canadians Fighting the Great War 1914–1916* (Toronto: Penguin, 2007), 645; Mark McKenna, "Anzac Day: How Did It Become Australia's National day?" in Marilyn Lake and Henry Reynolds, eds., *What's The Matter With Anzac: The Militarisation of Australian History* (Sydney: University of New South Wales Press, 2010), 126–28.

12 Tim Cook, "The Politics of Surrender: Canadian Soldiers and the Killing of Prisoners in the Great War," *Journal of Military History* 70, no. 3 (July 2006): 637–65.

13 J. L. Granatstein, *The Last Good War: An Illustrated History of Canada in the Second World War, 1939–1945* (Vancouver and Toronto: Douglas and McIntyre, 2005), viii; *The Greatest Victory: Canada's One Hundred Days, 1918* (Don Mills, ON: Oxford University Press, 2014), 193.

14 Never Forgotten National Memorial, nfnm.ca. The foundation's flashy website was underwritten by $100,000 in public money.

15 For the context of this misleading quotation from the uber-imperialist Ross, see McKay and Swift, *Vimy Trap*, 272n5.

16 "'This was Canada at its best': Remembering the fallen 100 years after Vimy," *Globe and Mail* (Toronto), Apr. 9, 2017.

17 The most renowned of them was soldier Charles Yale Harrison, whose harrowing *Generals Die in Bed* (Toronto: Annick Press, 2014, originally published New York: Morrow, 1930) caused considerable controversy. Contrary to a much-reported legend, Harrison's brilliantly deadpan depiction was received with enthusiasm by many of his fellow veterans. See Jonathan Scotland, "And the Men Returned: Canadian Veterans and the Aftermath of the Great War" (Ph.D. diss., University of Western Ontario, 2016).

18 Ernie Regehr, *Disarming Conflict: Why Peace Cannot Be Won on the Battlefield* (Toronto: Between the Lines, 2015).

19 "'We fought like lions,' Trudeau says of our soldiers as monument unveiled," *Globe and Mail* (Toronto), June 9, 2016.

This National Film Board of Canada photograph shows Corporal Frank Walsh with his family as he prepares to leave as part of the UN peacekeeping force in the Middle East in 1956. "Official" photos like this one offered Canadians an image of peacekeeping linked to family and sacrifice rather than danger and controversy.

PEACEKEEPER

Kelly Ferguson

***Reconciliation.* This is the official name of the** peacekeeping monument erected in Ottawa in 1992. Located between the National Gallery of Canada and the American Embassy, the monument depicts three peacekeeping soldiers, two men and one woman, on a ridge surrounded by the debris of war. They stand at the highest point, surveying the land below. One holds binoculars. Another employs communications equipment. The third stands stoically with a rifle slung over his shoulder. Below them is a quote from former diplomat and prime minister Lester B. Pearson. It reads, in part, "We need action not only to end the fighting but to make the peace." Like many other peacekeeping commemoration efforts, it offers a selective representation of Canadian peacekeeping—one that avoids the complicated reality of war.[1] These peacekeepers, after all, have not engaged their weapons.

The title of the monument is almost certainly meant to allude to Canadian peacekeepers' attempts to reconcile warring interests in divided communities around the globe. But it is also an apt reminder of the difficulties Canadians have faced in attempting to reconcile the popular mythology surrounding

Reconciliation: The Peacekeeping Monument resides in downtown Ottawa. Built in 1992, the monument was one of the first public efforts to commemorate Canada's peacekeeping past.

Canada's military interventions with an otherwise harsh and sometimes disturbing reality. Equally, it ought to remind us that there are competing visions of Canada's military history (and duty) that offer very different assessments of peacekeeping's proper place in official stories about Canada's military history—visions that have proven impossible to reconcile.

A major defining moment for the symbol of the Canadian peacekeeper was the 1956 Suez Crisis that pitted Egypt's president, Gamal Abdel Nasser, against the British government.[2] Britain's decision to pull financial support for the Aswan High Dam prompted Nasser to nationalize the Suez Canal Company, which had been controlled by British and French investors and was a key tool in linking the various parts of the British Empire through trade.[3] By the end of October 1956, France, Britain, and Israel, which had joined in the conflict to support its own stakes in the region, had sent troops to Egypt.[4] While

Canada was not directly implicated in the conflict, many English Canadians argued that the country had a moral responsibility to help the Empire.[5] But a combination of concerns, including Commonwealth disunity and a lack of support from the United States, convinced Prime Minister Louis St. Laurent and his top diplomat, Lester B. Pearson, to demur.[6] Instead, Pearson—at the time Canada's secretary of state for external affairs, and head of Canada's delegation to the United Nations—worked to develop the first large-scale United Nations peacekeeping force. By mid-November, the United Nations Emergency Force had landed in Egypt, where it eventually oversaw a ceasefire. Pearson would receive the Nobel Peace Prize in 1957 for his work at the United Nations and his role in the crisis.

The Suez mission came at a transitional moment for English-Canadian identity. During the first half of the twentieth century, many English Canadians identified closely with Britain. But these ties were weakening as the Empire itself was waning. The transformation occurred slowly during the 1950s and early 1960s. Indeed, while the Emergency Forces initiative was cheered at the United Nations, many Canadians were critical of the mission and considered the government's reaction to be nothing less than an abandonment of the country's moral duty to support the Empire.[7] The Liberals would end up losing votes in the Maritimes, Ontario, and British Columbia, and thus the 1957 election itself—in part because of this perceived betrayal.[8] As the century progressed, however, English Canadians increasingly embraced an image of Canada as an autonomous "peacekeeping" nation.

At the same time the United States had emerged as a world power—one that, by the 1960s, suffered from an image problem. Cold war military policies, including the threat of nuclear conflict and the controversial Vietnam War, spawned massive protests, both at home and across the border in Canada. American military initiatives combined with racial tensions during the civil rights movement to undermine the United States' claim to be a shining example of liberal democracy. While increasing numbers of English Canadians were keen to see their country distance itself from Britain, many were also anxious to avoid increased interdependence with the United States. Peacekeeping became a way for Canada to set itself apart from both Britain and the United States as a "middle power" within the Cold War international landscape.

This was in many ways a distinct, if only slowly realized, departure from the "warrior nation" mentality of the First and Second World Wars, which posited the notion that Canada's military history involved a proud tradition of warfare and fighting.[9]

Despite their perceived "victory" in the Suez crisis, Canadian peacekeepers continued to serve in Egypt into the 1960s, with President Nasser demanding the United Nations remove their troops in 1967.

Indeed, as peacekeeping developed as a key symbol of Canadian identity, the narratives of the First and Second World Wars shifted away from the "warrior nation" theme, and were instead reframed as part of the story of the "Peaceable Kingdom."

The idea of the Peaceable Kingdom, promoted and developed by Canadian cultural critics like Northrop Frye and William Kilbourn, framed Canada as a country defined by peace, one that had rarely experienced war or domestic unrest, and instead had pursued military ventures primarily to help others, usually in support of peace and stability.[10] The notion of the Peaceable Kingdom was frequently contrasted with the bloodier history of the United States.[11] While this actively ignored Canada's foundational violence of colonialism and conquest, the idea of the Peaceable Kingdom was popular; it connected the "good versus evil" narratives of the World Wars with Cold War ideals of "liberal democracy." This selective story was rendered tangible through Canada's involvement in specific peacekeeping missions, especially its efforts in Cyprus.

By 1964, Canada had already established itself as an active participant in United Nations missions, but it was the country's involvement in Cyprus that would catch the Canadian public's imagination. The UN launched this mission in response to unrest between the minority Turkish Cypriots and the majority Greek Cypriots following the island's independence from British rule. As a conflict between fellow NATO members Turkey and Greece, this was of particular interest to Canada and its Cold War allies keen to maintain a united front against communism.[12]

Almost immediately, filmmakers and cultural commentators alike used the Cyprus campaign as an example of Canadian "exceptionalism," arguing that Canada was meant to protect others and promote peace and stability around the globe. Documentaries and commentaries presented UN peacekeeping troops, and Canadian regiments in particular, as professional,

strong, and well organized.[13] Frequently these cultural interventions portrayed Canadian troops as the "best" peacekeepers, often praising their skills and preparedness.[14] UN success in Cyprus was a point of pride not only because of its impact in that particular nation, but also because it was crucial for the credibility of future peacekeeping efforts.[15]

Not everyone supported this line of thinking.[16] While the Canadian military, for example, continued to emphasize traditional military values of duty, heroism, and responsibility,[17] some young men viewed peacekeeping as less "manly" than the more aggressive military activities pursued by the United States. Hence the concern expressed by a Canadian diplomat in 1966 that the United Nations' reputation was not compelling enough to convince young men to join the Canadian Armed Forces.[18] There were even reports of young Canadians travelling to the United States to voluntarily fight communism in Vietnam, rather than serve as peacekeepers in Cyprus.[19]

The 1970s and 1980s saw a decline in popular commentary about peacekeeping missions and their connection to Canadian national identity—in part because of the extended duration of the Cyprus campaign and the international prominence of the Vietnam War.[20] Moreover, under Prime Minister Pierre Trudeau, the Canadian government reoriented its efforts away from international and peacekeeping initiatives to focus on internal, national-unity endeavours—though Liberal governments would occasionally embrace opportunities to strategically highlight their party's connection to positive peacekeeping legacies, particularly after Pearson died in 1972.[21]

Canada nonetheless continued to participate in peacekeeping missions, and most Canadians viewed peacekeeping as a positive part of Canadian identity and the country's role in international affairs. French Canadians also viewed peacekeeping favourably—in part because the practice marked a clear departure from Canada's earlier ties with British imperialism.[22] In the 1990s, however, missions in Somalia, Rwanda, and Bosnia challenged this popularity.

In 1992, the United Nations formed a peacekeeping mission to help bring stability to Somalia after the country was wracked by civil war and famine. Canada, alongside twenty other nations, participated in this military intervention. The mission, however, was met with controversy. Indeed, media reports quickly suggested that it was failing to provide relief to the country's suffering population.[23] But even these failures soon took a back seat to reports of Canadian soldiers' transgressions. In 1993, Canadian troops shot two Somalis in the back. This incident was followed two weeks later by the death of Somali prisoner Shidane Abukar Arone. Arone, who was sixteen years old, had been transferred to Canadian custody under the control of Master Corporal Clayton Matchee who, with Private E. Kyle Brown, tortured and beat the teenager to death.[24]

The Somalia Affair, as the controversy came to be known, complicated the ideal of the Canadian peacekeeper. As a nation proud of its image as the Peaceable Kingdom, and proud of its peacekeeping legacy, the violence in Somalia left many Canadians struggling to hold on to these old narratives. While some condemned the violence and demanded accountability,[25] others viewed Somalia as an exception and were keen to distinguish between past peacekeeping missions, and what they called Canada's "peace enforcement" campaign in Somalia.[26] Others blamed the incident on a few "bad apples" and continued to champion peacekeeping as a worthy pursuit.[27]

The Somalia Affair, in many ways, brought to the fore issues that were already part of Canadian peacekeeping. The idea of peacekeeping, as well as the Peaceable Kingdom, relied on an "us" versus "them" mentality, with Canadians seeing themselves as an example of civility in relation to the "chaos" of the developing world. Peacekeeping was meant to confront this "savagery." This narrative, both patronizing and steeped in racism, allowed for observers to rationalize the events in Somalia. According to this view, Canadian peacekeepers were "saving" the countries in which they were deployed, with the violence directed at the local population simply an unfortunate side effect.[28]

The 1990s also saw Canadian peacekeepers struggling with failure in missions to Rwanda and Bosnia. The rising ethnic violence and tensions in Rwanda had developed into a full-scale civil war in the early part of the decade. In response, the United Nations moved to launch a peace mission and, in 1993, the UN Assistance Mission for Rwanda began.[29] Within a year of the mission's deployment, however, Rwanda would experience a region-wide genocide, in which over half a million people would lose their lives. The UN's failure to stop the genocide highlighted around the world the limitations of peacekeeping.

From 1992 to 1995, Canadian troops in Bosnia also suffered very public failures, including a 1995 incident in which UN peacekeepers were taken hostage. These reversals were routinely broadcast into Canadian living rooms.[30] Following so quickly on the Somalia controversy, the Rwanda and Bosnia missions further destabilized the dominant perception of peacekeeping and made it less appealing to Canadians and their governments. Indeed, the late 1990s would see Canada cut military spending and move away from peacekeeping initiatives.[31]

Yet throughout the 1990s and 2000s, Canadians continued to commemorate the work done by Canadian peacekeepers during the twentieth century on coins and in monuments, books, and films. One of the first efforts to commemorate Canada's peacekeeping legacy was *Reconciliation: The Peacekeeping Monument*, which was conceived, developed, and erected in Ottawa before the controversies of the 1990s.[32] Other tributes included folksinger Stompin' Tom Connors's 1991 song "Blue Berets," which

In 2000, Canada Post released this stamp, titled "Lester B. Pearson: On Guard for World Peace." It was one of many widely circulated commemorative tributes to Canadian peacekeeping produced in the early 2000s.

included the lines, "Yes we are the Blue Berets / We're always proud to say / We'll stand between the mighty and the frail." Performing the song at concerts throughout the early 1990s, Connors urged Canadians to support their peacekeepers.[33]

In the years that followed, other commemorative efforts attempted to support an understanding of peacekeeping that steered clear of the Somali, Rwandan, and Bosnian controversies. In 1995, for example, *Reconciliation* was included on a commemorative one-dollar coin.[34] Similarly, in 2001, the Canadian ten-dollar bill featured a commemorative image titled, *Remembrance and Peacekeeping*, which was composed of various reminders of Canada's military history, including part of John McCrae's poem, "In Flanders Fields," a female peacekeeper, and a veteran alongside subsequent generations of Canadians. The phrase, "in the service of peace," also inscribed on *Reconciliation*, appeared at the top of the bill. Such images effaced earlier distinctions between Canada's longer history as a "warrior nation" during the First and Second World Wars and modern peacekeeping.[35] Together, the bill and the coin reinforced a representation of peacekeeping that seemed to actively discourage Canadians from coming to terms with the controversies of the 1990s.[36]

One person who refused to steer clear of the controversies surrounding peacekeeping was Lieutenant-General Roméo Dallaire. Dallaire had been an eager, if inexperienced, choice to lead the UN mission in Rwanda and returned from the ordeal suffering from post-traumatic stress disorder.[37] His harrowing tales and blunt assessments of government and bureaucratic failures, particularly those detailed in his 2004 book *Shake Hands with the Devil: The Failure of Humanity in Rwanda*, foregrounded the complications of peacekeeping and made him a national hero.[38]

While peacekeeping commemoration continued apace, with the government instituting National Peacekeepers' Day in 2008,[39] in practice Canada moved away from peacekeeping. When the Conservative Party gained power in 2006, Prime Minister Stephen Harper embraced and promoted a military history of Canada that emphasized the "warrior nation" perspective. The government focused on a story of Canada that celebrated those who fought on the side of "good" during the World Wars, the Cold War, and in support of the British Empire.[40]

This shift produced a backlash that was seen most clearly in debates surrounding Canada's participation in the War on Terror and the US mission in Afghanistan. New Democratic Party leader Jack Layton, for example, lamented what he saw as a tragic shift in foreign policy: "For nearly five decades Canada has pursued peace in nations around the world and brought hope to lives torn apart by war.... We must not allow that legacy of good work to falter in the growing shadow of the Bush administration's Operation Enduring Freedom."[41]

In reality, direct military intervention, rather than peacekeeping, fit more easily within a comprehensive survey of Canada's past endeavours. Many of Canada's past military interventions had been in non-peacekeeping contexts, and humanitarianism was often employed selectively as a justification for Canadian intervention in other countries.[42] Canada was also a major arms exporter—the fifth-largest in the world in 2003—and frequently supplied weapons to countries with dismal human rights records.[43] Even during the Vietnam War, when Canada had claimed moral superiority by not entering the conflict, it still supplied arms to United States' forces and did that country's bidding at the International Control Commission, established in 1954 to implement the Geneva Accords.[44]

The 2015 federal election saw the Liberal Party return to power after a decade of Conservative rule, and with it a stated desire to employ the Canadian military in the service of the United Nations.[45] Yet despite its early statements, the Liberal government quickly reined in expectations. In August 2016, the government unveiled a $450 million plan for future UN deployments,[46] but within a year it backtracked when it delayed a high-profile peacekeeping mission to Africa[47] and announced a need to increase the country's "hard power" military capabilities.[48] In 2017, Canada remained a minor contributor to UN missions, ranking seventy-first in the world.[49]

Canada's experiences with peacekeeping since 1956 have been complicated and, at times, controversial. The practice helped

Released by the Bank of Canada in 2001, this "Remembrance and Peacekeeping"–themed ten-dollar bill linked the imagery of the "warrior nation" with that of the "Peaceable Kingdom."

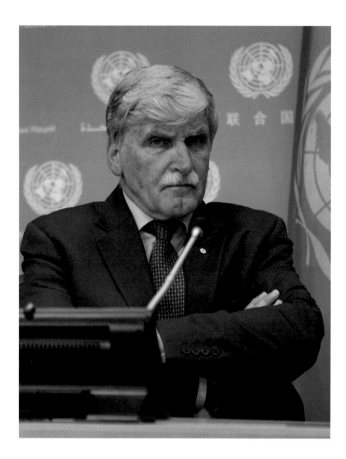

Roméo Dallaire, Canada's most famous peacekeeper, has had schools and streets named in his honour. An outspoken critic of the international community's failure to prevent genocide in Rwanda, Dallaire has encouraged Canadians to grapple with the failures of the UN's 1994 mission to that country without abandoning the notion that peacekeeping is a positive and necessary endeavour.

Canadians to shape an identity that was separate from the British Empire and distinct from the United States. But while many Canadians viewed peacekeeping positively, the country's history of militarism, violence, and racism remained, particularly as controversies arose. Should Canada renew its interests in peacekeeping, the country will need to continue to reckon with the complicated history of the practice itself as well as the competing narratives of Canadian military history. Reconciliation, after all, requires reflection and forthright discussion rather than selective and comforting stories.

NOTES

1   Zachary Abram, "In the Service of Peace: The Symbolic Power of Peacekeeping in Canada," *The Dalhousie Review* 92, no. 1–2 (2012): 194.
2   While Canada participated in UN missions prior to the Suez Crisis, notably Korea in 1947 and the India-Pakistan ceasefire in 1949, the 1956 mission marked the beginning of peacekeeping's role as a significant part of the national consciousness. See Colin McCullough, *Creating Canada's Peacekeeping Past* (Vancouver: UBC Press, 2016), 5–10; Ian McKay and Jamie Swift, *Warrior Nation: Rebranding Canada in an Age of Anxiety* (Toronto: Between the Lines, 2012), 198.
3   Michael K. Carroll, *Pearson's Peacekeepers: Canada and the United Nations Emergency Force* (Vancouver: UBC Press, 2009), 7–9.
4   Ibid., 21.
5   José E. Igartua, *The Other Quiet Revolution: National Identities in English Canada, 1945–71* (Vancouver: UBC Press, 2006), 116.
6   Carroll, *Pearson's Peacekeepers*, 12.
7   Igartua, *The Other Quiet Revolution*, 116.
8   Carroll, *Pearson's Peacekeepers*, 55.
9   McKay and Swift, *Warrior Nation*, 12.
10 Robert Lecker, "'A Quest for the Peaceable Kingdom': The Narrative in Northrop Frye's Conclusion to *The Literary History of Canada*" *PMLA* 108, no. 2 (1993): 581.
11 William Kilbourn, *The Making of a Nation: A Century of Challenge* (Toronto: The Canadian Central Library, 1965), 120.
12 McKay and Smith, *Warrior Nation*, 230.
13 *You Are Welcome Sirs, to Cyprus*, dir. Richard Gilbert (National Film Board of Canada, 1964).
14 *Postmark U. N. E. F.*, directed by Richard Gilbert (National Film Board of Canada, 1965).

15 David Van Praagh, "Martin Restates Canada's Faith in UN's Bid for Cyprus Peace," *Globe and Mail* (Toronto), July 22, 1964.

16 McKay and Swift, *Warrior Nation,* 12.

17 "Your Son and the Armed Forces," *Maclean's,* Oct. 1, 1969.

18 Marilyn Cooper, "Most Canadian Men Would Rather Fight…" *Globe and Mail* (Toronto), Nov. 21, 1966.

19 "The Canucks that Fight for Uncle Sam," *Maclean's,* Oct. 1, 1967.

20 William Frye, "Peacekeeping Can Hinder Rather than Help Peacemaking," *Toronto Star,* July 23, 1975; J. L. Granatstein, "Peacekeeping Image has Changed since the Blue Berets Palmy Days," *Toronto Star,* Jan. 20, 1973.

21 Colin McCullough, *Creating Canada's Peacekeeping Past,* 15; "Peacekeeping, Oil, and Electioneering," *Canadian Forum,* Jan. 1974.

22 McCullough, *Creating Canada's Peacekeeping Past,* 12.

23 Grant Dawson, *"Here is Hell": Canada's Engagement in Somalia* (Vancouver: UBC Press, 2007), 4.

24 Ibid., 157.

25 "A Sad Silence on Somalia," *Globe and Mail* (Toronto), Apr. 5, 1997.

26 Lewis M. Mackenzie, "Letters to the Editor: Canada's Honour," *Globe and Mail* (Toronto), Nov. 15, 1994.

27 John Craig Eaton, "Somalia and the Canadian Forces," *Globe and Mail* (Toronto), July 9, 1997.

28 Sherene Razack, *Dark Threats and White Knights: The Somalia Affair, Peacekeeping and the New Imperialism* (Toronto: University of Toronto Press, 2004), 17.

29 Veterans Affairs Canada, "The Canadian Armed Forces in Rwanda," veterans.gc.ca/eng/remembrance/history/canadian-armed-forces/rwanda.

30 A. Walter Dorn, "Canadian Peacekeeping: Proud Tradition, Strong Future?" *Canadian Foreign Policy* 12, no. 2 (2005): 7.

31 McKay and Swift, *Warrior Nation,* 253.

32 Paul Gough, "'Invicta Pax' Monuments, Memorials and Peace: An Analysis of the Canadian Peacekeeping Monument, Ottawa," *International Journal of Heritage Studies* 8, no. 3 (2002): 218.

33 John O'Callaghan, "A Whole Lot of Stompin' Going On," *Globe and Mail* (Toronto), Aug. 27, 1993.

34 Abram, "In the Service of Peace," 194.

35 David Jefferess, "Responsibility, Nostalgia, and the Mythology of Canada as a Peacekeeper," *University of Toronto Quarterly* 78, no. 2 (2009): 714–15.

36 Abram, "In the Service of Peace," 194.

37 Dorn, "Canadian Peacekeeping," 13–14; Carol Off and Romeo Dallaire, "Romeo Dallaire's new memoir 'Waiting for First Light: My Ongoing Battle with PTSD'," *CBC Radio,* Oct. 27, 2016, cbc.ca/radio/asithappens/as-it-happens-thursday-edition-1.3824230/romeo-dallaire-s-new-memoir-waiting-for-first-light-my-ongoing-battle-with-ptsd-1.3824235.

38 Off and Dallaire, "Romeo Dallaire's new memoir."

39 See Veterans Affairs Canada, "National Peacekeepers' Day," veterans.gc.ca/eng/remembrance/history/canadian-armed-forces/peacekeeping; Michael K. Carroll, "Peacekeeping: Canada's Past, But Not its Present and Future," *International Journal* 71, no. 1 (2016): 167.

40 McKay and Swift, *Warrior Nation,* 27.

41 Hon. Jack Layton, NDP, House of Commons Debates, May 17, 2006, ourcommons.ca/Parliamentarians/en/PublicationSearch?View=D&Item=&ParlSes=39-1&oob=&Topic=53765&Per=&Prov=&Cauc=&Text=peace&RPP=15&order=&targetLang=&SBS=0&MRR=150000&Page=7&PubType=37.

42 Todd Gordon, *Imperialist Canada* (Winnipeg: Arbeiter Ring Pub, 2010), 302.

43 Ibid., 306, 307.

44 "Beyond Peacekeeping," *Canadian Forum,* Feb. 4, 1973; McKay and Swift, *Warrior Nation,* 211.

45 Liberal Party of Canada, "Promoting International Peace and Security," liberal.ca/realchange/promoting-international-peace-and-security/.

46 Murray Brewster, "Liberals Commit $450M, up to 600 troops to UN Peacekeeping Missions," *CBC News,* Aug. 26, 2016, cbc.ca/news/politics/canada-peacekeeping-announcement-1.3736593.

47 Bruce Campion-Smith, "Canada's Decision on Peacekeeping Mission is now Delayed for Months," *Toronto Star,* May 12, 2017.

48 Mike Blanchfield, "Canadian Diplomacy Needs 'Hard Power' Says Freeland," *Maclean's,* June 6, 2017.

49 United Nations, "Summary of Troop Contributing Countries by Ranking," June 30, 2017, un.org/en/peacekeeping/contributors/2017/jun17_2.pdf.

This 2008 Canada Post stamp marked the hundredth anniversary of the publication of Lucy Maud Montgomery's *Anne of Green Gables*.

ANNE OF GREEN GABLES

Michael Dawson and Catherine Gidney

A red-headed, hot-tempered orphan named Anne (with an "e"!) and a picturesque rural landscape featuring a green-latticed white farmhouse dominate imaginary depictions of Canada's Prince Edward Island. Since the publication of Lucy Maud Montgomery's *Anne of Green Gables* more than a hundred years ago, Anne's image has transformed the small village of Cavendish, PEI from a little-known rural hamlet into the island's major tourist attraction. Government marketing strategies, along with stage, film, and television depictions, ensure that Anne remains one of Canada's most recognized and beloved cultural representations—both at home and abroad. But it was the book—and the character—that started it all. In the words of one young reader, "I've loved that red-haired girl.... After ... read[ing] a few pages I regain strength and dignity. Anne is my greatest friend...."[1]

Anne of Green Gables is the story of a young orphan whose joyful spirit, imagination, and optimism have drawn in generations of readers. Adopted by Matthew and Marilla, aging siblings who had hoped instead to secure a young orphan *boy* to help them on the family farm, Anne breathes life into their dreary home, often

A PEI highway sign directs tourists to Green Gables.

upending their disciplined routine in the process. Set in the late nineteenth century, the book follows Anne's integration into her adopted household and the local community as she overcomes doubts about her character and respectability.

The storyline follows Anne's (mis)adventures with her bosom friend, Diana Barry, as well as her scholastic rivalry with Gilbert Blythe—a relationship that gets off on the wrong foot when, in an attempt to gain her attention, he makes fun of her hair by calling her "Carrots." She responds by cracking a school slate over his head. Anne perseveres despite continual slights from the locals, and through her determination eventually wins over some of her most ardent detractors, including Diana's mother and the gossipy Mrs. Lynde. Through the support and dedication of Miss Stacy, the teacher of Avonlea's one-room schoolhouse, Anne and a number of her classmates successfully pass the entrance exams that enable them to complete their schooling in Charlottetown where Anne wins a prestigious college scholarship. Anne's education is put on hold following Matthew's death; she ultimately decides to support Marilla by teaching in Avonlea. Gilbert facilitates this opportunity by vacating the town's lone teaching position—a gesture that *finally* kindles their romance. Follow-up volumes trace Anne's adventures in Avonlea's one-room schoolhouse, her life at college, her marriage to Gilbert Blythe, and motherhood.[2]

The Anne novels evoke the values and ideals of a more traditional, agrarian society, one mythologized as a tight-knit, Anglo-Celtic Presbyterian community based on hard work, independence, and Christian duty. Montgomery's love of PEI and its landscape permeate the stories, and in her portrayal of the region she offers her readers an idyllic rural setting. This occurs most directly through Anne's actions, for the title character is forever romanticizing and mythologizing the landscape—and thus assigning alluring characteristics to various locations. As a result, "the Avenue," a road through bridging apple trees in blossom, becomes the "White Way of Delight," and "Barry's Pond" is turned into the "Lake of Shining Waters."[3] Written at a time of rapid industrialization and urbanization, the story's rural setting, "traditional" values, and romantic storyline provided readers with healthy doses of nostalgia and escapism.

Not surprisingly, community and nationhood in Anne's world are viewed through a lens that erases the Indigenous Mi'kmaq, scorns the region's French-speaking Acadian population, and overtly expresses nativist fears of outsiders.[4] Speaking to her neighbour, Mrs. Lynde, about the difficulty of finding good farm help, Marilla refers to "those stupid, half-grown little French boys."[5] Mary Joe, a "broad-faced French girl" engaged by Mrs. Barry to look after her children during a brief absence, is quite immobilized in the face of a sick Minnie Mae: "helpless and bewildered, quite incapable of thinking what to do, or doing it if she thought of it."[6] When Anne buys some hair dye from a peddler that turns her hair green rather than the promised black, Marilla admonishes her: "I told you never to let one of those Italians in the house!" When Anne retorts that he was a "German Jew" working to bring his family over from Germany, the narration quickly points to the faulty dye as a symbol of the peddler's general dishonesty.[7]

For some observers, Anne represents a process of imperial acculturation: Anne is an impoverished Anglo-Celtic Canadian who, with education and Marilla's firm hand, can be integrated into the community.[8] She is also herself part of that process of colonialism through her renaming, and thus marking, of

the landscape.[9] Moreover, Anne's exportation has been part of a process of Westernization; this is seen most clearly in the publication of the book in Japan and its inclusion in the Japanese national school curriculum in 1953, where it was used as an extension of the Americanization efforts undertaken after the Second World War under the Allied occupation.[10] Yet equally, *Anne* can be read as a recognition of "the positive power of difference,"[11] or of imagination as "a liberating force in the face of oppression."[12]

Anne's spirit embodies the ideal of the "new girl" in contrast to the imperial "ideal girl" that dominated much British literature of the time. The latter placed girls on the margins of society, hidden within the domestic world of the home and engaged in sewing, reading, and other virtuous activities. The new girl, in contrast, took centre stage, was both passionate and independent in character, and pushed back against constraining

Signs near Green Gables encourage visitors to follow in Anne's footsteps.

CANADA'S ROYAL WINNIPEG BALLET

ANNE OF GREEN GABLES

WEDNESDAY, JANUARY 24 TO FRIDAY, JANUARY 26
DU MERCREDI 24 AU VENDREDI 26 JANVIER 1990

Opera 20:30 Opéra

Anne's stage adaptations included a 1990 production
by the Royal Winnipeg Ballet at the National Arts
Centre in Ottawa.

gender and community norms. As such, she expressed an early form of twentieth-century feminism. Some commentators have linked the "new girl" trope to turn-of-the-century expressions of Canadian nationhood, seeing Anne as a metaphor for Canada: a youthful and vigorous nation carving out its own cultural identity.[13]

Published to critical acclaim in 1908, *Anne of Green Gables* sold more than nineteen thousand copies in its first five months of circulation, and it was eventually translated into more than thirty languages.[14] The character of Anne spawned a major entertainment industry, with three Hollywood films released between 1919 and 1940. *Anne of Green Gables: The Musical*, first produced in 1965, is the longest-running musical in Canadian history. Kevin Sullivan's 1985 *Anne of Green Gables* television miniseries broke Canadian viewership records and, along with the 1987 sequel, it went on to be translated into multiple languages and broadcast around the world. It was followed by Sullivan Entertainment's sentimental television series *Road to Avonlea* (1990–96), co-produced by the CBC and the Disney Channel, which secured unprecedented ratings in English Canada. More recently, Breakthrough Entertainment produced three made-for-television movies for YTV, while 2017 saw the CBC and Netflix collaborate on a grittier Anne series reflecting contemporary therapeutic concerns, from bullying to post-traumatic stress disorder, along with a more realistic representation of the life of an orphan. These numerous stage, musical, and television adaptations continue to bring Anne to new audiences.[15]

Montgomery's story proved particularly popular in Japan—and not just because of the postwar Allied occupation. In 1939, Hanako Muraoka received a copy of the novel from a New Brunswick missionary. She spent the war years secretly translating the book, which was published in Japanese in 1952, setting the stage for that nation's love affair with the book's title character. Indeed,

Anne's popularity in Japan has taken many forms, including a 1979 anime television production, several musicals, five volumes of Anne-themed comic books, and numerous Anne-related books on topics ranging from potpourri to quilting to the landscape of Prince Edward Island. There is also a nursing school in Okayama, the School of Green Gables, which boasts distinctly Canadian-looking buildings and whose students explicitly take Anne as a role model. In 1993, the Canadian World theme park opened in Hokkaido featuring a replica of Green Gables and a variety of Anne-related activities.[16]

Anne of Green Gables proved equally popular in Poland, particularly during periods of reconstruction after the First and Second World Wars.[17] It was among that nation's most popular novels in the 1920s and 1930s, and just a year after the end of the Second World War, Poles republished and feverishly purchased the first three volumes of the *Anne* series. Jerzy Wyszomirski, a member of the Polish underground army and hero of the Warsaw Uprising, publicly supported this endeavour. It was not simply Poland's cities that needed to be rebuilt, he argued, but its values, including joy and optimism. Anne's romantic spirit, he suggested, offered a model for Poles to embrace.[18] When communist authorities outlawed *Anne*, along with many other popular "girls' novels," children responded by circulating them clandestinely—sometimes even gluing pages together and rewriting missing parts by hand. "We Polish girls needed the cheerfulness of 'Anne'," remembered one schoolgirl.[19]

In the character of Anne, Montgomery had offered up a protagonist whose spirit was not bound by local practices. Hence the novel's appeal to multiple and diverse audiences. Japanese adults, confronted with the task of postwar reconstruction, considered Anne to be a role model for children because of her positive, optimistic spirit.[20] Iranians exposed to the story in the 1990s found comfort in the book's emphasis on familial duty and community bonds.[21] Equally, the element of nostalgia contained within *Anne of Green Gables* continues to speak to a modern international expatriate community seeking a sense of home. One volunteer for the Canadian Universities Service Overseas carried the book with her to Nigeria in the early 1980s, where she loaned it to a ten-year-old girl who was the daughter of two teachers from India. The girl memorized passages from *Anne*, even acting them out one day on the Mambilla Plateau. As an adult living in Bahrain, she came to long for the vast spaces of "lonely emptiness" that she frequented in her youth—a connection forged by her experience of reading about PEI's pastoral beauty while living on the Plateau. In today's globalized world, the book's focus on themes of "belonging" and "home" continue to resonate.[22]

Readers' connection with the story's setting has fuelled Prince Edward Island's tourism industry. Many Anne fans desire to capture the imaginary, to walk it, to touch it, to reach out and grasp what is illusory. Not surprisingly, almost immediately after the publication of the novel, tourists began to search out Green Gables—the home Anne shared with Matthew and Marilla. Montgomery loosely modeled the fictional house on the home owned by her MacNeill cousins, though the actual house had no gables, green or otherwise, nor a green roof, and was, in fact, somewhat run down. In the 1920s, the Webb family (MacNeill descendants residing in the house) opened the premises to tourists.[23] In the mid-1930s, the federal government expropriated the Webbs' land in order to create a national park.[24] It was with an eye to maximizing tourist visits in the late 1930s and early 1940s that authorities fitted the house with green gables and shutters. In 1950, several years after the Webbs had vacated the property, park authorities reopened the house, replete with late-nineteenth-century furnishings.[25] A 1996 fire forced a restoration and redecoration—undertaken with some help from the blueprints used to design the theme park in Hokkaido.[26]

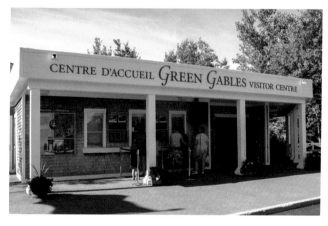

The Green Gables Visitor Centre welcomes thousands of "Anne" fans every year—and encourages them to tour "Anne's" home.

The desire to see Anne's house has played a key role in boosting PEI's tourism accounts. Indeed, "[t]he verbose orphan ... towers over the island like some pigtailed colossus," reported the *Boston Globe* in July 2000. "Only potatoes and lobsters surpass her in economic value."[27] Anne has become an industry on the island—so much so that when the Heirs of L. M. Montgomery Inc. registered "a trademark on L. M. Montgomery's name, associated images, and characters" just before the author's work would have entered public domain in the late 1980s, the province entered into a seven-year legal battle over licensing rights, resulting in the creation of the Anne of Green Gables Licensing Authority. As a result, the heirs ultimately had to split licensing royalties with the province.[28]

Much was at stake in that battle. Montgomery's characters are used to lure tourists, bolster business, and "sell products ranging from tourist accommodation to pizza."[29] Indeed, Anne is used to market a significant array of souvenirs, from candy to dishes, toys to clothing. There is also an abundance of textual adaptations—picture books, easy readers, colouring and pop-up books—that extend Anne's influence. Government marketing strategies promote this form of literary tourism, both in Canada and abroad. And Anne's image is also used to sell PEI products unconnected to Montgomery or her fictional creations. Even the local Cows Ice Cream company sells clothes featuring a cow adorned with a straw hat and red pigtails, à la Anne.[30]

Beyond marketing, the success of the PEI tourist industry owes much to the fact that Anne's house, its grounds, and the pastoral landscape that surround it still reflect what Montgomery captured more than a century ago. That success is also based on a particular image of Anne—a red-headed sprig of a girl. Those wishing to alter that image best beware. The online retailer Amazon discovered this in 2013 after reproducing a box set of the first three Anne novels featuring a buxom, precocious-looking

From fridge magnets to beverages to dolls, Anne's red pig tails are instantly recognizable on a wide variety of consumer items.

blonde on the cover. News coverage dubbed the remake "Anne of Sweet Valley High," sparking a flurry of condemnation.[31] "Anne is a redhead," lamented one fan, "and not the sexpot portrayed ... here."[32]

This was not the first time Anne's sexuality produced newspaper headlines. In 2000, many readers had been similarly alarmed when reports circulated of English professor Laura Robinson's suggestions that Anne's friendship with Diana Barry was "homoerotic" while her "stormy relationship" with fellow teacher Katherine Brooke in *Anne of Windy Poplars* was "informed by sadomasochism." Talk-radio hosts across the country took up the issue, with audiences frequently charging that the professor was taking the novel out of its historical context.[33]

In 2016, Anne's image again made headlines when abortion rights activists enlisted a strikingly similar visage (partially covered with a menacing blue bandana and labelled "Karats") in their campaign to convince the PEI government to provide women with access to abortion services. Abortion opponents, including the PEI Right to Life Association, immediately took issue with the use of an image from an "adopted fictional character" who is "the epitome of the unexpected blessings of choosing life."[34] Karats forcefully disagreed: "Anne was a fierce, out-spoken girl who understood hardships and overcoming adversity, and she brilliantly imagined a world where she was in control of her life and the choices she made."[35]

Reaction to the use of Anne's image makes clear readers' attachment to the story. Montgomery's work draws on powerful themes that transcend time and location. Anne embodies the power of imagination, the spiritedness and promise of youth, the desire for community or belonging, the struggle with difference, and the search for home. Such ideals are brought into sharp relief when contrasted with Montgomery's own life experience,

A poster from Karats's campaign to secure abortion services for women on Prince Edward Island. The hashtag "#Hey Wade" was directed toward Premier Wade MacLauchlan.

which was profoundly shaped by the influence of Anglo-Celtic Presbyterian respectability, an unhappy marriage, and the limited opportunities for women at the time.[36]

In 1935, Montgomery was inducted as an officer into the Order of the British Empire, clear recognition of her significance as a Canadian author. Still, her work faced scorn from male literary critics who considered it naive and dismissed it as romantic girls' literature.[37] Though enjoying great popularity, her work remained largely ignored within academic circles, only to be later rediscovered by female literary scholars.[38]

At the time of Montgomery's death in 1942, Canadian literary giant Robertson Davies wrote that "nations grow in the eyes of the world less by the work of their statesmen than their artists. Thousands of people all over the world are hazy about the exact nature of Canada's government ... but they have clear recollections of *Anne of Green Gables*."[39] Some seventy-five years later, such recollections, fashioned by literary and television experiences and the considerable efforts of tourism promoters, continue to ensure that Anne remains a prominent symbol of Canada for Canadians and non-Canadians alike.

Our thanks to Laura Robinson, Sue Fisher, and our *Symbols of Canada* collaborators for their feedback and suggestions—and to Joshua Adams for his excellent preliminary research!

NOTES

1   Anne Rogala quoted in Barbara Wachowicz, "L. M. Montgomery: At Home in Poland," *Canadian Children's Literature* 46 (1987): 26.
2   L. M. Montgomery would go on to write seven other novels featuring the character of Anne: *Anne of Avonlea* (1909); *Anne of the Island* (1915); *Anne's House of Dreams* (1917); *Rainbow Valley* (1919); *Rilla of Ingleside* (1921); *Anne of Windy Poplars* (1936); and *Anne of Ingleside* (1939).
3   Irene Gammel and Elizabeth Epperly, "L. M. Montgomery and the Shaping of Canadian Culture," in Gammel and Epperly, eds., *L. M. Montgomery and Canadian Culture* (Toronto: University of Toronto Press, 1999), 7.

4 Cecily Devereux, "'Canadian Classic' and 'Commodity Export': The Nationalism of 'Our' *Anne of Green Gables*," *Journal of Canadian Studies* 36, no. 1 (Spring 2001): 22–3.

5 L. M. Montgomery, *Anne of Green Gables* (New York: Bantam Books, 1979), 6.

6 Montgomery, *Anne of Green Gables*, 142.

7 Montgomery, *Anne of Green Gables*, 217.

8 Devereux, "'Canadian Classic' and 'Commodity Export',*"* 24.

9 Brooke Collins-Gearing, "Narrating the 'Classic' on Stolen Ground: *Anne of Green Gables*," in Jane Ledwell and Jean Mitchell, eds., *Anne Around the World: L. M. Montgomery and Her Classic* (Montreal and Kingston: McGill-Queen's University Press, 2013), 170.

10 Irene Gammel with Andrew O'Malley, Huifeng Hu, and Ranbir K. Banwait, "An Enchanting Girl: International Portraits of Anne's Cultural Transfer," in Irene Gammel and Benjamin Lefebvre, eds., *Anne's World: A New Century of Anne of Green Gables* (Toronto: University of Toronto Press, 2010), 177–81.

11 Laura M. Robinson, "'A Born Canadian': The Bonds of Communal Identity in *Anne of Green Gables* and *A Tangled Web*," in Gammel and Epperly, *L. M. Montgomery and Canadian Culture*, 29.

12 Jane Urquhart, *Extraordinary Canadians: Lucy Maud Montgomery* (Toronto: Penguin, 2012), 58.

13 Pearce, "Constructing a 'New Girl'," 230–8.

14 On early acclaim, see Gammel and Epperly, "L. M. Montgomery and the Shaping of Canadian Culture," 10; Carole Gerson, "Seven Milestones: How *Anne of Green Gables* Became a Canadian Icon," in Gammel and Lefebvre, *Anne's World*, 24.

15 Gerson, "Seven Milestones", 21–7; Benjamin Lefebvre, "*Road to Avonlea*: A Co-production of the Disney Corporation," in Irene Gammel, ed., *Making Avonlea: L. M. Montgomery and Popular Culture* (Toronto: University of Toronto Press, 2002), 174–85.

16 After the theme park went bankrupt in 1997, the city turned it into a public park. See Yoshiko Akamatsu, "Japanese Readings of *Anne of Green Gables*," in Gammel and Epperly, *L. M. Montgomery and Canadian Culture*, 205–7; Terry Dawes, "Why Anne of Green Gables is Big in Japan," *Huffington Post*, Mar. 5, 2014, huffingtonpost.com/terry-dawes-anne-of-green-gables-japan_b_4899252.html.

17 Irene Gammel et al., "An Enchanting Girl," in Gammel and Lefebvre, *Anne's World*, 169–71.

18 Wachowicz, "L. M. Montgomery: At Home in Poland," 10–11.

19 Ibid., 11.

20 Akamatsu, "Japanese Readings of *Anne of Green Gables*," 207.

21 Gammel et. al., "An Enchanting Girl," 169–71.

22 Margaret Steffler, "Anne in a Globalized World: Nation, Nostalgia, and Postcolonial Perspectives of Home," in Gammel and Lefebvre, *Anne's World*, 150–51, 153, 161.

23 Clare Fawcett and Patricia Cormack, "Guarding Authenticity At Literary Tourism Sites," *Annals of Tourism Research* 28, no. 3 (2001): 694.

24 Alan MacEachern, *Natural Selections: National Parks in Atlantic Canada, 1935–1970* (Montreal and Kingston: McGill-Queen's University Press, 2001), ch. 4.

25 Fawcett and Cormack, "Guarding Authenticity at Literary Tourism Sites," 694.

26 Akamatsu, "Japanese Readings of *Anne of Green Gables*," 211n3.

27 Colin Nickerson, "A Tempest Under Anne's Gables," *Boston Globe* July 1, 2000.

28 Laura Robinson, "'Outrageously Sexual' Anne: The Media and Montgomery," in Jean Mitchell, ed., *Storm and Dissonance: L. M. Montgomery and Conflict* (Newcastle, UK: Cambridge Scholars Publishing, 2008), 313–16, and 323n7.

29 Shelagh J. Squire, "Literary Tourism and Sustainable Tourism: Promoting 'Anne of Green Gables' in Prince Edward Island," *Journal of Sustainable Tourism* 4, no. 3 (1996): 125.

30 Squire, "Literary Tourism and Sustainable Tourism," 125–6. On the effects of globalization on Atlantic-Canadian literature more generally, see Herb Wyile, *Anne of Tim Hortons: Globalization and the Reshaping of Atlantic-Canadian Literature* (Waterloo: Wilfrid Laurier University Press, 2011).

31 Phil Han, "Anne of Sweet Valley High?" *CTV News*, Feb. 6, 2013, ctvnews.ca/entertainment/anne-of-green-gables-gets-blonde-makeover-in-the-new-cover-1.1145610.

32 "Fans see red over blonde Anne of Green Gables," *Calgary Herald*, Feb. 7, 2013.

33 Stephanie Nolan, "Does lesbianism underlie Anne of Green Gables?" *Globe and Mail* (Toronto), May 31, 2000. See also Cecily Devereux, "Anatomy of a 'National Icon': *Anne of Green Gables* and the 'Bosom Friends' Affair," in Gammel, *Making Avonlea*, 32–42, and, Robinson, "'Outrageously Sexual' Anne," 317–19.

34 "A militant Anne of Green Gables is on posters promoting abortion access in Prince Edward Island," *National Post* (Toronto), Jan. 29, 2016.

35 "Karats speaks: Militant doppelgänger of Anne of Green Gables takes abortion fight coast-to-coast," *National Post* (Toronto), Feb. 11, 2016.

36 Urquhart, *L. M. Montgomery*, 157–61. For a full biography see Mary Henley Rubio, *Lucy Maud Montgomery: The Gift of Wings* (Toronto: Doubleday Canada, 2008).

37 Urquhart, *L. M. Montgomery*, 51–6, 161.

38 Mavis Reimer, "Suggestions for Further Reading: A Guide to the Research and Criticism on *Anne of Green Gables*," in Mavis Reimer, ed., *Such a Simple Little Tale: Critical Responses to L. M. Montgomery's* Anne of Green Gables (Metuchen, NJ and London: The Children's Literature Association and Scarecrow Press, 1992), 178–9.

39 Robertson Davies quoted in Mary Rubio, "*Anne of Green Gables*: The Architect of Adolescence," in Reimer, *Such a Simple Little Tale*, 65.

Tourists approaching the Canadian or "Horseshoe" Falls.

NIAGARA FALLS

Karen Dubinsky

As a tourist destination, **Niagara Falls has** become famous for being famous. At first, the plantation-owning southern United States provided the bulk of elite visitors, who were drawn by the relatively temperate northern climate in the summer. During the nineteenth century, the Falls quickly became an item to check off for European and other visitors doing the North American grand tour. Changes in transportation and the economy brought middle- and later working-class visitors by the carload, who amused themselves at the water's edge as well as at the vast array of commercial amusements that grew around the natural spectacle. The opening of casinos in recent decades has helped to maintain a frantic pace.

So Niagara Falls has enjoyed centuries of celebrity, yet its cultural meaning is eclectic. The imaginary geography of Niagara Falls has never been single or consistent; it has always meant different things to different people. And it has always been far more than a rare and mesmerizing natural phenomenon. For its millions of observers, it has been, over time, a place to commune with God, nature, and technological progress; a place to ponder the virtues of civilization—in both human and

Visitors at Niagara Falls, Ontario.

non-human forms—over wilderness; and a giant aquatic toy to play alongside.[1] Some years ago I spent time researching how the place became an amiably risqué place for couples to celebrate heterosexual citizenship through the ritual of the honeymoon.[2] It is clearly a visible, high-profile symbol *in* Canada, and has adorned souvenirs of Canadian vacations for over a century. But odd though it may seem, it has rarely been symbolic *of* Canada. In Canada, at least, narratives of the Falls have generally eclipsed strictly national meanings. That's not as paradoxical as it might appear.

One obvious reason is that Niagara Falls is not located solely in Canada. Falling water is nothing if not transnational, and of course the Falls are shared between Canada and the United States. In paintings, particularly in the nineteenth century, depicting bald eagles, the stars and stripes, and flag-draped young women standing before the Falls, many Americans tried to define and celebrate the waterfall in national terms, appropriating it for the spirit of their country.[3] But because the Falls were shared, and furthermore because the Canadian Horseshoe Falls was the larger and more visually compelling of the two distinct waterfalls that make up this natural phenomenon, American nationalist claims were difficult to sustain.

The American visitors who commented specifically on the Canadian Falls often did so jokingly, expressing remorse or envy.

The American and Bridal Veil Falls (left) and the Canadian or "Horseshoe" Falls (right).

Novelist William Howells admitted that he watched "the mighty wall of waters" on the Canadian side "with a jealousy almost as green as themselves." An anonymous scribbler in a public comment album on the Canadian side expressed the same sentiment in verse: "My pride was humbled and my boast was small, for England's King has got the fiercest Fall." American president John Quincy Adams turned the Canadian-American border into an act of God. "It was as though," he wrote, "Heaven had considered this vast natural phenomenon too great for one nation."[4] Perhaps this stands as yet another example of the fact that Canadians and Americans perform nationalism differently. Canadian writer Agnes Machar's patriotic delight that "our Canadian falls are the grandest" was a boast taken up by surprisingly few Canadian visitors.[5]

We ought not to scoff too much at John Quincy Adams's musings that Niagara's greatness exceeded national boundaries. People visited Niagara to see, of course, but also to think, reflect and, throughout the nineteenth century in particular, to write. Visitors filled their diaries, letters, postcards, and occasionally publications, with fervent and stirring tributes to Niagara's majesty. A visit to Niagara Falls was, for many, not unlike a visit to a church or shrine. And, as in church, on-site comportment was critical. Over the nineteenth century, as industrial and commercial development—factories and hydroelectric plants,

Even at night the "American" and "Canadian" waterfalls compete for visitors' attention.

as well as small-scale enterprises offering an assortment of pastimes and attractions—crowded around the waterfall, a preservation campaign arose with the aim to "Free Niagara." Two important leaders in this campaign, which was composed of intellectuals, artists, and a few politicians, were Frederick Law Olmstead, designer of New York's Central Park, and Harvard professor Charles Eliot Norton. Hoping to spread the message that Niagara's tourist industry and the visitors it attracted were destroying the place, Olmstead and Norton hired popular journalist Jonathan Baxter Harrison to spend the summer of 1882 at the waterfall. Harrison's newspaper reports and book, *The Condition of Niagara Falls and the Measures Needed to Improve Them*, laid out the concerns and philosophy of the Niagara preservation campaign. His book in particular read like a detailed instruction manual on the right and wrong way to appreciate Niagara. The spiritual and moral elevation of the waterfall was, for Harrison and his backers, paramount:

It offers to those who are weary from toil of any kind, of hand or brain, or from the wearing, exhausting quality which is so marked in modern life ... a vital change, the relief and benefit of new scenes and new mental activities and experiences consequent upon observing them.... There is a quickening and uplifting of the higher powers of the mind, an awakening of the imagination; the soul expands and aspires ... self-respect becomes more vital.[6]

This explains why the cultural elite of the day considered the amusements and curiosity shops around the Falls "debasing, vulgarizing and horrible in the extreme."[7]

The other part of this story—and, indeed, of all so-called preservation campaigns around Niagara through the years—was a deep mistrust of the local tourist industry. This animosity towards what *The Canadian Magazine* termed the "sharks, hucksters and pedlars" around Niagara was based in large measure around class and racial animosities about black tour guides, Jewish museum owners, and Indigenous souvenir vendors.[8] Niagara was never "freed." By eventually nationalizing the area around the Falls, it was simply placed in different, more culturally acceptable hands. It had become a matter of national duty, expressed, as nationalism usually is, in racial terms. A popular American sporting magazine explained its enthusiastic support for the preservation campaign in these terms: "The two great branches of the English-speaking people—the British and the Americans— share in the control of Niagara; the Canadian province of Ontario and the American State of New York are simply their trustees."[9]

The idea that the waterfall was shared was rarely expressed in terms of co-operation or cross-border friendship. Niagara's iconography, in tourist art and material culture, occasionally displayed twinned Canadian and American imagery, usually in the form of flags, but this was rare.[10] However, by virtue of geography and history, the place could not be contained in strictly national terms. The campaign to "harness" Niagara for hydroelectric development revealed how the place was imagined in terms of empire rather than nation. Early hydro promoters used military metaphors to describe their attempts to "conquer" Niagara, turning the story of industrial development into a heroic and mystical "epic" of man against nature.[11] The waterfalls themselves had long been feminized, at least in the imagination of many painters and travel writers. Thus many writers imagined the success of hydro developers at Niagara using the symbols and language of white male conquerors everywhere. As one writer enthused, "man has accomplished here, with Nature

The Clifton Hill district of Niagara Falls, Ontario, boasts a wide variety of kitschy attractions, including the Movieland Wax Museum and beavers in canoes selling pastries.

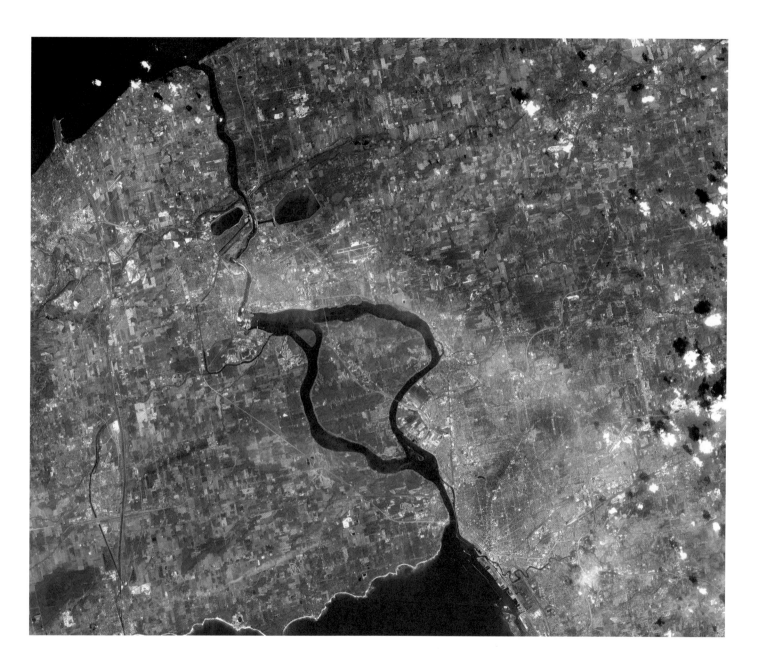

With enough perspective, the national identity of the Falls
is rendered irrelevant—as with this view from space.

as his handmaiden, some of the greatest achievements of any age." The Canadian Steamship Lines evoked the spirit of what it termed "yesterday's Indian," the Maid of the Mist (a white fantasy "Indian princess") to praise the developers. "The hunting grounds of her fathers are peopled by a new race of strong, virile men. To them, the earth is their destiny, the things of the earth their heritage; this wonderful natural phenomenon but a potent natural force to be brought under human control."[12] By proclaiming electrical development as the manifest destiny of white men, Niagara Falls became symbolic not of a specific nation, but of something much larger.

Such grand imperial claims waxed and waned over Niagara's history, conforming to familiar ideas of technological and economic development across the nineteenth and twentieth centuries and observable around the world. Through the twentieth century, the heroic vision of imperial progress that accompanied (and underwrote) hydroelectric development faded into the dull roar of consumer capitalism: roadside motels and lodges, large-scale hotels, mom-and-pop restaurants, and a head-spinning array of amusements and curiosities (many of which continued to evoke "yesterday's Indian," such as the 1960s-era "Indian Village" that invited visitors to take themselves "back in time").

As mass tourism exploded after the Second World War, Niagara came to symbolize something else: the sleazy, tacky, "honky tonk" clip joint. Gone were the grand tributes to British or American masculine achievement over nature; this generation had other economic issues on its mind. Old national rivalries re-emerged, but not around the debate over which waterfall was more magnificent. Rather, the small-scale entrepreneurs who were fighting losing battles with multinational hotel companies and chain restaurants—which would dominate the landscape from the 1960s to today—engaged in high-pitched struggles for customers across both sides of the border.

Canadian entrepreneurs claimed that their American counterparts told lies about Canada in order to keep American visitors to themselves: for example, that accommodations in Canada were fully booked; that Americans were not allowed to bring their cars to Canada; that naturalized Americans could lose their citizenship by visiting a foreign country. Fake "information booths" sprang up around Niagara Falls, New York, which directed visitors away from Canada but also promoted specific lodging on the American side, for which they earned kickbacks. On the Canadian side, "officially" dressed taxi and tour-bus operators flagged down motorists as if to caution or detain them but actually to sell them motel rooms. A century of rivalries between the tourist industries in both countries hit a particularly low point in 1989, when, in its annual tourist map, the visitor's bureau on the American side omitted any references to Canada, or even to the bridges crossing the river.

I spent years thinking and writing about how the Niagara Falls honeymoon drew on centuries-old ideas of romance, danger, gender, and sexuality, which then gave way to the overt commodification of romance in the twentieth century. I also learned about the many ways Niagara has been imagined and depicted by visitors: as wildness, the sublime, and a reflection of Anglo-Saxon technological superiority. But another framing of the Falls caught my attention more recently, this one from an unlikely source: Cuban poetry. I began researching and teaching in Cuba after my work on Niagara was completed. I was surprised at how much interest my new Cuban colleagues had in Niagara. Of course, international visitors had been coming to the Falls for centuries, so it wasn't surprising that Cubans knew about the place. But they knew it for something that, despite a decade of Niagara research, I had never heard of. In 1824, Cuban poet José María Heredia penned a poem titled "Níagara." Exiled at the youthful age of nineteen for his activities in support of Cuban

The Heredia plaque.

independence from Spain, Heredia settled in the United States and made his way to Niagara to visit the Falls, which fascinated and inspired him.

Scholars have claimed that Heredia's poem helped to establish him as the first Romantic poet in the Spanish language. It was quickly translated into English, and it received some fame in both languages. But in Cuba the poem's popularity soared, particularly when, a few decades later, José Martí—another Cuban national hero who was also a poet and also in exile in the United States—sang its praises and termed Heredia "el primer poeta de América"—the first poet of the Americas. For generations, and even today, Heredia's Niagara poem is taught, memorized, and recited by Cuban school children as part of their national cultural canon. Heredia's impact in Canada and the United States is less profound, but he lives on at Niagara.

His presence was inscribed and noted in Canada in 1955, when the Cuban contingent to the International Scout Jamboree gifted a plaque to its host city, Niagara Falls. The plaque, given four years before the Cuban Revolution of 1959, identified Heredia as an "exiled patriot" and "sublime singer of the wondrous greatness of Niagara Falls." The plaque is located at Table Rock, near the brink of the Falls. This original plaque, having been worn down over time, was replaced with great fanfare in October 1989 by another visiting Cuban poet, Eliseo Diego, at a ceremony that included Cuban and Canadian officials as well as Canadian literary figures (and a message from Margaret Atwood). The current plaque includes fragments of the poem and quotes José Martí that Heredia's work "awoke an ever-burning passion for freedom" in the hearts of all Cubans.[13] My work in Cuban studies now involves helping to co-ordinate an exchange agreement between Queen's University and the University of Havana, which includes annual visits from Cuban scholars, artists, and musicians. As host, I am obliged and delighted to accompany those of my Cuban colleagues who request trips (and most do) to the Falls. First on their Niagara itinerary is the Heredia plaque, which they admire and photograph; from memory, they recite a few lines.

That people from another nation, culture, and language might enjoy a visit to Niagara in order to reflect on one of their own national figures tells us a great deal about both the fictitiousness and the durability of nations. It is a truism of cultural theory and history that readings of cultural texts are multiple but not infinite or equal; some stories have more power than others. Perhaps one of the most interesting aspects of Niagara—along with the mesmerizing spectacle of water rushing over rock—is how it has offered up such a wide array of stories over the years.

NOTES

1   Patrick McGreevy, *Imagining Niagara: The Making and Meaning of Niagara Falls* (Amherst: University of Massachusetts Press, 199); Patricia Jasen, *Wild Things: Nature, Culture and Tourism in Ontario, 1790–1914* (Toronto: University of Toronto Press, 1995); William Irwin, *The New Niagara: Tourism, Technology and the Landscape of Niagara Falls, 1776–1917* (University Park: Pennsylvania State University Press, 1996).

2   Karen Dubinsky, *The Second Greatest Disappointment: Honeymooning and Tourism at Niagara Falls* (Toronto: Between the Lines and New Brunswick, NJ: Rutgers University Press, 1999)

3   Elizabeth McKinsey, *Niagara Falls: Icon of the American Sublime* (Cambridge: Cambridge University Press, 1985), 39.

4   William Howells, "Niagara First and Last," in Howells, Mark Twain, and Nathaniel Southgate Shaler, eds., *The Niagara Book: A Complete Souvenir of Niagara Falls* (Buffalo, NY, 1893), 9; George Menzies, *Album of the Table Rock, 1846; A Souvenir of Niagara Falls* (Buffalo, NY, 1864), 1.

5   Agnes Machar, *Down the River to the Sea* (New York, 1894), 25.

6   Jonathan Baxter Harrison, *Certain Dangerous Tendencies in American Life* (Boston, 1880), 8–9.

7   Dubinsky, *The Second Greatest Disappointment*, 90.

8   E. A. Meredith, "The Queen Victoria Niagara Falls Park," *The Canadian Magazine*, (July 1897): 7.

9   *Outing and the Wheelman* 5, no. 6 (March 1885): 458.

10 See, for example, Virginia Vidler, *Niagara Falls: 100 years of Souvenirs* (Utica, NY: North Country Books, 1985).

11 H. V. Nelles, *The Politics of Development* (Montreal: McGill University Press, 1974), 218–23.

12 Canada Steamship Lines brochure (1915), 8; E. T. Williams, *Niagara, Queen of Wonders* (Boston: Chapple, 1916), 1.

13 This story of Heredia and his legacy is drawn largely from Keith Ellis, *José María Heredia and "Niagara Falls"* (Havana: Editorial José Martí, 2010).

A group of "Raging Grannies" make their position on the public-private health-care debate crystal clear at a Friends of Medicare rally at the Alberta legislature in 2009.

UNIVERSAL HEALTH CARE

Cheryl Krasnick Warsh

"Mommie, what is a Canadian?" asks a child in a recently posted internet cartoon. "It's an unarmed North American with health insurance, sweetie," the mother responds.[1] Popular representations of ostensibly essential Canadian characteristics include food, sport, flora, fauna, and military exploits—but also, in the case of universal health care, public policy. Like many other Canadian symbols, universal health care (or Medicare as it's officially known) is highlighted as a mark of differentiation from, and superiority to, the United States, where citizens may receive haphazard and unequal medical coverage, if they receive medical coverage at all. According to one woman from St. Albert, Alberta, our health-care system "speaks to Canadians' superior imagination."[2]

Universal health care is widely viewed as the most cherished social policy in Canadian history. Indeed, poll results consistently demonstrate Canadians' affinity for Medicare. In 2009, 86.2 percent of Canadians favoured "strengthening public health care rather than expanding for-profit services."[3] In 2012, 94 percent of respondents considered Medicare to be "an important source of collective pride." In contrast, only 60 percent deemed

This 1958 stamp acknowledged the growing link between medical care and Canadian national identity.

the *Charter of Rights and Freedoms* "very important," while the monarchy scored a paltry 39 percent.[4]

Medicare's popularity belies its complexity. It encompasses federal and provincial jurisdictions and layers of stakeholders, including physicians, nurses, other health professionals, hospital administrators, finance departments, and citizen-users. It pits bean-counters against spenders, the old against the young, and even the imbibers, smokers, and tokers against the clean-livers. Yet it is a symbol jealously guarded by the Canadian population as a fundamental right of every citizen.

Medicare has a heroic origin story, one based in twentieth-century politics. Its portrayal as a contrast to (inferior/heartless/ unequal) American health care has evolved to the point where Canadian Medicare is presently raised by warring political factions in the United States as either a bugaboo or a beacon. In reality, Canadian Medicare is an over-used, top-heavy, creaky structure whose cracks may well turn into sinkholes. But woe betide any government that threatens its core principles: universality, portability, public administration, comprehensiveness, and accessibility. Indeed, the symbolic construction of Medicare directly shapes political agendas across the country.

Unlike many of the symbols included in this collection, which developed in an organic, albeit haphazard, fashion over time, the symbolism of Medicare has been carefully nurtured by one particular political faction: the Co-operative Commonwealth Federation (CCF) and its successor, the New Democratic Party (NDP), along with these parties' historians and a sympathetic left-leaning press. The origin of Medicare has been characterized as a battle between the forces of light (the Saskatchewan CCF government) versus the forces of darkness (the Liberals, the Conservatives, the Canadian Medical Association, and representatives of Big Business).

In reality, the establishment of Medicare was the result of an evolutionary process incorporating the intellectual, political, technological, and cultural advancements of many individuals from many countries over several decades. A public health-care system was first established in Great Britain by a Labour Party government in 1948, and other Western nations followed suit after the Second World War. The idea of Canadian public health-care had been floated in Liberal Party election platforms since the 1920s, although, unlike old age pensions, mother's allowances, and unemployment insurance, this vital piece of the social safety net was not implemented.

Medicare is venerated in large part as the crowning achievement of Saskatchewan's CCF premier T. C. (Tommy) Douglas, and this narrative is intertwined with the Cult of the Hero. Douglas's iconic status was confirmed as recently as 2004, when CBC Television viewers chose him as the "Greatest Canadian."[5] But why Saskatchewan and why Douglas? In Saskatchewan, the most rural of the Prairie provinces, the need for communal effort led to the creation of the Wheat Pool and other forms of mutual co-operation.[6] Indeed, it was in Swift Current, in 1941, that a prototype of Medicare was established, whereby residents in the town and nearby communities could pay a tax and access medical services.[7]

And why Douglas? He has been correctly characterized as "the right man in the right place at the right time."[8] Diminutive, pugnacious, and fearless, Douglas travelled to every riding of his province, parlaying the sermonizing skills he honed in front of his Baptist congregation in Weyburn (Douglas was an ordained minister) to put a human, and humane, face to his socialist government during the Second World War and early Cold War. His oft-quoted recounting of his impoverished childhood in Scotland, and his dependence, due to his family's lack of funds, on a charitable physician to save his leg, rang true with a generation of Canadians who experienced the Great Depression and suffered their own losses from inadequate or expensive health care.

Yet even the iconic Douglas was found to have feet of clay, and his humaneness to be racially relative: in 1933 he wrote a thesis for a master's of social work degree at McMaster University that advocated eugenic measures to deal with what he called "sub-normal" families.[9] While in the many hagiographic biographies this unfortunate blemish on Reverend Douglas's ivory image is either omitted or glossed over with a brief statement that he recanted these views when he observed the Nazi atrocities in Europe, it also has been ignored in the public narrative, including the 2004 CBC Greatest Canadian competition.

By the 1990s, Tommy Douglas's image was perhaps the most recognizable popular and official representation of Canadian Medicare. Hence this 1998 stamp.

There has been push-back, however, particularly when the left-wing narrative oversteps hagiography to engage in partisan slander. This was most evident in the 2006 biographical television miniseries *Prairie Giant*, which took great liberties with the historical record. In the drama, Douglas's political rival is Jimmy (J. J.) Gardiner, federal minister of agriculture in Mackenzie King's postwar Liberal government. Every hero, after all, requires a villain, and Gardiner is portrayed as Darth Vader in a business suit, spitting on communists and immigrants, setting the Mounties on the strikers in the tragic Estevan miners' strike, and attempting to bankrupt the province of Saskatchewan out of pure spite. It made for great theatre, but since many

The Saskatchewan Medical Association meets amidst the 1962 doctors' strike.

of the protagonists' families and colleagues were still alive and took issue with the depiction of Gardiner, it made for less than great history.

But real battles in the national Medicare saga established its symbolic power, beginning with the 1962 Saskatchewan doctors' strike. After winning his fifth term on a Medicare platform, Douglas took up the leadership of the national NDP. He left Medicare's implementation to his lieutenant, Woodrow Lloyd, whose government enacted Medicare legislation modelled after the British National Health Service—itself symbolic "proof" of British superiority over America. When the Saskatchewan Medical Association withdrew its services, the hysteria exhibited by the affected populace, the macho stand-off between government and physicians, and the airlift of British physicians as saviours or scabs (depending on one's political inclinations), were journalistic fodder reminiscent of any number of Western films.[10]

After Saskatchewan Medicare's proven success, other Canadians demanded this benefit for themselves. Since the 1930s, Canadians increasingly characterized health care as a human right.[11] By the 1940s, this viewpoint was taken up by the Canadian labour movement and farmers' parties during radio debates with representatives of the Canadian Medical Association (CMA).[12] At this point, Douglas exits the Medicare narrative and other actors come to the forefront, although with the unglamorous task of negotiating among the federal and provincial governments and the CMA.

At Confederation in 1867, issues such as health, education, and social welfare were considered of "local" interest, and as such were enshrined in the *British North America Act* (Canada's first constitution) as the purview of the provinces. However, by the 1930s, after the losses of the Great War and the worldwide influenza pandemic, as well as the human costs of the Great Depression, the Canadian population embraced a social welfare agenda, as signaled by the emergence of the federal CCF/NDP and the cherry-picking of its platform by Mackenzie King's Liberals. Nor did the right ignore the growing will of the people. Saskatchewan Conservative John Diefenbaker, who led a minority government in Ottawa (1957–63) amidst decades of Liberal rule, appointed Supreme Court Justice Emmett Hall to head the Royal Commission on Health Services.

In his report, Justice Hall included a defence of Medicare that best encapsulates its place as a national myth:

> The value of a human life must be decided without regard to whether the person is a producer or not. Health services must not be denied to certain individuals simply because the latter make no contribution to the economic development of Canada or because he cannot pay for such services. Important as economics is we must also take into account the human and spiritual aspects involved.[13]

With language like this, the Hall Report "took much of the wind out of the opponents of Medicare,"[14] particularly since Justice Hall did not retire back to the judiciary, but publically campaigned for the implementation of a national health-care

system. By the time the Hall Report was published in 1964, the Pearson Liberals were back in power. They instituted hospital care and then full medical coverage in 1966. Medicare thus became associated with all that was benevolent, optimistic, and dynamic as Canada burst upon the world stage amidst a sustained period of economic prosperity and its 1967 Centennial celebrations.

Medicare, which is the only symbol in this collection explicitly based on social justice, represents a superb meshing of public interest and political astuteness. It also reflects the changing and gendered composition of the electorate. The emergence of the woman voter put social-justice issues front and centre, and the nineteenth-century suffragist platform of protection of home and family evolved into the popular—and therefore vote-winning—mother's allowances, government support for education, and public hospital and health insurance. Health care is, literally, a motherhood issue, and the fact that it is recognized as such by Canada's governments is evident in the statistics. To date, nine of the twenty-four federal health ministers have been women. Judy LaMarsh became just Canada's second female cabinet minister when she served as health minister in the Pearson government. When Canadian newspapers printed stories of families devastated by illness, LaMarsh wrote about her mother's cancer "swiftly swallowing" her father's life savings.[15] In our post-Oprah age, where "sharing" has become routinely expected of public figures, we should not underestimate the extent to which this intimate story from a lone female politician resonated with Canada's women voters.

By the 1980s, due to the constitutional framework whereby every province implemented its own Medicare scheme, many provinces were permitting user fees and extra-billing for services insurable under the plan. The provinces and the CMA argued that these were safety valves supporting an under-funded, albeit tremendously well-used, system, and they encouraged specialists to

Calgary Herald cartoonist Tom Innes offers an interesting role reversal of the traditional doctor-patient relationship. The sickly, scared patient represents the provinces facing funding cutbacks, while the doctor is Monique Bégin, the female health minister wielding a giant needle that will deliver "Pain . . . Pure Unadulterated Pain!"

remain in Canada by supplementing their incomes. Such powerful lobbies were met with opinion-makers looking to save the basic principles of Medicare by appealing to the public.

At the forefront of this response was another powerful female health minister, Monique Bégin, who served in two Pierre Trudeau administrations.[16] Bégin's second term coincided with the release of the second Hall Commission Report, which passionately defended Medicare as a core Canadian value, stating that Canadians fully understand "that the pain of illness, the trauma of surgery, the slow decline to death, are burdens enough for the human being to bear without the added burden of medical or hospital bills penalizing the patient at the moment of vulnerability."[17]

Under Bégin, the Department of National Health and Welfare responded with the 1983 publication of *Preserving Universal Medicare: A Government of Canada Position Paper*. This document was requested by twenty-three thousand Canadians, and the department subsequently provided funds for communities to hold town hall meetings on Medicare's future. The Liberal government had brilliantly galvanized the popular will, as reflected in surveys finding that Canadians across the country overwhelmingly supported Medicare while rejecting user fees and extra-billing.[18] After twenty-five years, Medicare was well and truly a national policy—a development underscored by the tabling of the 1983 *Canada Health Act*, which added "accessibility" to Medicare's original four core principles of universality, portability, public administration, and comprehensiveness.

The *Act* specifically outlawed extra-billing for procedures covered by the government plan, and it included a clause that any extra-billing would be clawed back in reduced federal transfer payments to the provinces. Despite ferocious opposition from provincial leaders in British Columbia, Alberta, and Ontario, as well as the CMA, the House of Commons unanimously passed the *Act*; as Brian Mulroney, new leader of the Progressive Conservatives and soon to be prime minister, stated, "Medicare is a sacred trust which we will preserve."[19]

Popular respect for physicians, which had peaked in the mid-twentieth century with advancements in surgery and the creation of magic bullets for a variety of diseases, reached rock bottom in 1986, when Ontario's doctors went on strike in response to the passage of the *Act*. As physicians either left the country—primarily for what was perceived as the greener pastures of the United States—or joined the CMA in its legal challenge of the *Act*, the profession discovered, as its members had feared when Medicare was first launched, that they were now popularly regarded as one more party at the public trough, and a greedy one at that.

In the years that followed, special-interest groups ranging from unions to health administrators called upon the federal and provincial governments to reform Medicare and eliminate wait-lists while controlling costs. Canadian nationalists on the left, notably Mel Hurtig and Maude Barlow, raised the spectre of this Canadian symbol being threatened by American economic imperialism during the free trade election of 1988. They warned that American private health companies might operate freely in Canada, but Canadians were largely satisfied with government assurances that Medicare would be protected.

Protected, perhaps, but the underlying tensions at play in sustaining a universal health-care system have not been resolved. Hence, like all popular symbols, there are cracks in the veneer. The same generation who benefitted most from the institution of Medicare, the aging baby boomers, now demand similar entitlements from a two-tier system allowing those with money to jump the queue for needed surgeries and other therapies in an unwieldy, wasteful financial structure bursting at the seams. The pre-Medicare doctors, who were vilified as greedy and uncaring, are now nostalgically remembered as upstanding community members who made house calls and took chickens and other bartered goods from cash-strapped patients. Contemporary physicians, on the other hand, particularly those involved in primary care, are perceived as chafing at their status as civil servants while wistfully eyeing American incomes.

A crack in the inviolability of the ban against extra-billing came with the Supreme Court of Canada's judgment in *Chaoulli v. Quebec (AG) 2005*. The Court found that the Quebec *Health Insurance Act* and the *Hospital Insurance Act* prohibiting private medical insurance violated, because of long wait times for certain surgical procedures, a Quebecer's right to life and security of the person under the Quebec *Charter of Human Rights and Freedoms*.[20] While the Court's decision only applied to Quebec, it reverberated throughout the country—effectively highlighting the tension between individual rights and a health-care system that ostensibly aims to provide equal access to all Canadians. Not everyone was pleased. Writing to the *Globe and Mail*, one woman described the decision as "shameful" because it promises to "subvert the equality-based principles of Medicare" by introducing a

two-tier system based not on need but on one's ability to pay.[21] And that, argued another letter writer, is hardly Canadian: "The idea that every citizen is entitled to health care regardless of ability to pay is as true to the Canadian soul as water is wet."[22] Yet wait times seem to be increasing: in 2016, wait times ranged from 4.1 weeks for medical oncology to 38 weeks for orthopedic surgeries (including common hip and knee replacements). Access to procedures also varied widely, with an average of 38.8 weeks in New Brunswick and 15.6 weeks in Ontario.[23]

Chaoulli v. Quebec (AG) was followed by another case, currently before the British Columbia Supreme Court, concerning Dr. Brian Day's private Cambie Surgery Centre of Vancouver, which is testing the ban on doctors charging privately for services.[24] Representatives of the various interests used heated rhetoric to emphasize the stakes involved. Dr. Day cited one of the plaintiffs who became paralyzed after waiting twenty-seven months for spinal surgery, while representatives of both Canadian Doctors for Medicare and the BC Nurses' Union argued that the case was about "profit and not patients," and that "public health care, the jewel of Canada's health-care system, [was] a core value of our society and we have to defend it."[25]

This Tommy Douglas statue in Weyburn, Saskatchewan was unveiled with great fanfare in 2010. Sculptor Lea Vivot included maple leaves in Douglas's breast pocket and at his feet, symbolizing, perhaps, that he belongs to all of Canada.

Despite its popularity as a Canadian symbol, Canada's health-care system is a tarnished icon. In a 2017 study of eleven affluent nations, Canada ranked third-last in terms of "access, equity and health-care outcomes. It scored particularly poorly in the areas of infant mortality, access to after-hours medical care, and affordability of dental visits and prescription drugs.[26] Tommy Douglas's status as the face of Canadian Medicare speaks to a simpler time when it was easier to make a revolution than to run the new republic afterwards.[27] As public policy, Medicare is the victim of multiple health plans, competing jurisdictions, ballooning costs, and intractable inefficiencies. But as a symbol, Medicare is cherished and protected by Canadians across the country.

Thanks to Diana Pearson, my research assistant.

NOTES

1 See "Mommie, what is a Canadian?" Mar. 18, 2017, possom.postach.io/post/mommie-what-is-a-canadian.

2 Doris Wrench Eisler, letter to the editor, *Globe and Mail* (Toronto), June 13, 2005.

3 Physicians for a National Health Program, "New Poll Shows Canadians Overwhelmingly Support Public Health Care: Group Says Advocates of Private System are Out of Touch with Most Canadians," press release, Aug. 12, 2009.

4 Bruce Cheadle, "Universal Health Care Much Loved among Canadians, Monarchy Less Important: Poll," *Canadian Press*, Nov. 25, 2012.

5 "The Greatest Canadian of All Time Is . . . ," (CBC Television, Nov. 29, 2004), cbc.ca/player/play/1402807530.

6 C. Stuart Houston, *Steps on the Road to Medicare: Why Saskatchewan Led the Way* (Montreal and Kingston: McGill-Queen's University Press, 2002), 125.

7 Ibid., ch. 6.

8 Ibid. 7.

9 Angus McLaren, *Our Own Master Race: Eugenics in Canada, 1885–1945* (Toronto: University of Toronto Press, 1990), 166. Douglas's racist past was again resurrected by journalist Peter McMartin in "Before the Greatest Canadian Vote, Tommy Douglas Had Darker Past," *Vancouver Sun*, Oct. 25, 2016.

10 Doris French Shackleton, *Tommy Douglas* (Toronto: McClelland and Stewart, 1975), 243–4.

11 See "Bennett and the Premiers," in *Making Medicare: The History of Health Care in Canada* (Canadian Museum of History, 2010), historymuseum.ca/cmc/exhibitions/hist/medicare/medic-2h06e.shtml.

12 "Fundamental Principles," in *Making Medicare: The History of Health Care in Canada* (Canadian Museum of History, 2010), historymuseum.ca/cmc/exhibitions/hist/medicare/medic-3h11e.shtml.

13 Justice Emmett Hall, *Report of the Royal Commission on Health Services* (Ottawa: Queen's Printer, 1964), ch. 12.

14 Tom Kent, *A Public Purpose* (Kingston and Montreal: McGill-Queen's University Press, 1988), 364.

15 Walter Stewart, *The Life and Political Times of Tommy Douglas* (Toronto: McArthur and Co., 2003), 233.

16 The Justin Trudeau government's original federal minister of health, Jane Philpott, was the first physician to occupy that role.

17 Malcolm G. Taylor, *Health Insurance and Canadian Public Policy: The Seven Decisions That Created the Canadian Health Insurance System and Their Outcomes*, 2nd ed. (Montreal and Kingston: McGill-Queen's University Press, 1987), 430.

18 "Building Public Support for Medicare," in *Making Medicare: The History of Health Care in Canada* (Canadian Museum of History, 2010), historymuseum.ca/cmc/exhibitions/hist/medicare/medic-7h08e.shtml.

19 House of Commons Debates, *Hansard* (Dec. 9, 1983), 44.

20 David Spurgeon, "Canadian Supreme Court upholds right to take out private health insurance," *British Medical Journal* 330, no. 7505 (June 18, 2005): 1408.

21 Martha Jackman, letter to the editor, *Globe and Mail* (Toronto), Mar. 8, 2006.

22 Bruce Lyth, letter to the editor, *Globe and Mail* (Toronto), June 13, 2005.

23 Carmen Chai, "Q & A: How long are medical wait times in Canada by province and procedure?" *Global News*, Nov. 23, 2016, globalnews.ca/news/3084366/q-a-how-long-are-medical-wait-times-in-Canada-by-province-and-procedure/.

24 Yvette Brend, "Epic Court Battle over Private Health Care Rages in B.C. Courts," *CBC News*, Feb. 12, 2017, cbc.ca/news/Canada/British-Columbia/Cambie-Surgeries-Healthcare-Canada-Public-vs-Private-System-BC-Dr-Brian-Day-1.3977566.

25 Rupinder Brar of the CDM and Gayle Duteil, president of the BCNU, were quoted in Sunny Dhillon, "Constitutional Challenge against Canada's Health-Care System Begins," *Globe and Mail* (Toronto), Sept. 6, 2016.

26 Kelly Grant, "Canada ranks third-last in study of health care in 11 rich countries," *Globe and Mail* (Toronto), July 26, 2017.

27 Vincent Lam, *Tommy Douglas* (Toronto: Penguin, 2011), 153–4.

In the early 1980s, Bob and Doug McKenzie
helped make "eh" a national phenomenon.

EH?

Steven High

What can be more Canadian than saying "eh," eh? Appending those two letters to almost any sentence can transform a firm statement into a (usually rhetorical) query and, in the process, identify the speaker as a stereotypically polite Canadian in need of reassurance. A term that emerged organically through conversation can now be found emblazoned on T-shirts, bumper stickers, and coffee mugs. In 2017, to show its support for Canada's one hundred and fiftieth anniversary, Kentucky Fried Chicken briefly transformed itself from KFC to K'ehFC, while the Chapters bookstore chain sold tea towels and T-shirts carrying the phrase "150 Years On the Eh Team!" Like "G'day" in Australia, the term has come to reflect and symbolize a national identity.

While the word has been associated with the way Canadians speak for some time, it only became iconic in the early 1980s thanks to Bob and Doug McKenzie. Part of a comedy skit on the popular *Second City Television* program, or SCTV, these fictional "hosers" sported parkas and toques while drinking beer and eating donuts and back bacon. They talked about all things Canadian while peppering their speech with "eh." It was a national

KFC Canada ✓ @kfc_canada · Jun 26
We decided to change our name for #Canada150 🍁. Turn on sound to find out
how it's pronounced. #KehFC 🇨🇦

HAPPY CANADA 150
from
K'ehFC

💬 9   🔁 36   ♡ 45

A fully commodified expression of Canadian identity.

phenomenon. When the duo arrived in Regina, they were swamped by hundreds of toque-wearing fans. An appearance in Toronto forced police to close a major highway "as thousands of well-liquored fans staged an impromptu parade."[1] For a time, the lyrics to their introductory theme song, "Coo loo coo coo, coo coo coo coo," could be heard in schools across the nation, as could the exaggerated "eh."

Actors Rick Moranis and Dave Thomas came up with the idea for "The Great White North" skit after CBC Television insisted on two additional minutes of "identifiably Canadian content" each week. Moranis and Thomas thought it was a bit of a joke, as *SCTV* was taped in Canada and used a predominantly Canadian crew and cast. So they invented an unscripted parody of what it means to be Canadian—and it took off. The show was soon picked up by a major TV network in the United States, the duo's comedy album sold more than one million copies, and a feature film soon followed. Bob and Doug could henceforth be seen in commercials shilling everything from pizzas to lube jobs.

Out of this steaming cauldron of commercialism, "eh" emerged as a marker of Canadian speech. It joined other iconic Canadianisms like "chesterfield" (not "couch"), prescribed Canadian spellings ("-our" endings instead of "-or"), as well as phonetic markers of linguistic difference such as "Canadian raising": the phenomenon whereby Canadians pronounce news as "newse" and roof as "rewf" (rather than the American "nooze" or "ruf"). Collective identities rely on what Sigmund Freud once called the "narcissism of small differences," exaggerating whatever small markers of national difference there are. Language is often central to this political construction of difference. To understand the emergence of "eh," we therefore need to understand the post-1945 invention of Canadian English and the central role played by Canadian lexicographers and linguists.

Ever since the emergence of the modern state in the sixteenth century, and certainly since the American Revolution of 1776, nation-states have sought to distinguish themselves from one another. In the immediate aftermath of the American Revolution, Noah Webster advocated the abandonment of his country's linguistic ties to Great Britain. "As an independent nation," he wrote, "our honor requires us to have a system of our own, in language as well as in government."[2] Webster's spelling book of 1783, and his dictionaries of 1806, 1828, and 1840, prescribed changes to American spelling, including the conversion of -our and -re endings to -or and -er. Henceforth, his compatriots claimed to speak "American English."

Canada went through a similar period of linguistic nation-building in the 1950s and 1960s, between the release of the final report of the Royal Commission on National Development in the Arts, Letters and Sciences, chaired by Vincent Massey, in 1951 and Canada's Centenary Year in 1967. While the English language has been spoken in northern North America since the earliest European settlement of Newfoundland, Canadian English as a recognized national language, distinct from British and American varieties, is a recent innovation. Linguists discovered Canadian English in the mid-1950s, and they sought to make Canadians aware of its existence in the 1960s. Canada was not alone in this regard, as many other English-speaking countries produced national dictionaries at this time: Jamaica (1967), South Africa (1978), The Bahamas (1982), and Australia (1988). Canada, and the discovery of "eh" as a national marker, was thus part of a post-colonial rush to establish symbols of national linguistic difference.

A self-confident Canadian pillow case.

Until that happened, however, the prevailing wisdom was that Canadians and Americans spoke with the same North American accent. But in a pioneering 1956 article in *Saturday Night* magazine, boldly entitled "Canadians speak Canadian," Calgary-based linguist M. H. Scargill challenged those who would deny the existence of Canadian English: "What a narrow view," he declared. "Who discovered insulin, pray, and named it from the Latin? Who experimented with and named the splake? And since when have Americans or British freely discussed Clear Grits, Digby Chickens, Socreds, the Land of Little Sticks, separate schools, nitchies, longlinermen?" To convince the naysayers, he called for an authoritative dictionary of Canadian English, without which, he lamented, Canadian English teachers were forced to use "books based on British or American usage." Other linguists shared Scargill's passion.

In the 1950s and 1960s, a band of lexicographers in the Canadian Linguistic Association set out to show that Canadians did, in fact, speak English with a distinctly Canadian accent. At first, this generation of Canadian linguists felt it more important to cut Canada's linguistic ties to Great Britain than to the United States. Briticisms were associated with Canada's colonial past as well as a more general upper-class pretense. The antipathy for the British accent, English professor Walter Avis noted, represented a "rejection by a former colonial people of British attitudes after a century and a half of domination of Canada by Britishers whose condescending ways and superior airs have come to be associated connotatively with British speech and mannerisms."[3] Strong words, indeed.

The dictionary movement produced a series of Canadian dictionaries, starting in 1962 with Canada's first bilingual dictionary. *The Canadian Dictionary/Le dictionnaire canadien* sought to bridge Canada's linguistic divide. It was published at a fortuitous moment in Canadian history, as official bilingualism was about to become

Grafitt(eh).

the law of the land. Unveiled to great fanfare, the *Toronto Daily Star* enthusiastically proclaimed the book a dictionary for Canada: "Here is the Canadian language, both French and English."[4]

Despite the sale of two hundred thousand copies by 1975, the bilingual dictionary fell victim to a changing political climate in Quebec, wherein the provincial government came increasingly to play the role of language guardian, defender of the purity of the French language. Many Québécois now felt that some anglicized words used in everyday Canadian French should not have been included in the dictionary.[5] The move toward a "purer" form of French and away from slang, or *joual*, meant that the *Canadian Dictionary* was seen as sub-standard. Thus, in the context of a growing nationalist movement in Quebec, the inclusion of anglicisms associated with language loss and assimilation made the dictionary unacceptable to the Quebec government for use in schools.

The next dictionary project had more commercial success. In 1959, the Ontario Ministry of Education announced its intention to replace imported school dictionaries with Canadian ones; foreign dictionaries, the ministry declared, were not doing the job. To make this point, the government's spokesperson cited a laughably inept British dictionary definition of hockey as a "game played with a ball and a stick." With public interest in Canadian English duly aroused, and a ready market guaranteed, the publishing house of W. J. Gage Limited of Toronto, at the time Canada's premier textbook publisher, agreed to sponsor the *Dictionary of Canadian English* for Canadian schools. Walter Avis and Harry Scargill were hired to produce a set of three graded school dictionaries based on the American E. L. Thorndike and Clarence L. Barnhart dictionary. It would be customized for the Canadian market.

After the dictionaries appeared, between 1962 and 1967, journalists across the country were thrilled by the discovery that Canadians had their own way of saying things. One observer called the dictionary the most significant contribution to "Canadian letters in the past 300 years. At last we have a language and a fascinating one!"[6] Another saw the dictionary as evidence of the nation's coming of age and as a "refreshing assertion of Canada's growing national character."[7] The *Charlottetown Patriot*, in turn, noted that the dictionary helped "the nation in our search for a Canadian identity."[8] Virtually all columnists and book reviewers concluded by saying that the dictionary should be in the homes, offices, and classrooms of every Canadian.

But how Canadian was this national dictionary? Its origins in the American dictionary were rarely mentioned in media reports; to have done so would have been to question the book's Canadianness. When it was mentioned, the media was careful to emphasize its many Canadian features. The retention of the original illustrations, however, resulted in some awkwardness.

Coff(eh) mug.

For example, the caption under a US marine read: "Marine: Canada has no marines."[9] Perhaps more revealing is the fact that the dictionary editors frequently opted for American spelling. Hence, readers were instructed to employ "labor" rather than "labour," "program" instead of "programme," "judgment" in place of "judgement," and "defense" rather than "defence." However, British spelling was retained in other cases, such as "cigarette," "theatre," and "analyse."[10]

At an early point in the dictionary's production, Avis conceded that even his nine-year-old son refused to accept the shorter American spellings.[11] Apparently, Ontario's curriculum, and thus his son's teachers, advocated British forms for the most

part. Avis realized that the dictionary makers risked dampening teachers' interest in their project if they went too far in recommending American spellings. Indeed, the tenacity with which English-Canadian educators clung to British spelling traditions, bolstered by the nationalism of the time, was not to be reasoned with. Just as the bilingual dictionary fell victim to the changing political winds in Quebec, the *Dictionary of Canadian English* soon found itself under attack for recommending American spelling. Given the growing unpopularity of America's war in Vietnam, the desire to differentiate Canada from the United States intensified during the 1960s. In linguistic terms, this trend could be seen in the push to expunge American spelling from Canadian English. Once provincial school boards began to insist on British spellings as a sign of Canadianness, dictionary publishers had no choice but to follow suit.[12] Gage abandoned its increasingly vulnerable position in the mid-1990s and switched to British spellings "in light of current trends."[13]

In 1967, the campaign to recognize and codify Canadian English culminated in the publication of a fourth volume in the Gage series, the *Dictionary of Canadianisms on Historical Principles*, which provided a comprehensive record of words invented or used in Canada. It defined a Canadianism as a "word, expression, or meaning which is native to Canada or which is distinctively characteristic of Canadian usage though not necessarily exclusive to Canada." The linkage between language and national identity was paramount in Scargill's eyes: "Don't wave the flag," he told his fellow citizens, "speak Canadian to prove you are one."[14]

Each entry in the *Dictionary of Canadianisms* was supported by historical quotations, usually the earliest and most recent quotations on file. The entries can be grouped into several subheadings. Words describing geographical features, including flora and fauna, are most frequent. Words of Indigenous origin also appear in abundance, part of a much wider cultural borrowing and appropriation. French terms such as *aboiteau*—Acadian for dike, dam, or sluice gate—appeared in large numbers alongside everyday slang phrases such as "main drag," defined as "the principal street of a village or town; the main street of a city."[15] Canada's rich political history was also on display, with words like "acclamation" and "advance poll" and party names such as "Clear Grits" and "Socreds." Words associated with the fur trade, mining, logging, farming, and the railway likewise made their appearance. Sports-related vocabulary, particularly words associated with hockey (such as "deke": a fake shot or movement), pepper the dictionary. A few Canadianisms for consumer items were also identified. The word "chesterfield," Canadian for couch or sofa, for example, loomed large in the linguistic imagination. Avis was particularly fond of telling the story of a Canadian in an American department store who asks to see the chesterfields only to be shown the cigarette counter. The chesterfield story

A verbal idiosyncrasy as national pride: the Eh team.

served as a linguistic marker, or shibboleth, that told Canadians that there was such a thing as Canadian English.

The Canadian media heralded the *Dictionary of Canadianisms* as a fitting tribute to Canada on its Centennial. Indeed, the Canada that emerges in the citations included with each entry—one of exploration and settlement, the fur trade and farming, Indigenous people, railways, logging, and mining—fit the contemporary thirst for public commemoration. Largely left offstage, however, are words derived from urban Canada, from immigrant groups other than the French and the English, from industry or the working-class experience.

The crest of the wave of Canadian English lexicography broke in the late 1960s. The first generation of linguistic nationalists had run out of steam and the second generation were more interested in syntax and pronunciation than in collecting Canadianisms. The wave of Canadian cultural nationalism also ebbed, as the world became more interconnected with new digital technologies and the rise of the internet. In 2008, the research unit that produced the *Canadian Oxford Dictionary*—the last of Canada's research-driven print dictionaries—was shut down, a victim of free online dictionaries.

The *Dictionary of Canadianisms* contained thousands of entries, but not one for "eh." Its absence was noted by the media, as the term was already widely associated with Canadian speech. Such criticism prompted Avis to make the case against the word in a 1972 article entitled "So eh? Is Canadian, eh?"[16] He noted that entries for "eh" were commonplace in American and British dictionaries, none of which identified the word as Canadian. For example, the *Oxford English Dictionary* (OED) traces the word back to 1567 and cites Oliver Goldsmith's 1773 play *She Stoops to Conquer*: "Wasn't it lucky, eh?" The OED suggests that "eh" originates in Middle English interjections such as *ey, ei* and *a*, or was adapted from the French *eh*. In terms of its current usage, the

OED defined two principal meanings: "interjectional interrogative particle, often inviting assent to the sentiment expressed," and the "ejaculation of sorrow."

The debate did not die there. Linguistics professor Sandra Schecter revisited the issue in 1979, asserting that the word had become central to Canadian identity, as evidenced by its frequent appearance in popular consumer culture, from T-shirts to coffee mugs.[17] A 2004 survey of Canadians found ten distinct uses of "eh," ranging from a statement of opinion or fact to a question, command, or exclamation, an insult or accusation, or telling a story (the narrative "eh"). The narrative "eh" also surfaced regularly in Canadian literature, such as in the work of Stephen Leacock, Morley Callaghan, Farley Mowat, Mordecai Richler, Margaret Laurence, and Robertson Davies.

More recently, linguist Derek Denis has argued that "eh" was used differently in Canada than elsewhere: as a technique to confirm the attention of the listener and as part of a declaratory statement.[18] He has suggested as well that within Canada, "eh" was associated with the speech patterns of rural or blue-collar men and women, such that it now has a second meaning for urban Canadians. Bob and Doug McKenzie may have been spoofing not only what it is to be Canadian, but also a social category deemed less educated and sophisticated: the Canadian redneck. The timing here is important, as blue-collar and rural Canada was in crisis in the 1970s and 1980s with the closure of mills and factories and farm foreclosures. The public embrace of "eh" might thus be best understood as an example of the mounting triumphalism of the ascendant urban middle class, or cultural representatives, as it denigrated all things working class as backward and retrograde. Or, perhaps, the embrace of class stereotypes was a form of resistance to the same—such as the ways that gays and lesbians appropriated the word "queer" during the same period. Either way, the timing of "eh's"

M(eh)rry Christmas.

emergence as the primary linguistic marker of national distinction seems significant.

Today, "eh" has an entry in the *Canadian Oxford Dictionary* as well as the online *Canadian Encyclopedia*. But linguists believe that the traditional tolerance for linguistic variance (the double standard) in Canada is fast disappearing. American pronunciation has largely supplanted British pronunciations of such words as "leisure" and "schedule." Even the use of "chesterfield" is on the wane. Some say that the patriotic "eh" is being supplanted

A sand(eh) beach.

When its use and its meaning was explained to him, Syrian refugee Mohammad Albrdan promised to use "eh" in a sentence to impress his high school English teacher. In the background is the Fredericton walking bridge, once leased by the Canadian Pacific Railway.

by "right" and "so" among young Canadians. According to the *Windsor Star*: "'Eh' is dying. It's not dead yet, but the vultures are circling. More precisely, the vultures are circling, right? 'Right' has moved in, elbowing 'eh' out of the way among young, urban speakers of Canadian English."[19] Whether Canadians use "eh" or not in their everyday lives, it remains a playful and widely recognized symbolic marker of Canadianness in the twenty-first century.

Parts of this chapter were previously published as "The 'Narcissism of Small Differences': The Invention of Canadian English, 1951–67." Permission granted by the Publisher from *Creating Postwar Canada* edited by Magda Fahrni and Robert Rutherdale © University of British Columbia Press 2007. All rights reserved by the Publisher.

NOTES

1 Jonathon Gatehouse, "Take off, eh! Eh?" *Maclean's*, May 7, 2007.
2 Quoted in Henri Bejoint, *Tradition and Innovation in Modern English Dictionaries* (Oxford: Clarendon Press, 1994), 138.
3 Walter Avis, "The English Language: A Report," n.d. (1970?), File 2-16, Box 1, Series 1: Subject Files, Walter Avis, 3711.1. Queen's University Archives.
4 Editorial, "A Dictionary for Canada," *Toronto Daily Star*, Mar. 10, 1962.
5 Hand-written note, n.d. (1963?), McClelland & Stewart Collection. File: "Editorial Canadian Dictionary, 1958–63," McMaster University Library.
6 "Centennial Reader", *Winnipeg Voxair*, Jan. 2, 1968.
7 "Canada Month," *Canada Month*, Dec. 13–14, 1961.
8 Wallace Ward, "Canadians get a new identity," *Charlottetown Patriot*, Mar. 13, 1967.
9 H. Rex Wilson, "It's broader than beer parlor and baby bonus," *Globe Magazine*, Apr. 8, 1967.

10 "Summary of Spelling Principles for the Dictionary of Canadian English Series," File: "Jack Chambers, 1974–76," Box 1, Series I: Correspondence Files. 3726.3. Walter Avis Collection, Queen's University Archives.

11 Walter Avis to Canadian Linguistics Association, Feb. 25, 1959, Box 1, Series I: Correspondence Files. 3726.3. Walter Avis Collection, Queen's University Archives.

12 A study of how provincial departments of education (especially Ontario's) promoted British spelling is needed. Such a study could also examine school textbooks as well as elementary and high school curricula.

13 This news was welcomed by journalists. See Michael Valpy, "Over the hedge words: A look at Canadian English," *Globe and Mail* (Toronto), Nov. 21, 1996.

14 Dr. M. H. Scargill, Conference Speech at York University, Mar. 6, 1967, LRC 1991-041. 1.15. UVIC.

15 *Dictionary of Canadian English. A Dictionary of Canadianisms on Historical Principles* (Toronto: W. J. Gage, 1967), 1, 457.

16 Walter S. Avis, "So eh? Is Canadian, eh?" *Canadian Journal of Linguistics* 17, nos. 2–3 (1972): 89–104.

17 Sandra Schecter, "Eh? Revisited: Is It or Is It Not Canadian?" *The English Quarterly* 12, no. 4 (1979): 37–45.

18 Derek Denis, "The Social Meaning of Eh in Canadian English," *Proceedings of the 2013 Canadian Linguistics Association*, individual.utoronto.ca/derekdenis/Site/Derek_Denis_files/ms_proceedingsCLA2013.pdf.

19 "End of an era, eh?" *Windsor Star*, Dec. 19, 2013.

Poutine to go ... from La Banquise in Montreal.

POUTINE

Caroline Durand

Poutine is widely viewed as a specifically Cana-dian dish. In 2007, it was voted Canada's tenth-greatest invention—just four spots behind the artificial pacemaker and ten spots ahead of the birchbark canoe![1] Tourists visiting Ottawa in search of a "taste of Canadiana" are encouraged to try it. Historian Ian Mosby included it in his recent list of iconic Canadian foods.[2] And countless Canadians mercilessly criticized the Washington Capitals hockey franchise for its less-than-successful attempt to replicate the delicacy for its fans at a home game against the Toronto Maple Leafs in 2017.[3] And yet, more than one Québécois will argue that authentic poutine is a Quebec cultural phenomenon, and that labelling it "Canadian" is an act of cultural appropriation.[4]

Indeed, the dish is the subject of a cultural tug-of-war between Quebec and the so-called "rest of Canada." When the New York Fries restaurant chain established a world record for the largest poutine in Toronto in December 2004, Quebec newspaper columnist Denis Gratton was outraged. To establish such a record in Ontario, he argued, was dishonest because poutine was invented in Quebec.[5] Gratton must have been relieved when in

2015 a restaurant owner from Trois-Rivières crushed the Toronto record. At 4,410 pounds, this home-grown poutine record was more than three times heavier than its predecessor.[6]

The object of this dispute is deceptively simple. In its basic form, poutine consists of french fries topped with cheese curds and gravy. While many find this recipe mouth-watering, others wonder how people can possibly eat such a greasy and messy concoction. Until the late 1990s, it was the object of derision both inside and outside Quebec. But the last fifteen to twenty years have witnessed a radical change, both in poutine's status and in the social, cultural, and geographic scope of its consumption. Where does this passion for poutine come from, and how could this culinary mixture reach the level of contested national symbol? The history of poutine helps to answer these questions, while the recipe itself reveals what the dish means for Québécois and Canadians.

"A taste of Canadiana," according to Ottawa Tourism's website.

If poutine is enjoyed coast to coast, it holds a special significance in Quebec, where it was invented and where the dispute over its paternity remains unresolved. Both Fernand Lachance and Eddy Lajeunesse, from Warwick (near Victoriaville), and Jean-Paul and Fernande Roy, from Drummondville, claim credit for its invention. Tellingly, both creation stories share a common context: the commercialization of cheese curds (curdled milk) in the late 1950s and early 1960s in Quebec's dairy-producing region. Made in local dairies, fresh curds were then sold in small plastic bags at surrounding stores and greasy spoons. Restaurant patrons ate the cheese with other foods, and mixing curds and fries became a popular combination, with customers using gravy as a dip or topping to keep their food warm. Both stories stress the role of ordinary customers and workers in creating and naming the dish.[7] These elements are important in the mythology of poutine: it is folkloric in the most straightforward sense of the term, because it was invented by ordinary people in low-key eateries.[8]

The recipe soon made its way to larger centres. In 1972, a Quebec City restaurateur, Ashton LeBlond, added it to his menu. At first, his customers expressed skepticism, but LeBlond persevered, offering free samples to win them over. And it worked: today, poutine is the flagship item at the twenty-five Chez Ashton outlets.[9] By the 1980s, poutine became part of the Montreal restaurant scene, where it became a late-night snack. One of the city's most popular poutine diners, La Banquise, is open twenty-four hours a day and is busiest at night—when college and university students stream out of the city's bars in pursuit of the dish, which is reputed to help avoid a hangover.[10] Its reputation among students also accounts for much of its appeal outside Quebec. In 1993, students requested it at Kingston's Royal Military College.[11] By the mid-1990s, Canadian fast-food chains, such as Burger King, Harvey's, and McDonald's, boasted poutine options.

A horrible culinary disaster? The *Montreal Gazette*'s
Aislin has his say.

Headliners of the 2017 Festival de la poutine in
Drummondville, Quebec. At this annual festival
the public can sample the wares of twelve
poutiniers, and vote for their favourite in the
"golden fork" competition.

The 1990s marked a turning point in poutine's rise to cultural significance. As it gained popularity outside Quebec it became the subject of political commentary, both positive and negative. Renewed Quebec nationalism shaped this development. Many anglophones from outside the province likely experienced their first taste of poutine in 1995, when tens of thousands of people travelled to Montreal to participate in a "Unity Rally" designed to convince Québécois to vote "no" in the province's second independence referendum.[12]

Amidst this national unity crisis, outside observers developed an increased interest in Quebec culture. Some were curious and impressed; others expressed contempt and sometimes hatred. These conflicting feelings can be found in assessments of poutine in the 1990s. At first, the dish was used to deride the idea that

Quebec was a distinct society with a specific culture: poutine, it was argued, demonstrated the province's lack of refinement and its intellectual and artistic poverty. The most negative comments often came from where they were the least expected: from Quebec francophones and from French tourist guides.[13]

French tourist guides rarely had any praise for poutine. Indeed, most of them expressed either amusement or disgust. While many Québécois objected to these assessments, some concurred with the French: at a concert in Paris, singer-songwriter Robert Charlebois described poutine as "fries that caught a cold."[14] In an anti-nationalist political pamphlet published in 1992, titled La République de Poutine, François Dallaire imagined what an independent Quebec would resemble ten years after its separation from Canada. The picture he offered wasn't pretty, and he used poutine as an example of the province's lack of cultural prestige.[15] Just like the popular French spoken in Quebec, poutine was considered an embarrassing and bastardized cultural artefact when compared to an ostensibly more refined European cuisine.[16] Nevertheless, poutine had its champions. Among them were several anglophone journalists and columnists from Montreal who published enthusiastic articles profiling the best places to eat it.

While anglophones and francophones both partake in "poutinemania," the latter seem to lead the movement. Celebrity chefs like Martin Picard and Dany St-Pierre have devised upscale versions of the dish, and in doing so have secured praise from their peers.[17] Quebec musicians, including Mes Aïeux and Les Cowboys Fringants, have paid homage to the dish, as have the Vancouver folk/punk group the Dreadnoughts. In 2008, members of Les Trois Accords went so far as to create a very popular Festival de la poutine in Drummondville.[18]

Still, the stigma attached to this meal persists. In 2008, the president of Impératif français, an association dedicated to promoting francophone culture, was scandalized to learn that the Canadian Embassy in Washington had distributed invitations to a reception featuring French explorer Samuel de Champlain proudly displaying poutine.[19] Moreover, there are some Québécois, like Le Devoir columnist Francine Pelletier, who express no attachment to the dish and who associate it with a younger generation.[20] But despite these naysayers, since the early 2000s it is safe to say that poutine obtained its lettres de noblesse.

But how exactly can poutine be considered good, trendy, or comforting? This question is particularly relevant when one considers its nutritional qualities, or lack thereof. Poutine is routinely decried by dieticians and public health advocates as the epitome of unhealthy food. It is, after all, full of salt, fat, and starches, and for this reason it has been banned from some school cafeterias.[21] But it is worth remembering that dietitians do not have a monopoly on food appreciation. Even fat can be celebrated for its associations with a sense of belonging, nostalgia, and "a naughty moment of indulgence"[22]—characteristics that help to explain poutine's place in nightlife culture. Poutine's heaviness also makes it an excellent fit with Quebec gastronomy. Although the specific types of fats are not the same, traditional French-Canadian cuisine is very rich: cretons, tourtières, ragoûts, pea soup, and baked beans are all based on the abundant use of pork or lard—sometimes both. No wonder bacon is a popular side ingredient in poutine!

In fact, health has nothing to do with the decision to eat poutine: it is a comfort food, after all, one that boasts an addictive combination of fat, salt, and a hint of sugar—something that the giants of processed food are constantly trying to offer their consumers.[23] For many, the pleasure comes from the contrast of textures: the crispy fries and the soft cheese under the hot, thick gravy produce an evolving and dynamic tasting experience. As the cheese melts and the fries lose their crispiness, the taste changes, and each bite is different.[24]

Successful poutine recipes come down to blending good versions of the three main ingredients. The potatoes that give rise to the french fries have been a staple of the French-Canadian diet since the nineteenth century.[25] The fries, of course, are not particularly French-Canadian or Canadian in character. They have been a popular street food in France since at least the 1860s, when they became a common "working-class indulgence," as both a main course and a treat.[26] Their popularity comes, to a large degree, from their crispy texture, which was rarely found in traditional French cuisine, and from their richness, since fats remained expensive until quite late in the nineteenth century.[27]

But it is the cheese curds that make poutine unique. Quebec has produced cheese since the French colonial era, and its agricultural sector has been dominated by dairy since the second half of the nineteenth century. But in the middle of the twentieth century, cheese was not yet a very popular product. It was mostly seen as a substitute for more desirable meats, and as such was considered suitable for a wartime diet or the multiple lean days of the Christian calendar. In the 1950s, however, dairy farmers—facing growing competition (from such products as newly legalized margarine) and the shrinking British demand—sought new markets. Cheese curds came to the rescue: a new product designed to salvage something out of unsold milk.[28]

In time, many Québécois became truly passionate about cheese curds. In 2013, the daily newspaper *La Presse* asked its readers to name their favourite. More than twenty-five hundred respondents sung the praises of forty-five different cheese makers from regions such as Bas-Saint-Laurent, Saguenay-Lac-Saint-Jean, Estrie, and Charlevoix.[29] Preference for a certain cheese and a specific poutine often goes hand in hand in Quebec,

The fleur-de-lys on this can of poutine gravy produced by St-Hubert leaves no doubt: for this company, poutine is part of Quebec culinary culture.

and both are markers of local food production and regional identity. Cheese curds also mark social class. They lack refinement—both in the "curing" sense of the term and in terms of their position in a perceived cultural hierarchy. Serving them at a wine and cheese tasting would be perceived either as inappropriate and cheap, or as a joke. The irregular blobs are sold in plastic bags and eaten with one's fingers, and their rough appearance has given rise to an unflattering nickname: while their proper French name is *fromage en grains*, most people in Quebec also call them *fromage en crottes*—literally "cheese in the shape of turds," or simply "cheese turds." The scatological moniker underscores the fact that cheese curds and poutine are unpretentious foods, consumed with little regard for the standards of upper-class politeness and good taste.

Poutine's gravy content is the most elusive of the three basic ingredients to describe. The characteristics of classic poutine

The Whistle Stop Café in Peterborough, Ontario offers an impressive selection of poutine, which can be customized by adding ingredients from a long list of extras.

gravy are often defined in just a few terms: it is brown and thick enough to stick to the fries but thin enough to trickle. Often, such descriptions define good gravy in negative terms. Its taste should not hide the cheese; it should not be too salty, too spicy, or too sweet. Outstanding sauces are sometimes mentioned in descriptions and critiques, but a poutine can be called good without saying much about the sauce.[30] Originally, restaurants used the same sauces that they would serve with rotisserie chicken or a hot chicken sandwich, but countless variations are possible.[31] Certain ingredients can be highlighted, such as the meat that is used to make the stock, the addition of wine, or the degree of spiciness.

The variety of sauces is remarkable: besides the classic gravy, poutine can be made with barbeque sauce, spaghetti sauce (for an Italian poutine), and even Indian-style butter chicken sauce.[32] And if one were to list all the extra ingredients that can be added, the variations on poutine become endless: smoked meat, bacon, chicken, green peas, peppers, sautéed onions, any kind of sausage, ham, chilli, lobster, or foie gras. In Peterborough, Ontario, the Whistle Stop Café offers one hundred different poutines.[33] But lest we conclude that one can throw anything on a plate, cover it with sauce, and call it a poutine, in each case the architecture of the dish remains relatively standard: a crispy element combined with a dairy element, both covered in warm sauce.

Diversity may well explain poutine's wide adoption across Canada, as it can be adapted to include almost any cultural influence. Some stick to the original recipe, but others make very specific cross-cultural mixes that some observers identify as a "Canadian creole" cuisine.[34] Even in Quebec, poutine was "creolized" early, with the use of barbeque and spaghetti sauces coming from European and American culinary influences. One might even argue that poutine is itself a creole dish. Aside from the cheese curds, none of the ingredients are local: potatoes and fries, albeit very popular in Quebec and the rest of Canada, are also very American, British, French, and Belgian. Various sauces and adds-on are inspired by French or Indian cuisine. In fact, someone recently suggested that poutine might become a culinary classification of its own, just like sandwiches.[35] It can travel as far as customers and restaurateurs want it to go.

In the twenty-first century, poutine has become a vehicle for commercial success. The dish itself is a commodity, but one can buy canned poutine gravy, frozen poutine, poutine-flavoured potato chips, and all kinds of poutine-referencing consumer objects—often sold as souvenirs. Loto-Québec, the state-owned provincial lottery corporation, even launched a scratch ticket featuring the dish. But the most profitable venture remains operating one, or many, restaurants.

Ryan Smolkin, founder of the Ontario-based Smoke's Poutinerie chain, opened his first outlet in Toronto in 2008, successfully selling his favourite dish to a young and hip late-night crowd.

Gambling and poutine? Why not! This limited edition scratch ticket demonstrates Loto-Québec's proud sponsorship of the Festival de la poutine de Drummondville.

The chain is now present in forty-three Canadian and American cities.[36] Smoke's Poutinerie's success comes from its efficient operation and from the founder's capacity to capture several aspects of the history and symbolism of this famous food.

Smolkin grew up in Ottawa, in close proximity to Quebec, and he undertook plenty of research trips to Montreal to taste various versions of his flagship dish. In a 2012 interview, he expressed his love for Quebec and respect for the authenticity of the recipes found there. He also provides all his franchises with Quebec-made bacon, cheese curds, and sauces.[37] The decor of the restaurants and the design of the disposable containers they use is a nod to the reputation of the dish as "lumberjack cuisine," with the use of the black-and-red checkered pattern that was frequently worn by men cutting timber. The diversity of options (there are thirty poutines listed on the online menu) also displays how Smoke's Poutinerie contributes to the multicultural and

creole nature of the dish. Along with traditional versions, Smoke's offers a perogy poutine (popular in Winnipeg),[38] a butter chicken option, a Korean twist, and a Tex-Mex-inspired Nacho grande.[39] Finally, Smoke's embraces the Rabelaisian extravagance of the dish by organizing an annual poutine-eating championship.

Poutine's status has changed remarkably in the last couple of decades. It has been transformed from a derided, lower-class Quebec meal associated with cultural and material poverty to a dish that can be reinterpreted to fit the most formal occasions, including a White House state dinner.[40] It can even serve as a representation of Canadian society. In the words of Francine Pelletier:

> First Nations, like old roots, are the potatoes. Francophones, always there where you don't expect them, always intact despite miles of bad sauce, always surprising in this landscape, are the cheese curds. And the Anglophones are the big thick molasses that drown everything, like a sticky go-between that tries to hold this culinary maelstrom together, against all odds, wearing their heart—and their starch—on their sleeve.[41]

Poutine's simplicity, its popular origins, its messy, informal looks, and its ability to absorb almost any culinary heritage make it appealing to Canadians from all provinces and territories. This bodes well for its future. But the tendency to identify poutine as "Canadian" raises questions about the making and unmaking of collective identities. By insisting that poutine is Québécois, and not Canadian, by celebrating it and reinterpreting it, poutine connoisseurs underline the uniqueness and originality of Quebec popular culture. They refuse to see their favorite food become just one element in the Canadian smorgasbord. If poutine is now a distinctive and highly recognizable dish, the national label attached to it must be carefully affixed.

Smoke's Poutinerie in Ottawa. The lumberjack-inspired checkered pattern of Smoke's visual signature recalls the dish's humble French origins.

NOTES

1   See "The Greatest Canadian Invention," web.archive.org/web/
    20070216194414/http://www.cbc.ca:80/inventions/.

2   Ian Mosby, "We are what we ate: Canada's history in cuisines," *Globe and
    Mail* (Toronto), Mar. 15, 2017; Ottawa Tourism, "A taste of Canadiana in
    Ottawa," May 23, 2017, ottawatourism.ca/ottawa-insider/a-taste-of-
    canadiana-in-ottawa/.

3   Emma Prestwich, "Washington Capitals Tried To Pass This Off As Poutine,
    And Canadians Spoke Out," *Huffington Post Canada*, Jan. 4, 2017,
    huffingtonpost.ca/2017/01/04/washington-capitals-poutine_n_
    13956340.html.

4   Nicolas Fabien-Ouellet, "Poutine Dynamics," *Cuizine: The Journal of Canadian
    Food Cultures/Cuizine: revue des cultures culinaire au Canada* 7, no. 2 (2016):
    erudit.org/fr/revues/cuizine/2016-v7-n2-cuizine02881/1038479ar/.

5   Charles-Alexandre Théorêt, with Ève Derome and Raphaël Martin, *Maudite
    poutine! L'histoire approximative d'un plat populaire* (Montreal: Héliotrope,
    2007), 57–8.

6   Amélie Saint-Yves, "Trois-Rivières bat le record Guinness de la plus grosse
    poutine," *Journal de Montréal,* June 20, 2015.

7   The word "poutine" comes from old French regional dialects, and is used
    to designate several dishes, from desserts to leftovers combinations. In
    Acadian cuisine, *poutine râpée,* a combination of cooked and raw potatoes,
    remains a well-known cultural staple. See Théorêt, *Maudite Poutine!*,
    28–9, 55.

8   Théorêt, *Maudite Poutine!*, 14–31.

9   Émilie Laperrière, "Chez Ashton, la poutine contre vents et marées,"
    La Presse (Montreal), May 30, 2017.

10 Fabien-Ouellet, "Poutine Dynamics."

11 Théorêt, *Maudite Poutine!* 48–54.

12 Jean-Philippe Warren and Eric Ronis, "The Politics of Love: The 1995
    Montreal Unity Rally and Canadian Affection," *Journal of Canadian Studies/
    Revue d'études canadiennes* 45, no. 1 (2011): 5–32.

13 Théorêt, *Maudite Poutine!* 76–99.

14 Ibid., 63.

15 François Dallaire, *La République de Poutine* (Outremont, QC: l'Étincelle
    éditeur, 1992), 135.

16 Dallaire, *La République de Poutine*, 68–76.

17 Théorêt, *Maudite Poutine!* 150, 119–31.

18 Mes Aïeux have a song called "Hommage en grains" on their 2004 album
    En famille; the Dreadnoughts included "Poutine" on the 2010 *Polka's Not
    Dead.* Les Cowboys Fringants mention poutine in "Évangéline," included
    on *12 grandes chansons* (1997). The Drummondville *Festival de la poutine*
    has combined music and poutine tasting for the last ten years; see
    festivaldelapoutine.com.

19 Paul Gaboury, "Excuses et démisions réclamées," *Le Droit* (Ottawa),
    July 3, 2008.

20 Francine Pelletier, "La poutine et le patriotisme," *Le Devoir* (Montreal),
    July 5, 2017.

21 Fabien-Ouellet, "Poutine Dynamics."

22 Don Kullick and Anne Meneley, eds., *Fat: The Anthropology of an Obsession*
    (New York: Tarcher, Penguin, 2005), 6.

23 Michael Moss, *Salt, Sugar, Fat: How the Food Giants Hooked Us* (Toronto:
    McClelland and Stewart, 2013).

24 Fabien-Ouellet, "Poutine Dynamics."

25 Caroline Durand, *Nourrir la machine humaine: Nutrition et alimentation au
    Québec, 1860–1945* (Montreal and Kingston: McGill-Queen's University
    Press, 2015), 31–55.

26 Martin Bruegel, "Worker's Lunch Away from Home in the Paris of the Belle
    Epoque: The Fench Model of Meals as Norm and Practive," *French Historical
    Studies* 38, no. 2 (2015): 276.

27 Madeleine Ferrière, *Nourritures canailles* (Paris: Éditions du Seuil, 2007),
    402–11.

28 Lenore Newman, *Speaking in Cod Tongues: A Canadian Culinary Journey*
    (Regina: University of Regina Press, 2017), 102.

29 "Le fromage en grains préféré des lecteurs," *La Presse* (Montreal),
    Aug. 28, 2013.

30 mapoutine.ca.

31 Théorêt, *Maudite Poutine!*, 21.

32 Newman, *Speaking in Cod Tongues,* 82.

33 See whistlestoplife.com/.

34 Newman, *Speaking in Cod Tongues,* 70–90.

35 Fabien-Ouellet, "Poutine Dynamics."

36 smokespoutinerie.com/locations/.

37 Amie Watson, "Poutine for the rest of Canada," *Gazette* (Montreal),
    Mar. 17, 2012.

38 Maya Tchernina, "Company of the Year: Smoke's Poutinerie," *Foodservice and
    Hospitality*, Dec. 8, 2012.

39 smokespoutinerie.com/menu/.

40 Tom Sietsema, "State dinner will start with a gussied-up version of Canada's
    late-night party food," *Washigton Post*, Mar. 9, 2016.

41 "Les Amérindiens, telles de vieilles racines, sont les pommes de terre. Les
    francophones, toujours là où on ne les attend pas, toujours intacts malgré
    des kilomètres de méchante sauce, toujours suprenants dans ce décor, sont
    les grains de fromage. Et les anglophones, la grosse mélasse brune qui noie
    tout sur son passage, les intermédiaires un brin collants qui tentent de
    contenir ce maëlstrom culinaire vaille que vaille, la main sur le cœur et le
    féculent." Pelletier, "La poutine et le patriotisme. "

A familiar sight across the Canadian landscape, this sign welcomes consumers to one of over 3,500 Tim Hortons outlets in Canada.

TIM HORTONS

Michael Dawson and Catherine Gidney

On July 1, 2006—Canada Day—Tim Hortons opened a new branch of its doughnut- and coffee-serving restaurants—at the Kandahar Air Base in Afghanistan. What prompted this endeavour? Speaking to the assembled soldiers that day, Major-General Doug Langton made it clear that it wasn't a particular pastry or coffee recipe: "We hope this little piece of *home* will make your lives in Afghanistan just a little bit easier."[1] A decade later, the iconic franchise was front and centre as Canadians welcomed some twenty-five thousand Syrian refugees to *their new home*. Tim Horton appeared, alongside other "notable" Canadians, in a popular English-language workbook for new Canadians. The chapter on Horton provided a synopsis of the hockey-player-turned-entrepreneur's life, and to build vocabulary it encouraged readers to "guess the meanings" of key words such as "millionaire," "award," "donut," and "bagel." To facilitate their integration into their new communities, the exercise book informed them that "Coffee at Tim Horton [*sic*] has special words. You say the cream first, then the sugar"—hence "double, double" and "single, double," but only "at Tim Hortons, not at other coffee shops."[2]

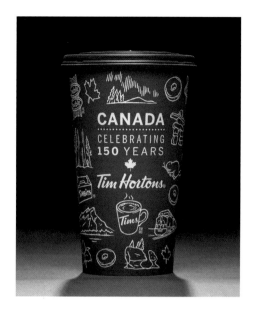

Tim Hortons in Kandahar, Afghanistan, on opening day, July 1, 2006.

A cup of Canadiana. Tim Hortons coffee cups sported a wide array of symbols to mark Canada's one hundred and fiftieth anniversary in 2017.

Whether supporting soldiers fighting overseas or welcoming newcomers fleeing violence in other countries, Tim Hortons features prominently in representations of what it means to be Canadian. But how did this happen? Less than forty years ago, Tim Hortons barely registered a blip on the fast-food radar, and despite theories to the contrary, there is no innate connection between doughnut or coffee consumption and Canadian identity. The answer, it seems, lies in the company's successful campaigns to promote a commodified or branded version of Canadian nationalism, one that draws upon established symbols such as the North and hockey to champion both local and national conceptions of community. Tim Hortons is not the first company to link its fortunes to an idealized understanding of what it means to be Canadian, but it may be the most successful.

From modest beginnings, Tim Hortons has grown to become perhaps the most recognizable fast-food chain in Canada—where, indeed, it boasts more franchises than McDonald's.[3] The first store opened in 1964 in Hamilton, Ontario, the product of a partnership between Tim Horton, then a successful defenceman for the NHL's Toronto Maple Leafs, and Jim Charade, a musician-turned-doughnut-store-owner, whose shop Horton regularly frequented. In 1966, entrepreneur Ron Joyce bought out Charade, becoming the first franchisee of the Tim Donut Ltd. corporation. Under Joyce's leadership the company showed slow but solid growth, opening 500 stores between 1964 and 1990, mainly in southern Ontario and the Maritimes. Thereafter, it grew exponentially, opening 1,500 stores in the next ten years. By 2011, it had doubled its number of stores to just over 4,000 outlets, covering mainly Canada and the northeastern United States. In 2010, when it opened its first outlet in Nunavut, Tim Hortons could truly be said to span the country from sea to sea to sea.[4]

In many ways this expansion fit a broader North American pattern of just-in-time delivery, fast-food franchising, and expanding service hours. Indeed, Canada's top doughnut store was modelled on its earlier American counterparts such as Mr. Donut and Dunkin' Donuts. The doughnut machine, an American invention, provided the basis for this new industry, while the logic of mass production facilitated its growth.[5] Whether the commodity on offer was hamburgers, chicken nuggets, or baked goods, the second half of the twentieth century witnessed an explosion of fast-food restaurants governed by detailed operations manuals designed to maximize profits and minimize inefficiencies by ensuring that consumers were served in a fast and predictable manner.[6] Ron Joyce attributed much of his company's early success to its ability to provide fresh products in a friendly manner in clean settings open twenty-four hours a day. Indeed, early Tim Hortons outlets catered to shift workers in Hamilton steel mills and other factories in southern Ontario. As the number of outlets grew, Tim Hortons became a convenient and accessible means for a quick snack and coffee, particularly, with the advent of the drive-through, on the way to work. But its ultimate success was due to its ability to cater to a broad market, from blue-collar shift workers to middle-class professionals, while maintaining a populist image.[7]

A key element of this success was the company's ability to draw upon existing Canadian iconography while establishing Tim Hortons as a symbol in and of itself. Early on, this meant capitalizing on Tim Horton's celebrity status as a professional hockey player. Horton featured prominently in the company's early marketing campaigns, and he routinely made public appearances to mark the opening of new stores. With time, though, the name "Tim Horton" has become largely disconnected from the

Tim Horton as a Toronto Maple Leaf, 1962.

company's co-founder. Indeed, for many customers today, Tim Horton is no more real than, say, Ronald McDonald or the smiling St-Hubert chicken.[8] But the restaurant's connection with hockey remains.

Over time, Tim Hortons came to be associated with parental attendance at early morning hockey practices—an experience understood to be less debilitating when one can draw upon a Tim Hortons coffee for a caffeine fix and to warm one's fingers. The company reinforced this connection to youth hockey by sponsoring "Timbit" leagues, named after the small, round doughnuts introduced in 1976.[9] Its television commercials similarly emphasized a link to Canada's official winter sport. One featured NHL star Sidney Crosby learning to skate on an outdoor pond. Another told the story of a strict Chinese-Canadian father adamantly insisting that his son should be engaged in his studies rather than playing hockey but proudly (and secretly) watching his son's games while drinking a Tim Hortons coffee. The company's sponsorship of televised hockey events, including outdoor NHL games and what's known as Hockey Day in Canada, further reinforced the connection.

While the store's eponymous founder provided a useful way to link its image to a popular Canadian symbol, its food offerings provided another. While New Zealanders and Australians argue over the provenance of pavlova and the French insist that theirs is the only true champagne, Canadians have routinely expressed their national identity by paying homage to the doughnut. Indeed, despite its American origins, the doughnut is routinely championed as Canada's "unofficial" national food. "If there's one thing that is distinct, that is ours," claims one Canadian, "I'd say it's doughnuts." "To criticize [the doughnut] is to criticize Canada," says another.[10] A popular explanation of why Canadians consume more doughnuts per capita than any other nation focuses on the country's harsh, northern climate;

Timbits as snack ... and hockey sweater for a racoon goalie on a parade float.

fatty foods and warm coffee, it is said, allow Canadians to endure long winters.[11] Central to such a claim is a certain level of anti-Americanism—a tendency to differentiate hardy Canadians from their softer American counterparts, or to contrast "authentic" Canadian experiences with ostensibly manufactured ones south of the border. Indeed, Tim Hortons has become a cultural "stand in" for the forty-ninth parallel, with the sheer number of doughnut shops on the Canadian side of the border serving as a forceful reminder that, despite the homogenization of North American culture, differences between Canadians and Americans do exist. Hence the Canadian government's decision to include a much-publicized visit to a Tim Hortons outlet on US secretary of state Condoleeza Rice's itinerary when she visited the country in 2006—a moment the press dubbed "double-double" diplomacy.[12]

While Tim Hortons is employed as a shorthand reference to Canada as a whole, it is also frequently used to express identification with smaller local communities. If there is a strong consensus that Canada is the world's foremost doughnut-consuming nation, there is no such agreement regarding which Canadian city is the country's "doughnut capital." Hamilton, St. Catharines, and Moncton appear to be leading contenders in a competition in which locals (and their journalist allies) combine quantitative and qualitative arguments. The former strategy routinely involves tabulating the number of local doughnut outlets, while the latter marshals arguments highlighting the respective town's "blue-collar" and "unpretentious" characteristics.[13] Even as coffee replaced doughnuts as the chain's main focal point, the stores' symbolism as authentic community meeting points remained intact.

In a country renowned for regional tensions it is this populist rhetoric that perhaps best explains how Tim Hortons is continuously championed as both a local and a national symbol. Indeed, the company's most famous advertising campaign, "Based on a True Story," employed iconic images and experiences of small-town Canada and astutely linked these to Tim Hortons. These television commercials, based on life stories gathered during an extensive customer-survey initiative, highlight "ordinary" Canadians' Tim Hortons routines. The first aired in 1996 and featured Lilian, an eighty-six-year-old native of Lunenburg, Nova Scotia who struggled to walk up a steep hill to have a daily coffee with friends at Tim Hortons. Others included horseback riders who regularly rode out of the mountains in Squamish, BC and hitched their horses outside the store as they grabbed a coffee; Cape Breton fiddler Natalie MacMaster and her crew regularly stopping at Tim Hortons while on tour; and a professional maker of curling ice who lived off of Tim Hortons coffee as he perfected the playing surfaces.[14]

These commercials are successful because they draw on and reinforce existing ideas about Canadian life and society: the simple delights of home, family, and friends; small towns and friendliness; northern climate and Saturday mornings at the rink.[15] And while they highlight individual acts of consumption, they contribute to a collective identity that not only links Tim Hortons to an idealized version of Canada but also makes Tim Hortons shops themselves a "site and source of Canadianness."[16]

The identification of Tim Hortons with "ordinary" Canadians convinced political operatives to coin the term "Tim Horton voter" to describe middle- or working-class families (in contrast to ostensibly pretentious and cosmopolitan Starbucks patrons). Tim Hortons would become a familiar stop for both Conservatives and Liberals as both parties jockeyed for position in the 2011 federal election campaign. The Conservatives proved far more adept—for example, by taking advantage of a photograph of a Starbucks cup on Liberal leader Michael Ignatieff's bus to support their claims that he was elitist and out of touch with mainstream Canada.[17]

That the name of a doughnut shop had come to feature prominently in the country's political discourse signalled just how successfully the company had managed to identify its products and services with key elements of mainstream political culture. By the 1990s Tim Hortons had joined Roots clothing and Molson

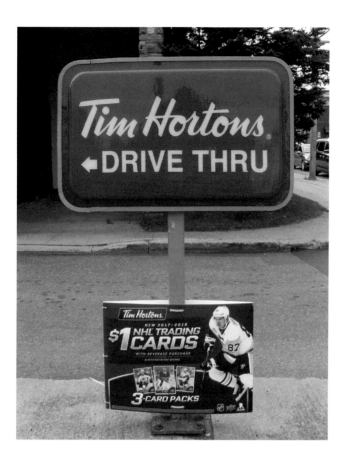

A product of North American fast-food and automobile culture, Tim Hortons has maintained its connection with Canada's official winter sport by a variety of means, including National Hockey League trading cards.

Canadian beer as perhaps the most prominent examples of consumer or "branded" nationalism in Canada. Other companies had emphasized the connection between their own profits and the national interest—the Hudson's Bay Company or the

Canadian Pacific Railway, for instance.[18] But in the late twentieth century, a combination of factors encouraged Canadians to express their patriotism through consumption like never before. On the one hand, the country's increasingly diverse population and its official support for a policy of multiculturalism discouraged mainstream expressions of ethnic nationalism. On the other, ongoing regional tensions (frequently expressed by the Eastern and Western provinces against Ontario and Quebec) and the continuing threat of Quebec separatism limited the appeal of civic nationalism. To fill this vacuum, Canadians increasingly turned to the practice of purchasing, consuming, and displaying their national pride.[19]

As the Canadian economy became more fully integrated into North American and then global trading networks, such expressions of patriotism frequently emphasized Canadian exceptionalism. Hence, the very successful Molson Canadian advertising campaign featuring "Joe," whose minute-long rant dispelling American misperceptions about Canada proudly championed, with increasing volume, the country's positive characteristics before declaring, "I am Canadian." Roots offered Canadians the opportunity to express their patriotism by sporting sweatshirts and cottage wear featuring beavers and maple leaves—a method of demonstrating national pride that reached new heights when the company secured the contract to outfit the Canadian team for the 1998 Nagano Olympics.[20] The act of ordering Tim Hortons doughnuts and coffee, then, was part of a marked trend toward branded nationalism in Canada—and one that left little room for irony. After all, in their quest to celebrate their national traits, Canadians were relying increasingly upon American and multinational corporations to express Canadianness. It was two young Americans, after all, who founded Roots in 1973; Molson merged with Coors to form Molson Coors in 2005; and US-based Wendy's corporation purchased Tim

Hortons in 1995 before selling its acquisition to Brazilian-owned Burger King in 2014.[21]

While the sheer volume of clothing, beer, doughnut, and coffee purchases suggested that Canadians had fully embraced branded nationalism, voices of dissent remained. Historian Catherine Carstairs lamented the fact that such practices left "Canadians with little sense of Canada's history or values," encouraged overconsumption, and did little to promote "tolerance, diversity and community."[22] Journalist John Stackhouse chose *Timbit Nation* as the title of a book arguing that Canada was in danger of losing its sense of purpose and identity. As director of the civic-oriented Dominion Institute, Rudyard Griffiths took direct aim at Tim Hortons by arguing that it represented "a backlash against ... diversity." The chain's uniformity, Griffiths argued, "is evocative of the darker side of our egalitarian worldview; the Canadian tendency to embrace conformity, blandness and studied mediocrity." Its growing popularity, he lamented, marked the "ascendency of a vapid 'feel good' nationalism."[23]

While these commentators focused on the cultural impact of the increasingly ubiquitous doughnut-and-coffee chain, others have decried the poor quality of the consumer experience it offers. There is no shortage of online commentaries lamenting the declining flavour of Tim Hortons coffee and baked goods.[24] One longtime customer received national media attention in 2015 when he vowed never to patronize the restaurant chain again. William Golding's complaints included "uneven service" and "the increasingly bland and industrial taste" of its food offerings. Fulsome devotion to a "procedure manual," he charged, left staff either unwilling or incapable of interacting professionally and empathetically with customers.[25] By 2017, a group of franchisees had taken note and were pointing an accusatory finger at the company's new owners. Frustrated with the parent company's decisions to cut costs, employ cheaper equipment,

and reduce corporate staff, the group formed the Great White North Franchisee Association—an apparent homage to fictional doughnut aficionados Bob and Doug McKenzie—in order to try to address their concerns and those of their customers.[26] Having leveraged the insights of mass production in the final decades of the twentieth century to gain not only a strong customer base but also its enviable status as a cultural icon, the logical extension of Tim Hortons' efforts—external corporate control and ever-increasing campaigns for efficiency—now risked alienating both its customers and its franchisees.

This dilemma was already on display on Christmas Day 2015 when a Tim Hortons drive-through restaurant in Truro, Nova Scotia boasted a lineup at least a hundred cars long. Asked to explain this phenomenon, one local resident opined, "It's almost like everybody's addicted to the Tim's coffee. *Home* brewed just isn't the same thing." Others saw the situation differently and expressed empathy for the employees, who, they assumed, were forced to work while many Canadians stayed *home* and enjoyed the day off.[27]

That a drive-through doughnut-and-coffee shop had become such a prominent Christmas Day destination says much about the popularity and symbolism of Tim Hortons in Canada. That locals wondered aloud about the ethics behind those services speaks to ongoing concerns about who benefits from a capitalist economy that prioritizes efficiency and convenience ahead of social justice and authenticity—as well as what is at stake when national identity is expressed through consumption. In January 2018, when Tim Hortons franchisees attempted to reduce workers' benefits in response to the Ontario government's decision to increase the province's minimum wage, protests and rallies across the country blasted the move as unfairly targeting vulnerable employees and betraying what Tim Hortons is supposed to stand for. A recent survey indicated that the company's annual

Is this discarded Tim Hortons cup a metaphor for the company's decline in the eyes of Canadians?

ranking for brand reputation in Canada had dropped precipitously from number four (in 2017) to number fifty.[28] Along with increased marketing opportunities, branded nationalism is clearly weighted with public expectations—especially when a company so successfully connects its image to Canadian symbolism that it becomes a symbol itself.

NOTES

1   Peter Pigott, *Canada in Afghanistan: The War So Far* (Toronto: Dundurn Press, 2007), 117. Emphasis added.

2   *10 Canadians I'd Like to Meet* (Toronto: Canadian Resources for ESL, 2011), 15–18.

3   Steve Penfold, "'Eddie Shack was no Tim Horton': Donuts and the Folklore of Mass Culture in Canada," in W. Belasco and P. Scranton, eds., *Food Nations: Selling Taste in Consumer Societies* (New York: Routledge, 2002), 49.

4   Ron Buist, *Tales from Under the Rim: The Marketing of Tim Hortons* (Fredericton, NB: Goose Lane, 2003), 30–9, 98,166; Douglas Hunter, *Double Double: How Tim Hortons Became A Canadian Way of Life, One Cup At A Time* (Toronto: HarperCollins, 2012), 3–5.

5   Penfold, "'Eddie Shack was no Tim Horton'," 49, 53.

6   Ibid., 59–60.

7   Ibid., 50, 54, 58; Buist, *Tales from Under the Rim* 39; Hunter, *Double Double*, 94.

8   Penfold, "'Eddie Shack was no Tim Horton'," 49–50.

9   Buist, *Tales from Under the Rim*, 79, 161.

10   Penfold, "'Eddie Shack was no Tim Horton'," 49–50.

11   Ibid., 49–51.

12   "Rice introduced to 'double-double' diplomacy," CBC News, Sept. 12, 2006,
     cbc.ca/news/canada/nova-scotia/rice-introduced-to-double-double-
     diplomacy-1.603412; Patricia Cormack, "'True Stories' of Canada: Tim
     Hortons and the Branding of National Identity," *Cultural Sociology* 2, no. 3
     (Nov. 2008): 370–1.

13   Penfold, "'Eddie Shack was no Tim Horton'," 56–8; "Moncton still Tim
     Hortons capital of Canada," CBC News, Nov. 24, 2016, cbc.ca/news/canada/
     new-brunswick/moncton-tims-king-of-canada-1.3864516.

14   Buist, *Tales from Under the Rim*, 140–64; Steve Penfold, *The Donut: A Can-
     adian History* (Toronto: University of Toronto Press, 2008), 185–6; Cormack,
     "'True Stories' of Canada," 375.

15   Penfold, *The Donut*, 186–8.

16   Cormack, "'True Stories' of Canada," 382.

17   Hunter, *Double Double*, 299–301.

18   Catherine Carstairs, "Roots Nationalism: Branding English Canada Cool
     in the 1980s and 1990s," *Histoire sociale/Social History* 39, no. 77 (May
     2006): 241.

19   Ibid., 237.

20   Ibid., 240–1, 244.

21   Ibid., 237, 243; Stephanie Nolen, "The Brazilian influence behind 3G's Tim
     Hortons deal," *Globe and Mail* (Toronto), Aug. 25, 2014.

22   Carstairs, "Roots Nationalism," 254.

23   Rudyard Griffiths, "A Timbit Nation?" *Winnipeg Free Press*, Aug. 15, 2006.

24   See, for example, the discussion in response to Calum Marsh, "How did
     Canada, the land most rich in donuts, become deprived of the Cherry Stick,
     its most priceless one?" *National Post* (Toronto), July 6, 2016.

25   Emma Loop, "Former Tim Hortons customer vows to give up his Timmies
     habit forever in scathing email rant," *National Post* (Toronto), Jan. 2, 2015.

26   Marina Strauss, "Tim Hortons outlets 'being destroyed' by cost-cutting,
     letter alleges," *Globe and Mail* (Toronto), Mar. 13, 2017.

27   Emphasis added. The store's owner insisted that all of the employees had
     volunteered to work that day. See "Tim Hortons lineup on Christmas Day at
     least 100 cars long in Truro," CBC News, Dec. 27, 2015, cbc.ca/news/canada/
     nova-scotia/christmas-day-tim-hortons-truro-1.3381155.

28   Katie Dangerfield, "Tim Hortons' reputation plummets in new survey—why
     Canadians may be fed up," *Global News*, Apr. 5, 2018, globalnews.ca/
     news/4124961/tim-hortons-brand-reputation-survey/.

ACKNOWLEDGEMENTS

Inspired by Richard White and Melissa Harper's *Symbols of Australia: Uncovering the Stories Behind the Myths*, this book is the product of a richly rewarding partnership between the editors, an enthusiastic collaboration among the contributors, and the valuable support of a wide range of institutions and organizations.

A Canada 150 Connections Grant from the Social Sciences and Humanities Research Council of Canada played a key role in facilitating a June 2017 workshop at St. Thomas University and the University of New Brunswick that allowed the contributors to share their ideas and to enhance and develop their chapters. To ensure the success of this endeavour, we sought financial and logistical support from our host institutions. We were overwhelmed by the response. At St. Thomas University, we received support from the Department of History, the Department of Sociology, the School of Education, the Office of Human Resources, the Department of Communications and Media Relations, the Office of the Deans, the Office of the Vice-President (Academic and Research), and the Office of the President. At the University of New Brunswick, we received equally generous support from the Department of History, the Office of the Dean of Arts, and the Office of the Vice-President (Academic). Darrow MacIntyre, Myfanwy Davies, and Colleen Kitts-Goguen of CBC New Brunswick took a keen and productive interest in our project, as did Clare MacIntyre of Edgewood Communications. To bring this project to completion, UNB provided a Grant in Aid of Publication from the Edwin Botsford Busteed Fund and a Grant in Aid of Scholarly Book Publishing from the Harrison McCain Foundation.

Our conversations in Fredericton were greatly enhanced by the presence of Cath Bishop, John Bodnar, Michael Boudreau, Bonnie Huskins, Erin Morton, Katie Pickles, and Richard White. We thank them for their insights and suggestions. (Cath, the opening line of the introduction is for you.)

Many thanks to Ryan Perks, our copy editor, David Vereschagin, our designer, and to the fabulous staff at Between the Lines, especially Amanda Crocker, Renée Knapp, David Molenhuis, and Jennifer Tiberio. Our thanks as well to the many organizations and individuals who agreed to make available the images used in this book—and to the archivists and librarians who helped us access so many photographs along the way. A special thank-you to photographer Jeff Crawford for providing us with so many fantastic images and to our research assistant, Isabella Horswill, for helping us locate suitable images from the Library and Archives Canada database.

By far our greatest debt is to the contributors. Thank you for your energy, your ideas, your diligence, your creativity, and for embracing this project as your own.

MD, CG, and DW
Fredericton, New Brunswick
April 2018

CONTRIBUTORS

Kristi A. Allain is associate professor of sociology at St. Thomas University. Her work examines the intersections of Canadian national identity, gender, aging, and physical culture.

Colin M. Coates teaches Canadian studies and history at Glendon College, York University.

Michael Dawson is professor of history at St. Thomas University. His teaching and research focus on national identity, tourism, consumerism, and sport.

Karen Dubinsky teaches in the Departments of Global Development Studies and History at Queen's University.

Jessica Dunkin is a writer and historian living in Chief Drygeese Territory (Treaty 8), home of the Wıìlìdeh Yellowknives Dene. Her first book, *Canoe and Canvas*, will be published by University of Toronto Press in 2019.

Caroline Durand is associate professor at Trent University. Her research and teaching interests include the history of food, French Canada, and Quebec.

Kelly Ferguson is a graduate of Carleton University's master's program in public history and an archivist at Library and Archives Canada.

Catherine Gidney is adjunct research professor in the Department of History at St. Thomas University. Her publications focus on the histories of education, gender, youth culture, health, and commercialism.

Alan Gordon is professor of history at the University of Guelph. He studies the political and cultural uses of the past in Canada and Quebec.

Patrice Groulx is a consultant, lecturer, and author in the fields of historical writing and heritage studies, focusing on Quebec and French North America.

Steven High is professor of history at the Centre for Oral History and Digital Storytelling, an interdisciplinary research unit of Concordia University.

Elizabeth L. Jewett is an environmental historian whose current research focuses on food and sporting landscapes. She is an adjunct faculty member in Canadian studies at Mount Allison University.

John Sutton Lutz is professor of history at the University of Victoria and the author of *Makúk: A New History of Aboriginal-White Relations*.

Ian McKay holds the L. R. Wilson Chair in Canadian History at McMaster University.

Cecilia Morgan is a professor in the Department of Curriculum, Teaching and Learning at OISE/UT. She has published extensively on the history of public memory and commemoration in Canada.

Gillian Poulter is associate professor of history at Acadia University. Her current research examines funeral rituals and the evolution of the funeral industry in Nova Scotia.

Jamie Swift, a Kingston-based writer and activist, is the author of some fourteen books. He lectures at the Smith School of Business at Queen's University.

Bill Waiser is distinguished professor emeritus at the University of Saskatchewan. *A World We Have Lost: Saskatchewan Before 1905* won the 2016 Governor General's Literary Award for Non-Fiction.

Cheryl Krasnick Warsh teaches the history of women, health care, and popular culture at Vancouver Island University. She is writing the biography of Dr. Frances Oldham Kelsey.

Donald Wright is professor of political science at the University of New Brunswick.

PHOTO CREDITS

INTRODUCTION

p.2.   Polar Bear, black bear, and moose. Photographs by Michael Dawson.

p.2.   Hudson's Bay Company Trading Post. Photograph by Michael Dawson.

p.3.   Maple leaf mural. Photograph by Michael Dawson.

p.4.   Birchbark canoe, Ottawa airport. Photograph by Michael Dawson.

p.4.   Inuksuit. Wikimedia Commons. Photograph by George Socka: CC BY 2.0.

p.4.   *Celebrating Flight* totem pole. Don Yeomans, 2007. Red cedar, canvas, and acrylic paint. Photograph by Michael Dawson.

p.5.   Beaver toy. Photograph by Jeff Crawford.

p.5.   Hockey bench and sculpture. Photograph by Michael Dawson.

p.6.   "Canada Vacations Unlimited" poster. Library and Archives Canada/Marc Choko collection/Accession No. R1409-38.

p.6.   Smoke's Poutinerie stickers. Photographs by Jeff Crawford.

BEAVER

p.8.   Vancouver Winter Olympics. ITAR-TASS News Agency/Alamy Stock Photo.

p.10. Stamp. Library and Archives Canada, R169-1129-4-E. © Canada Post Corporation 1851. Reproduced with Permission.

p.11. Five-cent piece. Image reproduced with the permission of the Royal Canadian Mint.

p.12. Cap badge. Reproduced with the permission of the Royal 22ᵉ Régiment.

p.13. Roots Canada logo. Design by Heather Cooper and Robert Burns. Reproduced with the permission of Roots Canada.

p.14. "Expose Yourself to CBC Radio" bumper sticker, 1975, Sean O'Sullivan fonds – RG 431. Brock University Archives, Brock University Library/CBC Still Photo Collection. Reproduced with the permission of the Canadian Broadcasting Corporation.

p.16. Kent Monkman, *Les Castors du Roi*, 2011. 96″ x 84″, acrylic on canvas; image courtesy of the artist.

CANOE

p.18. Emily Pauline Johnson in a Canoe, c.1890s. Photograph reproduced courtesy of the Brant Historical Society.

p.20. Soap dispenser. Photograph by Jeff Crawford.

p.21. Cartoon, Brian Mulroney canoeing with Robert Bourassa. Duncan McPherson, McCord Museum M2012.123.431.

p.22. Haida canoe. Photograph by Susan Clarke: CC BY 2.0.

p.22. Great Whale River, 1903. Chesterfield fonds – V007-L-36. Photograph reproduced courtesy of the Queen's University Archives.

p.23. Voyageur Canoe Pageant on its way to Expo 67. Library and Archives Canada/Centennial Commission fonds/a185522. © Government of Canada. Reproduced with the permission of Library and Archives Canada (2017).

p.23. Voyageur Canoe Pageant poster. Library and Archives Canada, Accession. No. 1983-33-1546.

p.25. Hicks' Boathouse. Photograph courtesy of John Hicks.

p.26. Sheet music. Edwin E. Goffe, "Out in Your Canoe," c. 1910 and Leo Edwards, "In a Little Canoe with You," c.1905. Images courtesy of the Adirondack Experience.

p.28. Todd Labrador. Photograph by Lori Craig-Labrador.

TOTEM POLE

p.30. A forest of totems at Skidegate, Haida Gwaii, in 1878; photograph by George M. Dawson. Image PN1020 courtesy of the Royal BC Museum and Archives.

p.32. Totem pole kitsch. Photograph by John Lutz.

p.33. Detail of the Grand Trunk Pacific Railway route in British Columbia showing "Indian Villages" along the Skeena where there were extant totem poles. (Chicago: Poole Brothers, 1907); courtesy of DavidRumsey.com.

p.33. Tourists examining Kitwanga totem poles in the 1920s. Image PN8371 courtesy of the Royal BC Museum and Archives.

p.34. The first drawing of a totem pole: Maquinna's house posts at Yuquot. *The Inside of a House in Nootka Sound by John Webber engraved by William Sharp* in James Cook, *A Voyage to the Pacific Ocean . . . in the Years 1776 . . . 1780* (London: 1785).

p.36. The Landsberg store selling totems and Indigenous art, Victoria, BC in 1901. Image PN9748 courtesy of the Royal BC Museum and Archives.

p.37. Exhibition of Canadian West Coast Art at the National Gallery of Canada, exhibition catalogue, 1927, Canadian Museum of History, IMG2013-0183-0040-DM.

p.38. Mt. Hurd framed with the Spesanish (Half-Bear Den) totem pole issued in 1928, Canadian Museum of History, IMG2018-0016-0001-DM.

p.39. Jasper Tea Room, Chateau Laurier, designed by Edwin Holgate in "Skeena River Totem Pole Style" and opened in 1929. Library and Archives of Canada, E010861279.

p.39. Totem Poles appear with other icons on the cover of *Canada Your Friendly Neighbour* (Ottawa: Canadian Government Travel Bureau, 1936).

p.40. Ellen Neel in her Stanley Park studio, 1953. City of Vancouver Archives, CVA 180-2361.

p.40. Totem in the Grand Hall of the Canadian Museum of History with its eye on Parliament. Photograph by John Lutz.

NORTH

p.42. *Isachsen*, 2018. Reproduced with the permission of aAron Munson.

p.44. Political Map of the Dominion of Canada, 1897. Library and Archives Canada, R11981-620-3-E.

p.46. Franklin Carmichael, *The Upper Ottawa, near Mattawa*, 1924. National Gallery of Canada. Accession no. 4271.

p.46. Lawren S. Harris, *Beaver Pond*, 1921. National Gallery of Canada. Accession no. 38020. Reproduced with the permission of Stewart Sheppard.

p.47. Jean Paul Lemieux, *Le visiteur du soir*, 1956, National Gallery of Canada. Accession no. 6504. Reproduced with the permission of Anne Sophie Lemieux.

p.48. Anne Murray on skis with Bonhomme, the ambassador of the Quebec City Winter Carnival. Library and Archives Canada, MIKAN no. 4443903.

p.50. Elisapee Ishulutaq (b. 1925, Pangnirtung), *Climate Change*, 2012. Inuit Art Foundation; reproduced with permission of the artist.

p.51. Skulls of members of the Franklin Expedition discovered and buried by William Skinner and Paddy Gibson. Library and Archives Canada, MIKAN no. 3191836.

LACROSSE

p.52. "Our Country & Our Game": emblem of the National Lacrosse Association of Canada, designed by John Henry Walker, c. 1867. McCord Museum M930.50.1.742.

p.54. *Messrs. Beers and Stevenson playing lacrosse, Montreal, QC, 1868.* McCord Museum I-35122.1.

p.56. "Lacrosse, Our National Game": words by James Hughes, music arranged by H. F. Sefton. Toronto: R. Marshall c. 1872–78. Library and Archives Canada Amicus No. 22914633; CSM6562-1C.

p.57. *Sakatis Aientonni, Baptiste Canadien, lacrosse player, Montreal, QC*, photographed by Notman & Sandham, 1876. McCord Museum II-41672.1

p.58. "The Canadian Lacrosse Team in England; Game at Kennington Oval, London, on the 5th Instant": illustration by James Inglis in *Canadian Illustrated News* vol. XIII, no. 26 (1876), 408. Library and Archives Canada, C-064421.

p.59. *La Crosse*: cover art for sheet music, c. 1867. Lacrosse sticks and a *ceinture fléchée* frame the image of an early game between an Indigenous and a white team. Library and Archives Canada AMICUS 20027694, CSM4026-1C.

p.60. *Female Lacrosse Player*: an altered sketch in one of the scrapbooks kept by Montreal sports enthusiast H. W. Beckett. Library and Archives Canada, Montreal Amateur Athletic Association fonds, MG28 I351, vol. 16, Scrapbook 2, 217; e008299381.

p.61. Canadian centenary postage designs. Top left: *Lacrosse the National Sport*, 1967. Library and Archives Canada, MIKAN 2272441, e003576113; top right: *La Crosse*, 1968. Library and Archives Canada MIKAN 2185989, s000546k; bottom: *Lacrosse National Game of Canada*, First day cover. Library and Archives Canada, MIKAN 3632985, e001218055.

HOCKEY

p.64. An outdoor hockey rink, 1956. Library and Archives Canada R1196-14-7-E/National Film Board Fonds e011176174.

p.66. The back of a $5 bank note. Bank note image reproduced with the permission of the Bank of Canada.

p.67. Paul Henderson, *The Goal Of My Life* book cover. Used by permission of Fenn/McClelland & Stewart, a division of Penguin Random House Canada Limited.

p.69. IIHF Women's World Championships, 2016. Andre Ringuette/HHOF-IIHF Images.

p.70. IIHF Men's World Championships, 2016 Andrea Leigh Cardin/HHOF-IIHF Images.

p.72. The cover of Roch Carrier's *The Hockey Sweater*. Used by permission of Tundra Books, a division of Penguin Random House Canada Limited.

p.73. Stamp. Library and Archives Canada, ITEMLEV34616. © Canada Post Corporation 1999. Reproduced with Permission.

ANTHEM

p.76. Mark Donnelly. Jason O. Watson (Sports)/Alamy Stock Photo.

p.78. *Thompson Indian version of "God Save the Queen" from Lytton, B.C.* Library and Archives Canada/Frederick Temple Hamilton-Temple-Blackwood, 1st Marquess of Dufferin and Ava fonds/e003525347.

p.79. *Now Then, All Together!* Department of the Interior, c. 1903-04. Library and Archives Canada, Accession. No. R1300-483.10V.

p.81. *Oh Canada! My Canada! Get Ready to Buy the New Victory Bonds*. Library and Archives Canada/National Film Board of Canada fonds/e010695735.

p.81. "O Canada, ton front est ceint de fleurons glorieux": ninth victory loan drive, October 20, 1945. Library and Archives Canada, Accession. No. 1983-30-1138

p.82. Drawing, cartoon. Toronto Baseball Fans Boo French in National Anthem (Aislin/Terry Mosher). McCord Museum M985.221.15.

p.83. Stamp. Library and Archives Canada, ITEMLEV10774. © Canada Post Corporation 1980. Reproduced with Permission

p.84. "Our Home on Native Land." Flickr. Photograph by Toban Black: CC BY-NC 2.0

FLAG

p.86. Backpack. Gari Wyn Williams/Alamy Stock Photo.

p.88. Prime Minister Lester B. Pearson. Library and Archives Canada, Duncan Cameron fonds, e011176702.

p.88. The Red Ensign. The Canadian Red Ensign at full mast in Northern Ontario, 2008. Wikipedia. Photograph by Necronaut. Public Domain.

p.89. The Pearson pennant lapel pin. Photograph by Jeff Crawford.

p.90. Maple Leaf of Canada evening dress. Canadian Museum of History, Maple Leaf of Canada evening dress, D-5915, IMG2009-0063-0110-Dm.

p.91. (left). Proposed flag design. Library and Archives Canada, Janina Lorzuczek/Department of the Secretary of State fonds, e011163963.

p.91. (centre). Proposed flag design featuring two igloos and a teepee. University of Saskatchewan, University Archives & Special

Collections, J. G. Diefenbaker fonds, series IX.C.277.13.ON.

p.91. (right). Proposed flag design "It's for the birds." University of Saskatchewan, University Archives & Special Collections, J. G. Diefenbaker fonds, series IX.C.277.10.2.ON.

p.92. *If you must know . . . I'm celebrating St. George's Day*. Library and Archives Canada, Leonard Matheson Norris fonds. Copyright: Estate of Leonard Norris. Reproduced with the permission of Stephen L. Norris.

p.94. *White Flag*. Reproduced with the permission of Emma Hassenahl-Perley.

FLEUR-DE-LYS

p.96. Hot air balloon. Sorin Papuc/Alamy Stock Photo.

p.98. Flag. Zoonar GmbH/Alamy Stock Photo

p.99. Charles Walter Simpson, *Jacques Cartier at Gaspé, 1534*. Oil on canvas laid on cardboard, 1927. Library and Archives Canada, Accession. No. 1991-35-3.

p.101. Postcard. Bibliothèque et Archives nationales du Québec (BAnQ) CP 3496 CON.

p.102. (top). Monument and rally. Photograph by Conrad Poirier, BAnQ P48,S1,P10706.

p.102. (bottom). Saint-Jean-Baptiste parade, 1946. Photograph by Conrad Poirier, BAnQ P48,S1,P13889.

p.104. Stamp. Library and Archives Canada R169-5; © Canada Post Corporation 1995. Reproduced with Permission.

p.104. Three flags in Montreal, 2017. Photograph by Alan Gordon.

MAPLE SYRUP

p.106. Maple syrup production. Wikimedia Commons. Photograph by M. Rehemtuall for QUOI Media Group. CC BY-SA 2.0.

p.108. (top left) Popcorn. Photograph by Jeff Crawford.

p.108. (top right) Maple Ice Wine. Photograph by Jeff Crawford.

p.108. (bottom left) Sugar maples. Photograph by Elizabeth L. Jewett.

p.108. (bottom right) Sugar maple. Photograph by Elizabeth L. Jewett.

p.109. *Sugar Making in Canada*. Library and Archives Canada/Peter Winkworth Collection of Canadiana at the National Archives of Canada/e000756690.

p.110. *Sugar-Making Among the Indians in the North*. Library and Archives Canada/Canadian Illustrated News, 1869–1883/vol.XXVII, no. 19. 296/Item Number: 458.

p.112. Oh Oh Canada Maple Candy Project. Photograph by Leah Decter. Reprinted with permission of Leah Decter.

p.113. *Canadians and the Duchess of Connaught's gift (Maple Sugar)*. Library and Archives Canada/Ministry of the Overseas Military Forces of Canada fonds/a022699.

p.114. Timothy Wilson Hoey, *Syrup*, O-Canada Series, 2017. Reprinted with permission of the artist.

CANADIAN PACIFIC RAILWAY

p.118. Photograph, 100-ton mountain engine on the CPR, near Field, BC, 1889, William McFarlane Notman. McCord Museum VIEW-2508.

p.120. (left). The last spike. Library and Archives Canada PA209978.

p.120. (right). Telegram. Library and Archives Canada, Manuscript Division, Macdonald Papers.

p.121. Cartoon. *Toronto Evening News*, June 20, 1885. Public domain.

p.122. Engraving. Canadian Pacific Railway Co., Land Grant in Manitoba and North West Territory. John Henry Walker. McCord Museum M930.50.2.233.

p.123. Colonization & Development poster. INTERFOTO/Alamy Stock Photo.

p.124. "Breaking his bonds" cartoon. *Grain Growers Guide*, October 20, 1916. Public domain.

p.125. CPR logo. NZ Collection/Alamy Stock Photo.

p.126. "Banff Spring Golf Course, scorecard," c. 1925. Artist: Unknown. Heritage Image Partnership Ltd / Alamy Stock Photo.

MOUNTIE

p.128. Royal Doulton bust. Photograph by Jeff Crawford.

p.130. (left) "A member of the RCMP poses in front of the Parliament buildings for snapshooting tourists." Ottawa, Ontario. October 1949. Library and Archives Canada, R1196-14-7-E.

p.130. (right) Musical Ride. Photograph by Sue Cole.

p.131. (left) Cover of T. Morris Longstreth, *The Scarlet Force* (Toronto: MacMillan, 1958). Photograph by Jeff Crawford.

p.131. (right) Cover of Kerry Wood, *The Queen's Cowboy* (Toronto: MacMillan, 1960). Photograph by Jeff Crawford.

p.132. *Northern Patrol.* Library and Archives Canada/Visual and Sound Archives Division film poster collection/e010779201.

p.133. *Nugget Shoe Shine The Very Best!* Library and Archives Canada/Morris Norman collection/e010757013.

p.134. Indigenous Mountie doll. Photograph by Jeff Crawford.

p.135. Minnie Mouse. Photograph by Jeff Crawford.

DOLLARD DES ORMEAUX

p.138. Louis-Philippe Hébert, *Dollard's Heroic Death at Long Sault*, 1895. Photograph by Jean Gagnon. Wikicommons. CC BY-SA 3.0.

p.141. The Dollard monument in Montreal's Parc Lafontaine at its inauguration, June 24, 1920. Photograph by Edgar Gariépy. Archives de a Ville de Montréal, BM-42, G0106.

p.142. "French Canadians, follow the example of Dollard des Ormeaux," 1914–1918. Library and Archives Canada, C-093228.

p.143. *Dollard*, 1921, detail from a print by Jean-Baptiste Lagacé. Private collection.

p.144. An April 1926 advertisement in *L'Action française.* Bibliothèque et Archives nationales du Québec, with the permission of *L'Action nationale.*

p.145. Robert La Palme, *La Presse* (Montreal), May 26, 1960. Bibliothèque et Archives nationales du Québec, with the permission of the Robert La Palme Foundation.

p.146. The Dollard monument in Montreal's Parc Lafontaine. Photograph by Camille Dufétel. *Journal de Montréal*, June 28, 2016.

LAURA SECORD

p.148. Stamp. Image courtesy of Jacob Van Vuuren and www.canadianpostagestamps.ca. © Canada Post Corporation 2012. Reproduced with Permission.

p.150. Aislin (Terry Mosher) cartoon, 1998. M2000.81.2, McCord Museum.

p.151. *Map of the Niagara Frontier, 1812–1815.* Adapted from George M. Wrong, *Ontario Public School History of Canada* (Toronto: Ryerson Press, 1922), 202.

p.152. *Mrs. James Secord*, c. 1865. Photographer unknown. MP-0000.2649, McCord Museum.

p.153. (left). Laura Secord monument, Queenston Heights. Photograph by Cecilia Morgan.

p.153. (right). Secord Company candy boxes, McCord Museum m996x.2.512.1-2.

p.154. (left) *Laura Secord Meets the Kahnawake Mohawk*, Henry Sandham, from J. E. Wetherell, *Handbook to Nelson's Pictures of Canadian History* (Toronto: Thomas Nelson and Sons, 1927).

p.154. (right). *Meeting Between Laura Secord and James FitzGibbon.* Lorne K. Smith, 1920. Library and Archives Canada, Acc. No. 1997-229-2, C-011053.

p.156. Laura Secord in the Angel Inn, Niagara-on-the-Lake. Poster by Mary Littlejohn Gillespie, c. 2000. Photograph by Cecilia Morgan.

VIMY RIDGE

p.158. Soldiers and horse. CWM 19920085-233, George Metcalf Archival Collection, Canadian War Museum. Reproduced with the permission of the Canadian War Museum.

p.160. Birth of a Nation cap. Photographs by Jeff Crawford.

p.161. Vimy monument. Photographs by Robert Vanderheyden.

p.164. $20 bill. Bank note image reproduced with the permission of the Bank of Canada.

p.166. Ottawa memorial. Photograph by Robert Vanderheyden.

PEACEKEEPER

p.168. Corporal Frank Walsh of the 1st Battalion, Queen's Own Rifles of Canada, preparing to serve for the United Nations Police Force in the Middle East. Library and Archives Canada/Department of National Defence/ PA-108139.

p.170. (left) *Reconciliation* monument. Wikimedia Commons. Photograph by Jean Gagnon. CC BY-SA 4.0.

p.170. (right). *Reconciliation* monument. Photograph by Kelly Ferguson.

p.171. Two Canadian soldiers scan the Egypt-Israel frontier during a desert patrol, Library and Archives Canada/Department of External Affairs/ PA-122737.

p.174. Stamp. Library and Archives Canada, ITEMLEV34639. © Canada Post Corporation 2000. Reproduced with permission.

p.175. $10 bill. Bank note image reproduced with the permission of the Bank of Canada.

p.176. Roméo Dallaire. Europa Newswire/ Alamy Stock Photo.

ANNE OF GREEN GABLES

p.178. Stamp. Library and Archives Canada, R169-1129-4-E. © Canada Post Corporation 2008. Reproduced with Permission.

p.180. PEI highway sign. Photograph by Michael Dawson.

p.181. "Haunted Wood" and "Lovers Lane" signs. Photographs by Michael Dawson.

p.182. Ballet poster. Former Royal Winnipeg Ballet Company dancers Laura Graham (1985–95) and Jorden Morris (1987–99). Photo courtesy of the Royal Winnipeg Ballet. Poster reproduced with the permission of the National Arts Centre. *L. M. Montgomery* is a trademark of Heirs of L. M. Montgomery Inc. Poster reproduced with the permission of the Heirs of L. M. Montgomery. Library and Archives Canada, Acc. No. 1990-100-2.

p.184. Green Gables and Green Gables Visitor Centre. Photographs by Michael Dawson.

p.185. (left). Fridge magnet. Photograph by Jeff Crawford.

p.185. (centre). Raspberry Cordial. Photograph by Jeff Crawford.

p.185. (right). Dolls. Michael Jenner/Alamy Stock Photo.

p.186. Access Now. Karats, Twitter post, January 30, 2016, 9:37 a.m., https://twitter.com/iamkarats/status/693488226003214336.

NIAGARA FALLS

p.188. Niagara Falls. Photograph by Pexels. Obtained from Pixabay. CC0 Creative Commons.

p.190. Visitors at Niagara Falls, Ontario. Wikimedia Commons, Public Domain. Photograph by JohnnyAlbert10.

p.191. The American and Bridal Veil Falls (left) and the Canadian or "Horseshoe" Falls (right). Wikimedia Commons. Photograph by ErwinMeir CC BY-SA 3.0.

p.192. (left) "American" Falls at night. Wikimedia Commons. Photograph by Safron Blaze. CC BY-SA 3.0.

p.192. (right) "Canadian" Falls at Night. Wikimedia Commons. Photograph by Eric Marshall. CC BY-SA 3.0.

p.193. Movieland and Beavertails. Photographs by Michael Dawson.

p.194. Niagara Falls from space. Wikimedia Commons. Public Domain. NASA Visible Earth.

p.196. The Heredia Plaque. Wikimedia Commons. Photograph by Themightyquill CC BY-SA 3.0.

UNIVERSAL HEALTH CARE

p.198. Raging Grannies. Flickr. Photograph by Grant Neufeld CC BY-NC 2.0.

p.200. Stamp. Library and Archives Canada, ITEMLEV32226. © Canada Post Corporation 1958. Reproduced with permission.

p.201. Stamp. Library and Archives Canada, R169-133-1-E. © Canada Post Corporation 1998. Reproduced with permission.

p.202. Saskatchewan Medical Association. George E. Dragan/Library and Archives Canada/PA-088485.

p.204. Cartoon. Tom Innes, *Calgary Herald*, July 27, 1983, Glenbow Archives, M-8000-1297.

p.206. (left) Tommy Douglas statue. Wikimedia Commons. Photograph by "Kamloops" CC BY-SA 3.0.

p.206. (right) Tommy Douglas statue (feet). Photograph by Jessica Hunter Photography.

EH?

p.208. Bob and Doug McKenzie. Entertainment Pictures/Alamy Stock Photo.

p.210. KFC Canada, Twitter post, June 26, 2017, 8:02 a.m., https://twitter.com/kfc_canada/status/879354147199475713.

p.211. Pillow case. Photograph by Jeff Crawford.

p.212. Garbage can. Flickr. Photograph by Alan Levine/CC BY 2.0.

p.213. Coffee mug. Photograph by Jeff Crawford.

p.214. Cooler bag. Photograph by Jeff Crawford.

p.215. Ornament. Photograph by Jeff Crawford.

p.216. T-shirt. Photograph by Jeff Crawford.

p.216. Beach. Photograph by Michael Dawson.

POUTINE

p.218 Poutine. Photograph by Sjschen. Wikicommons CC BY 3.0.

p.220. Ottawa Tourism. © Ottawa Tourism. Reproduced with the permission of Ottawa Tourism.

p.221. (left). *Haggis versus poutine*, Aislin (Terry Mosher), *Montreal Gazette*, July 2, 1987. © Musée McCord, M987.217.40.

p.221. (right) Poutine festival poster. © Festival de la poutine de Drummondville. Reproduced with permission.

p.223. St. Hubert poutine. © St-Hubert S.E.C. 2013. Reproduced with permission.

p.224. Whistle Stop Café. Photograph by Caroline Durand.

p.225. Loto-Québec. © Loto-Québec. Reproduced with permission.

p.226. Smoke's Poutinerie in Ottawa. Photograph by Michael Dawson.

TIM HORTONS

p.228. Tim Hortons sign. Photograph by Michael Dawson.

p.230. (left) Tim Hortons in Kandahar. Wikimedia Commons. Photograph by Staff Sgt. Brian Raley. Public Domain.

p.230. (right) Tim Hortons cup. Photograph by Jeff Crawford.

p.231. *Hockey Player Tim Horton—Toronto Maple Leafs* © Library and Archives Canada. Reproduced with the permission of Library and Archives Canada, Library and Archives Canada/Weekend Magazine collection/e002343748.

p.232. (top). Timbits. Wikimedia Commons. Photograph by Jiaqian AirplaneFan. CC BY 3.0.

p.232. (bottom) Parade float. Wikimedia Commons. Photograph by Loozrboy. CC BY 2.0.

p.234. Drive thru sign. Photograph by Michael Dawson.

p.236. Discarded cup. Photograph by Michael Dawson.

INDEX